From
Learning for Love
to
Love of Learning

A REISS-DAVIS CHILD STUDY CENTER
PUBLICATION

From Learning for Love to Love of Learning

Essays on Psychoanalysis and Education

RUDOLF EKSTEIN, Ph.D.

Director, Project Childhood Psychosis, Reiss-Davis Child Study Center; Training Analyst, Los Angeles Psychoanalytic Society and Institute; Clinical Professor in Medical Psychology, University of California at Los Angeles

and

ROCCO L. MOTTO, M.D.

Director, Reiss-Davis Child Study Center
Senior Instructor, Los Angeles Psychoanalytic Society and Institute

Foreword by Fritz Redl, Ph.D.

WITHDRAWN

BRUNNER / MAZEL Publishers • New York • 1969

THIS VOLUME IS DEDICATED TO

ANNA FREUD

Whose rich contributions to psychoanalysis, whose deep and compassionate interest in children, their parents and their teachers have inspired generations of professionals and researchers in our field.

THE CONTRIBUTORS

E. JAMES ANTHONY, M.D., Ittleson Professor of Child Psychiatry, Washington University School of Medicine, St. Louis, Missouri; Training Analyst, Chicago Psychoanalytic Institute, Chicago, Illinois.

BRUNO BETTELHEIM, PH.D., Rowley Professor of Education, University of Chicago; Director, Sonia Shankman Orthogenic School, Chicago, Illinois.

EDITH BUXBAUM, PH.D., Training Analyst and Chairman, Education Committee, Seattle Psychoanalytic Institute, Seattle, Washington.

RUDOLF EKSTEIN, PH.D., Director, Project on Childhood Psychosis, Reiss-Davis Child Study Center, Los Angeles, California; Training Analyst, Los Angeles Psychoanalytic Society and Institute; Clinical Professor of Medical Psychology, University of California at Los Angeles.

J. C. HILL, Inspector, East London Schools, London, England (retired).

LAWRENCE S. KUBIE, M.D., Consultant on Research and Training, The Sheppard and Enoch Pratt Hospital, Towson, Maryland; Clinical Professor of Psychiatry, University of Maryland School of Medicine, Baltimore, Maryland; Lecturer in Psychiatry, Johns Hopkins University School of Medicine, Baltimore, Maryland.

ROCCO L. MOTTO, M.D., Director, Reiss-Davis Child Study Center, Los Angeles, California; Senior Instructor, Child Analysis, Los Angeles Psychoanalytic Society and Institute.

G. H. J. PEARSON, M.D., Past Dean and Director, Child Analytic Training, Institute of the Philadelphia Psychoanalytic Association, Philadelphia, Pennsylvania; Professor Emeritus in Child Psychiatry, Hahnemann Medical College and Hospital, Philadelphia, Pennsylvania.

LILI E. PELLER, 1896-1966. Honorary member, Philadelphia Association for Psychoanalysis.

MARIA W. PIERS, PH.D., Dean, Chicago Institute for Early Education, Chicago, Illinois.

FRITZ REDL, PH.D., Distinguished Professor of Behavioral Sciences, Wayne University, Detroit, Michigan.

SYBIL T. RICHARDSON, ED.D., Professor of Education, San Fernando Valley State College, Northridge, California.

GEORGE V. SHEVIAKOV. Professor of Psychology, San Francisco State College, San Francisco, California (retired).

ALBERT J. SOLNIT, M.D., Professor of Pediatrics and Psychiatry, Yale University School of Medicine and Child Study Center, New Haven, Connecticut; Training Analyst, Western New England Psychoanalytic Institute, Springfield, Massachusetts.

RALPH TYLER, PH.D., President, National Academy of Education, Chicago, Illinois.

CONTENTS

CONTENTS

CONTENTS

ACKNOWLEDGMENTS

WE WISH TO EXPRESS our appreciation to the editors of the following journals and books for permission to reprint or quote material: "The Child, the Teacher and Learning" in *Young Children*; "The Unconscious Mind in Teaching" in *London Head Teacher*; "The Borderline Child in the School Situation" in Grune and Stratton's *Professional School Psychology*, edited by M. G. and G. B. Gottsegen; "Play and Mastery" in the 1969 Quadrangle Books (Chicago) publication by Maria W. Piers and Robert Coles. All other articles appeared originally in a slightly different form in the *Reiss-Davis Clinic Bulletin*.

We also wish to express appreciation to those individuals who have participated with us in the seminars and annual institutes for teachers on Psychoanalysis and Education. Participating with us as instructors in the seminars were: Phyllis Dupont Click, M.A., Director of Teacher Education, Center for Early Education; Gerald Aronson, M.D., Bernard W. Bail, M.D., Leonard H. Gilman, M.D., Arthur Malin, M.D., James M. Mott, M.D., Arthur J. Ourieff, M.D., Neal Peterson, M.D., Edwin F. Price, M.D., Kenneth Rubin, M.D., and Morton Shane, M.D., all instructors, Extension Division, Los Angeles Psychoanalytic Society-Institute; Elaine Caruth, Ph.D., Christoph M. Heinicke, Ph.D., Milton J. Horowitz, Ph.D., Mortimer M. Meyer, Ph.D., and Janet Switzer, Ph.D., members of the staff of the Reiss-Davis Child Study Center.

For the annual institutes, in addition to the instructors listed above, many individuals were most generous with their time as they served in the capacity of group discussion leaders. From the field of education were the following: Byron Burgess, Evangeline Burgess, Frances Houle Burnford, M.A., Jack Byrom, Ed.D., Helen Daitch, Helen P. Doak, Belle Dubnoff, M.A., Helen Fielstra, Shirley Garber, M.A., Allene Goldman, M.A., Sylvia Haber, Frances Hine, Ph.D., Donald Kincaid, Ed.D., Judith Kipper, M.A., Nadine Lambert, M.A., Sylvia Leshing, Florence Loeb, M.A., Jane Manning, Margaret Matthews, Donald McNassor, Jane Miller, Mary V. Minnie, June Patterson, Elta Pfister, Ph.D., Belle Rabinowitz, M.A., Sybil T. Richardson, Ed.D., Lewis Rubin, Ph.D., Wanda Schermerhorn, Harry Smallenberg, Ed.D., Marianne J. Wolman, Gertrude Wood, Ed.D. From the field of psychoanalysis and psychoanalytically oriented disciplines: Morris Beckwitt, M.D., Marvin H. Berenson, M.D., Justin Call, M.D., Barbara Carr, M.A., Richard R. Casady, M.D., Robert M. Dorn, M.D., Michael Dunn, Ph.D., Bernice T. Eiduson, Ph.D., Seymour W. Friedman, M.D., Abraham H. Gottesman, M.D., James S. Grotstein, M.D., Lyman Harrison, M.D., Peter D. Landres, M.D., Thomas Mintz, M.D., Hilda

Rollman-Branch, M.D., Leda Rosow, M.A., Margarete Ruben, Marshall D. Schechter, M.D., Bella F. Schimmel, M.D., Samuel J. Sperling, M.D., Carl Sugar, M.D., Helen Tausend, M.D., Heiman van Dam, M.D., Miriam M. Williams, M.D.

Contributing greatly to the interest and development of our overall efforts to bridge psychoanalysis and education was the willingness of the following outstanding educators and psychoanalysts to appear as program participants, some of them participating more than once: Stephen Abrahamson, Ph.D., Professor of Education, University of Southern California; Irving N. Berlin, M.D., Professor of Child Psychiatry, University of Washington, Seattle, Washington; Richard Bertain, Ph.D., Director, Secondary Schools and Principal, Culver City High School, California; Gaston E. Blom, M.D., Professor of Psychiatry, University of Colorado; Hanna Fenichel, Ph.D., Training Analyst, Los Angeles Psychoanalytic Society-Institute; John Goodlad, Ph.D., Dean, School of Education, University of California at Los Angeles; Milton J. Horowitz, Ph.D., Director, Division of Clinical Training, Reiss-Davis Child Study Center; Joseph Katz, Ph.D., Research Co-ordinator, Institute for Study of Human Problems, Stanford University, Palo Alto, California; Jacob S. Kounin, Ph.D., Education Research Project, Wayne State University, Detroit, Michigan; N. S. Metfessel, Ph.D., Department of Educational Psychology, University of Southern California; Fritz A. Schmidl, M.S., Clinical Assistant Professor Psychiatry (Social Work), University of Washington Medical School, Seattle, Washington; Eve Smith, Educator, Seattle, Washington; Ralph Tyler, Ph.D., Former Director of the Center for Advanced Study of the Behavioral Sciences, Palo Alto, California, and President, National Academy of Education, Chicago, Illinois.

The co-sponsorship arrangements between the Reiss-Davis Child Study Center and the Los Angeles Psychoanalytic Society-Institute have been the mainstay of our endeavors. More recently the affiliation has included the Center for Early Education and for a brief interlude there was also an affiliation with the Education Extension of the University of California at Los Angeles. The continuing interest and cooperation of these participating institutions have helped in the support and the advance of our work.

This book could not have been brought to completion without the very able editorial assistance of Sylvia B. Harary. In preparation of preliminary drafts of manuscripts, we are grateful for the work of Clara Ballinger. A very special debt of gratitude is expressed for the loyal, devoted and "beyond the call of duty" contribution of Greta L. Solomon whose typing and retyping of the manuscript along with all the correspondence between the authors, the numerous contributors and publisher was always carried on with diligence and responsibility.

Foreword: It's About Time

FRITZ REDL

IT'S ABOUT TIME we recovered from the sins of the past. In this volume, Motto and Ekstein begin with a classic: nowhere else have I found such a lucid and realistic account of the history of the efforts of psychoanalysis and education to come to grips with each other. Since I was part of the historical epoch which they describe and analyze, I may be allowed to summarize and be less polite about it. Most of these efforts seem to me to be the sins of the past we ought to junk for good, never mind how understandable or even important it was to have committed them in the first place.

SIN No. 1: *Escape into Delusional Thought.* This phase was actually of very short duration. The idea that "the liberation of the child" from adult pressures was all that was needed was a delusion hung onto only before analysts started taking work with children seriously. It was punctured for good when child analysis came to grips with the real lives of children, rather than with reconstructions from couch fantasies of neurotic adults. By the way, this sin we got punished for more than we deserve. For, we, remorseful that we ever claimed it, abandoned it fast. But the "general public" picked up the very delusion we discarded and is still cultivating it or fighting it as though it was our theory now. I suggest we bury this silly issue for good: permitting and setting limits are not controversial theories. They are both realistic issues that need to be integrated in varying patterns in the life of each child.

SIN No. 2: *Throwing Crumbs from the Tables of the Rich.* This one I remember more vividly still, though the mere thought of it makes me blush. It is understandable enough. Impressed with the rich findings brought up from the depth of the earth, where they had been hidden from view for centuries, one was easily misled into a somewhat condescending missionary zeal: if those poor teachers only "knew more" about what goes on in the "unconscious" of their charges, what a real and beneficial job they could do! Our schools and homes would stop producing the neuroses we struggled with if only the adults who dealt with children knew what we know. . . . But remember, please, by this purposely overdrawn statement I do not want to imply that there aren't some crumbs which would be good for all involved to have, or that the spread of knowledge, where it is not yet available, isn't a worthwhile task. What bothers me about that phase we went through, way back when, is rather the incredible naïveté with which we indulged in gestures like this, as though they would suffice for the enormous tasks before us.

SIN No. 3: *Let's Pick Us a Few Indians and Make Good House Indians Out of Them, That Ought to Take Care of It All.* Being lucky enough to have been picked for a "good Indian," I can witness to the enormous value of such an approach—provided I can also be permitted to criticize the shortsightedness that came with it. For, obviously, teachers analyzed and then, to boot, trained in whatever might be useful to them or what might make them good helpers on cases in analysis, are a commodity devoutly to be wished. Only—it is as far from solving the problem of education or schools as the giving of Christmas baskets is from a solution of the problems of social welfare. And there was another hitch that came somewhat as a surprise: for many a good House Indian developed a strong knack for continuing life in that comfortable House, and a good many did not want to go back to the rough life on their reservation or in the sticks.

SIN No. 4: *Let's Set up a New Enterprise, Psychoanalysis and Co.,* which means the educators are partners, for the treatment of the sick. By the way, as long as we look at this combine as an outfit created for the treatment of the sick, this is no sin. On the contrary, it probably constitutes the most important and beneficial gain in the field of child therapy this century can be proud of. However, if you look at it in terms of what it means for bringing psychoanalysis and education closer together, it is obviously bound to fail. While it admits educators into a new role as partners in therapy and prevention, it does not come to grips with the issues of teaching and education per se. In fact, by being such a successful and important therapeutic device, it has contributed to our blindness toward the real problems, as yet untouched.

As far as psychoanalysis and education in their interrelationships are concerned, the real issues are still before us. It seems to me that efforts like the Reiss-Davis Seminars and Institutes for Teachers reported on in this volume constitute one of the most effective steps toward burying the mistakes of the past—after learning from them.

However, recovering from the sins of the past is not enough. As this book demonstrates it is high time that we renew our efforts to take stock of the unfinished business, the challenge of the present and the future. It is a great temptation to try to begin spelling those out right now, at least as far as their visibility increases under the impact of previous study and research. Only, this is meant to be a preface, not the story itself. This much, however, should be said even within a modest framework: quite aside from what we have learned as to content from the analysis of adults as well as of children, and also from the joint experience of therapists and educators in our present-day clinical designs, great challenge seems to lie in the following directions.

(1) Teachers as well as parents do not deal with individuals in one-to-one relationships only. Much of their effort is bound to attempt to reach the individual while he is embedded in the psychological matrix of the group. Much educational leadership is, at least, "also" group leadership. The management of group behavior and the cultivation of group atmospheres which are supportive rather than detrimental to the task of learning as well as of growing, constitute task areas in their own right. It seems that the analytically oriented teacher operating in a classroom would have a unique chance to contribute to the study of group processes and what they do to individuals, especially if his eye is sharpened to those "inner events" which psychoanalysis has done so much to make visible to us.

(2) The process of learning weaves both cognitive as well as instinctual and affective events into an inextricable design. While the preponderance or dominance of the one or other of these factors has fascinated us in the past, much is yet to be learned about their unique interwovenness and about the optimum givens which are essential if constructive learning is to take place in the classroom group.

(3) Whether invited or not, all parts of a child's—and adult's—psychology "sit in" on the classroom scene. And, while our deeper zeal may be geared toward the "underlying" processes of growth and character formation, the classroom as well as the family room will invariably abound with the noise of overt behavior. Far from being "superficial," the task of managing the behavior of learners in groups or growers in the family-setting remains a nearly untapped area of enormous complexity. Only recently have we become more aware of the need to inspect techniques of educational and behavioral intervention with as depth-oriented an eye as we used to view the child's personality as such. The search for a psychoanalytically oriented pharmacopoeia of "behavioral management techniques" has moved from a vaguely perceived fantasy into the realm of attainable goals. It is obvious that the educator in the trenches of daily child life is as important a partner in such an undertaking as the psychoanalyst and his clinical colleagues.

(4) Anna Freud taught us about the necessity, in child analysis, to remain aware of the impact of the child's natural habitat as well as of parent and teacher behavior on the course of neurosis or its cure. This lesson has opened our eyes to the importance of taking not only the

children's "defenses" and ego functions more seriously, but also of increasing our push into knowing more about just which of the "environmental givens" do what to the child. Thus, from a statement of respect to environmental factors as they impinge on the treatment of neurotics, we have long since come to wish for a very specific psychoanalytically oriented analysis, not of the child or his parents only, but also of the very milieu factors with which both have to cope.

Since any one of these aspects, even if only modestly approached, will, of course, require the teamwork of clinical as well as educational personnel, it seems obvious that what has been undertaken by Motto and Ekstein and presented in this volume must be greeted as one of the most promising frameworks for renewed exploration of the old puzzle: psychoanalysis and education—where does each belong, what can they do for each other and what can they do for the child?

Editors' Introduction

The second field in which analysis has been widely, though much less systematically used for practical purposes is pedagogy. But here the situation, as to the problem of values, is different to begin with. In pedagogy there is no single goal accepted as unquestionably as is health in medicine. Social, moral, and other values are constantly to be considered. In the use of pedagogical techniques moral values cannot simply be put into parentheses, as they are in psychoanalytic technique. One has to face the differences in this respect between religious and nonreligious, between individualistic and conformist educational goals, between the aims of being a "good citizen" in a democratic or totalitarian society, and so on; yet there are, of course, also common elements in the ideas and practices of child rearing.

—Heinz Hartmann

THIS ERA, a time of great turmoil and social change, has been referred to by various authors as the age of unreason or as the time of anxiety. We are not sure whether we share this objective experience with all previous ages, or whether we actually are living under pressures much greater than the ones that earlier generations faced. But even if it were true that our anxieties—the dangers of escalations of local wars to widespread international conflicts; the eruptive nature of racial problems or the population explosions; the unrest of students and young people in general; the alarming threat of the atomic bomb as either an inner monster or an external danger—are greater than ever, we want to assume that the opposite is also true. Positive opportunities, such as the emancipation struggle of colonial peoples, the anti-poverty programs, the ambitions of a great society, the challenge to make our great cities livable and safe, also seem to be much greater.

In order to maintain the perspectives of a free and open society, we must not allow the current desire for mass solutions, the raw quest for power, the wish to find answers for the millions to overwhelm us. For along with such concerns, it behooves us to maintain an individualistic approach in the field of education. This book is dedicated to psychoanalysis and education. It is designed to strengthen and enlarge the living bridge between education and psychoanalysis. It is directed to psychoanalysts, educators and to professional workers in related fields. It is an expression of much work that has been carried on here at the Reiss-Davis Child Study Center. During the last decade, the authors of this volume have spent a great deal of time and effort in order to organize collaborative work between psychoanalysts and teachers as well as other professional people in the clinical and educational fields.

Only a modest reflection of these past activities, this book may be seen as a temporary summing up of our current thinking as well as a basis for further work. It absolutely abstracts the work of many contributors; lecturers and consultants, leaders of our Annual Institutes, instructors of our regular seminars and courses, hundreds of teachers, as well as other interested persons who took part in these training and research activities. All these collaborators from different professional fields who have been helping us through these years are named in our acknowledgment pages. There also are named the organizations, institutions, colleges, private and public schools, which united with us in this complex and difficult undertaking. Many of these helpers gave countless hours and remained permanently committed to the task. Some gave us time occasionally. Others came to us as guests in our yearly panels, and some participated in our permanent college courses. Often we met with teachers and organizations in other cities, even in other countries, and we came back enriched with new ideas and many more questions to be answered.

All this experience has been compressed in this little book. All the contributors whose chapters enrich our work brought their contributions directly to the Reiss-Davis Child Study Center which remained the hub of these efforts. Anna Freud, to whom the book is dedicated, came to our Center and the stimulus of her visit has much to do with our lasting commitment.

Psychoanalysis is usually thought of only in terms of a therapeutic technique. Actually, it is a basic psychological science, offering generic insights into human functioning, and as such invites use in many areas of human endeavor. Its main value lies in understanding individual psychic functioning and problems of external as well as internal stimuli for growth, for learning, for the acquisition of new psychic functions rather than only the study of psychopathology and malfunctioning.

As we establish educational goals for our children and our society, we move beyond the scientific issues. We find ourselves engaged in struggles through which we express our moral and social values as well. We emphasize that our endeavor reported here attempts to create that living bridge between scientific insight and educational and social application. The reader thus needs to keep in mind that we are talking about *truth* and *value*.

We think of psychoanalysis as a bulwark of individualism. We believe that the use of psychoanalytic principles and insights in the educational system, including the formal school system, indirectly strengthens the belief in the individual, defines his place in a free and open society and, in return, fortifies this very society.

The material contributed by educators and psychoanalysts certainly destroys the old fiction that sees the analyst in the ivory tower of his consulting room. While primarily interested in his patients, he nevertheless also sees the role of social institutions, and both seeks improvements and wants the opportunity to share his knowledge and insight with educators. But we also see that the teachers bring to the analysts their own insights into educational processes, their own view of maturation and development, so that the clinicians, in turn, can gain knowledge from the educators' observations and techniques. Thus it is that we may rightfully speak about the bridge between psychoanalysis and education, since we do not allow the chasm of separation to remain unspanned.

As we suggested earlier, many of the opinions expressed are based on value systems. One of the values projected in these papers is that of basing one's opinions on true information, on reflection and on insight. A good educational philosophy should be motivated by love and guided by knowledge.

He who is guided by knowledge, is motivated by love, identified with the needs of growing children and wants to help parents and teachers, must not abandon a concomitant responsibility. It is that of looking at the educational structures that society creates and having the courage to offer constructive criticism and suggestions for needed change. For this reason some sections of this book are concerned with the nature of the curriculum, how to improve it and how to arouse public support for better work and study conditions for teachers and pupils. Others deal with fostering research in the educational field and opposing trends which might pervert the school system from its goal of education and reflection in a free society, and make it into a melting pot of violent pressures of confrontation.

The book includes a large section on the new task in a changing society. The challenging question is asked as to whose property the public school system is. One becomes aware that only he who can use it truly owns a piece of property. The acquisition of the skill to use property indeed changes all *property rights*. One is reminded of Goethe's famous phrase: "What thou hast inherited from your fathers, acquire it to make it thine and thee."

But education can benefit from many new insights about the child. Anna Freud puts it this way: "I think one of the sources of error in this whole story which I am unfolding before you has been the fact that pieces of knowledge were applied in isolation, always the newest knowledge applied last; that we would have greater luck if we would take a wider view of the whole situation of the child and try to apply our idea of the whole structure of the personality to education, not only knowledge either of his instinctive part (the id), or of his conscience, or even of the fight between the two." The knowledge of the child's growing personality or organization has permitted us to develop new concepts about learning and teaching readiness, about learning and teaching resistance, and has given us generic insights into the issues of individuation, of identification, and the different modes of learning, characteristic for different phases in the development of the child. Large sections of the book are to illustrate these modes of learning, and to tackle the vital issue, the challenge of discipline, a problem of utmost importance in a society which faces a critical period when what is established is challenged without sound new goals for what ought to be established.

In order to allow room for constant growth, for creative and positive change, we have discussed our views, guided by Santayana's suggestion that "Those who do not know their past are condemned to repeat it." We therefore tried to offer historical perspectives, a history concerning the mutual relationships of education and psychoanalysis.

This history stresses the beginning in Europe in which one of the authors took part. It shows how these ideas traversed the ocean and came to the United States. The work of these ten years unites two analysts, one from Europe and one born in the United States. Both of them are today committed to a large extent to issues of professional education, the training of professional people, and have spent many years in the fields of education and training and the fields of educational and clinical administration, as well as research. It was a strange experience when we went back to Europe in 1968 to bring from America a chapter about the application of psychoanalysis to education. Some of the Europeans experienced as new and strange what had originally come from there.

In this sort of civilization ideas and values have their ebb and flow. In times of rising anxiety, of social stress, there may be little room for truly democratic options, for an education that looks at the individual, for a psychology that looks at the inner man, for a school system that develops personalities rather than trains primarily for functions to be executed. As we bring this book to the public, we think it might well be true that we run against the tides.

Perhaps our friends, teachers and clinicians, everywhere in this great land, might be but a handful. They might merely form little islands of professional activity. In moments of stress, when the social pressures remind one of raging ocean storms, we are apt to forget the existence of these islands and the beacon from their lighthouses. But it is the existence of the light on such islands that offers the promise of a fair mooring.

We think of this effort, the book and our total activities, in terms of maintaining connections between such islands, and in terms of building bridges among those of us interested in the individual child, the individual parent and the individual teacher. We want to shape our contribution into an experiment based on our love for freedom and our psychoanalytic knowledge of the mind. That knowledge comes from collaborative research in psychoanalysis and education which can give us the tools for our commitments to society and its new generation. The book is also for those who are willing to swim with us against the tide.

RUDOLF EKSTEIN, PH.D.
and ROCCO L. MOTTO, M.D.

December 22, 1968

PART I: Historical Perspectives

. . . the relationship of psychoanalysis to education is complex. In a first approach the inclination may be to characterize it as one between a basic science and a field of application. Psychoanalytic propositions aim at indicating why human beings behave as they do under given conditions. The educator may turn to these propositions in his attempts to influence human behavior. The propositions then become part of his scientific equipment which naturally include propositions from other basic sciences. *In any relationship between a more general set of propositions and a field of application outside the area of experience from which these propositions were derived, a number of factors must be taken into account. The more general propositions, in this instance those of psychoanalysis, must be formulated in a way that permits their operation in a field, here that of education.* The process of application is likely to act as a test of the validity of the propositions or of the usefulness of their formulation. Hence we are dealing not merely with a process of diffusion of knowledge from a "higher" to a "lower" level, from the more "general" to the "applied" field but with a *process of communication between experts trained in different skills in which cross-fertilization of approaches is likely to occur.*

—ERNST KRIS

CHAPTER 1

Psychoanalysis and Education – An Historical Account

RUDOLF EKSTEIN and ROCCO L. MOTTO

THROUGH MOST OF THE HISTORY of psychoanalysis we find bridges which lead from the area of psychoanalysis to the area of education. There has always been a strong relationship between these two endeavors, although a changing one. The changes occurred both in terms of the readiness of a specific social scene to make use of psychoanalysis in different areas of application, and the readiness of psychoanalysis itself to become available to special fields of application. The degree and the nature of this mutual readiness depend on social as well as on certain scientific issues. It will be our purpose here to trace the historic development of the relation of these two fields in order to learn about the social and scientific climate which gave rise to different experimentation. This paper may thus throw some light on questions that confront us today as we wish to explore the ways in which experts in both fields may be able to collaborate.

Our concern is not merely with the contribution of psychoanalysis to the prevention of pathology, but rather to the facilitation of positive growth. We do not wish to think of education as a preventive force, but rather as a force which releases growth potentials and fosters development and maturation in a positive way. Perhaps our review will allow us to see whether we merely express a semantic difference in a more optimistic mood, or whether we might add another important dimension to psychoanalysis beyond the therapeutic and preventive application.

The first reception of psychoanalysis in medicine, as well as in the social sciences and the field of education, was a hostile one. Consequently, we find a paucity of direct attempts to deal analytically with the child before the first World War, and even fewer attempts to apply analysis to problems of education or parent guidance. Beyond

3

Freud's "*Little Hans*" (1909) and the outstanding exception of Hug-Hellmuth's work, we find but few traces of such interest in the literature which reach into the pre-war period. During the post-war era there was a resumption of psychoanalytic work, and we find suddenly an avalanche of contributions—a situation not unlike the immense growth of psychoanalysis in America after the Second World War. One has the impression that the end of the military holocaust released positive forces permitting the questioning of old educational institutions and methods. The questioning fostered experimentation in the field of education, and thus offered an opportunity for psychoanalysis to extend its contributions.

As we quote from the literature we do not mean to be exhaustive. Instead, we hope to give representative samples in order to follow the psychoanalytic climate as it affects educational experimentation. In Switzerland, an island of peace, Oskar Pfister addressed the pedagogues as early as 1916 in a summer course of the Swiss Pedagogic Society. He spoke to them on the issue "What Does Psychoanalysis Offer to the Educator?" In this address he described psychoanalysis as a form of education and suggested that Freud was a great pedagogue. He referred to psychoanalysis, as did Freud and many others, as *Nacher-ziehung*.

After the war a number of educational experiments, usually in connection with war orphans or with children who faced a variety of difficulties, were made and described by their respective originators. Bernfeld (1921) reports on *Kinderheim Baumgarten*: a "serious experiment with new education." Hoffer collaborated in this pioneering educational experiment in 1919. In an account of Willi Hoffer's contribution to teaching and education, Ekstein[23] reports that Friedjung, a Viennese pediatrician and psychoanalyst, and also one of the Socialists in an enlightened city administration, had reviewed Bernfeld's book and commented on the deep commitment of the author and his colleagues. He described the experimental Kinderheim Baumgarten, an attempt to bring Freud's teaching to an educational community composed of 300 orphaned children. Friedjung maintained that in spite of very unfortunate conditions the effort succeeded. Bernfeld described how a mob of wayward, bitter children was transformed into a community of self-respecting youngsters through the help of psychoanalytically trained educators who were able to effect the mobilization of repressed libido previously fixated in narcissism.

Hoffer, in his last paper (1965), returns to that early effort. He suggested that youth movement experiments, which started in Kinderheim Baumgarten, actually created a blueprint for Kibbutz education. Hoffer, back from the war, had helped Bernfeld open this home for

Jewish war orphans, and he offers a touching account of their passionate struggle against impossible odds. One of Hoffer's paragraphs shows how he has grown beyond the bitterness expressed in Bernfeld's book, and indicates that we frequently face the same struggles today.

What was the outcome of the experiment, one will ask? In fact, those who had come with Bernfeld to Baumgarten, including all the teachers, left the home on the 15th of April, 1920, and parted from the children. It was not possible to carry on without a self-sacrifice beyond our intentions. Bernfeld has given an account of the reasons, as he and we felt and saw them. Throughout the six months of the Bernfeld Baumgarten there was an unending battle between the "administration" and the education staff. Today I would say it was the fault of neither side, but the mésalliance ought never have happened. The two sides had started from opposing viewpoints, and there was a mutual deafness which made communication and understanding impossible, though on the surface we managed to co-operate; the children themselves sensed the gap, and—naturally, we say today—took sides.[43]

Hoffer also states in this paper that Bernfeld's ideas came to life again in Israel's Kibbutz education of the early twenties. He comments that although Bernfeld may be unknown there today, he is one of the architects who produced a blueprint for their educational system, now known throughout the civilized world.

Schmidt (1924) also offers a report about a children's home, one in Moscow, and thus describes "psychoanalytic education in Soviet Russia." Aichhorn's famous Wayward Youth (1925) refers to his experience in a children's home with delinquent children; his experimentation goes back to his pre-analytical period but was understood and interpreted by him after he had received psychoanalytic training. These publications, between 1921 and 1925, refer to work of short duration. In spite of the writers' enthusiasm, which ran parallel to the new spirit in central Europe when revolutions replaced empires with republics, their experiments broke down because of external pressure and the lack of trained personnel. The liberation from dominating leaders led to a new society which Paul Federn, who was then very interested in the application of psychoanalysis to the child, analyzed in a publication of 1919. He described the new social scene as a fatherless society. In this contribution on the psychology of the revolution, he suggested that the father-son motive had suffered the most severe defeat. However, he thought that this motive was so basically and deeply anchored in family education and in inherited feeling deep inside of humanity that it would most likely prevent the success of a completely "fatherless society."[28]

This spirit of the post-war era influenced the thinking of analysts of those years for quite a long time and led to many enthusiastic publications, such as Wittels' The Liberation of the Child (1927), which ends:

> This will take a long time. In carrying out the new plan difficulties and unforeseen problems appear. But the fundamental thought is simple: Leave your children alone. Do not educate them, because you cannot educate them. It might be better if the teachers were to write a thousand times in their copy book, "I should leave the children alone!" instead of having the children write, "During school sessions one is forbidden to speak!" One speaks of the century of the child. But this will begin only when the adults will understand that the children have to learn less from them than they have to learn from the children.[74]

It is easy to see that at the time the basic contribution of psychoanalysis to education was a protest against the old forms of society, as typified by the Victorian age of suppression. Progressive education was seen as a liberation of the instincts, as a struggle against trauma, as favoring laissez-faire, with a minimum of intervention on the part of educators and parents. Much of the literature of those days, such as a contribution by Pfister (1929), was concerned with "the faults of parents":

> The Pädaanalyse (pedagogical analysis) fights, therefore, the education of categorical ordering and forbidding, which requires blind cadaver-like obedience without giving the child understandable reasons and without letting the child understand that the parents act not because of despotic needs, but because they are guided by consideration for the child's welfare.[57]

Those were the days in which there was a struggle against limits, and a constant fear of traumatization. As sophisticated a writer as Bernfeld, to whose credit is the first Psychology of the Infant (1925), sums up infancy as the phase of life which reaches "from the trauma of birth to the trauma of weaning."

It is not only naive enthusiasm as exemplified through Wittels' contribution, but sometimes also the somber recognition of limits of and for the educator which find reflection in the literature. Siegfried Bernfeld's Sisyphus or the Boundaries of Education (1925) describes as the two boundaries the unconscious forces in the child on the one hand, and the social forces on the other. These limit the educator and may frequently give him the feeling of a Sisyphus who faces endless and hopeless tasks. Bernfeld defined education as "the reaction of

Society to the facts of maturation and development." He thus forces us to take a look at societal forces as well as the inner forces of the child in order to move from a naive application of psychoanalysis to a more sophisticated one which includes those societal forces. Those familiar with this book will remember his invention of Citizen Machiavell(i), who was to be elected Minister of Education. Machiavell(i), knowing the insights of modern sociology as well as psychoanalysis, invents an educational system to serve a reactionary society by slowly molding the child into the willing tool of these future anti-Semitic, nationalistic and war-minded rulers.

In the meantime, psychoanalytic training organizations developed. Centers of influence, as far as the application of psychoanalysis to education was concerned, sprang up in many places. The first organized expression of a concentrated effort in relating these two fields was the *Zeitschrift für Psychoanalytische Pädagogik*, which first appeared in October, 1926, with articles by Meng of Stuttgart and Schneider of Riga. In later years we find, among other contributors, Aichhorn, Federn, Anna Freud, Friedjung, Hoffer, Storfer, Wittels of Vienna; Lou Andreas-Salomé of Gottingen; Marie Bonaparte of Paris; Chadwicke, Eder, Barbara Low of London; Ferenczi of Budapest; Furer of Zurich; Landauer of Frankfurt; Bernfeld and Müller-Braunschweig of Berlin; Piaget of Neuchâtel; Vera Schmidt and Wulff of Moscow; Tamm of Stockholm; and Zulliger of Bern. This *Zeitschrift* lasted until the invasion of Austria in 1938; its last editor was Willi Hoffer with the collaboration of Aichhorn, Federn, Anna Freud, Meng and Zulliger. There were at least six issues each year, and during some years the publishers brought out fifteen issues. The spirit of this journal is well described in Schneider's lead article in the first issue:

> Psychoanalysis as a therapeutic procedure, which undertakes to make conscious the unconscious and to restore subsequently the missed order, was always properly considered a pedagogical procedure. One spoke of Nacherziehung, of post-education. It was therefore in the nature of the matter that pedagogues began to utilize psychoanalytic procedures with educational intentions. . . .
>
> After all this we may say: Psychoanalysis serves the pedagogue once as "the science of the unconscious psyche" and enlarges for him the necessary psychological knowledge, and then gives him a new means of education, a procedure which is capable through interventions into the unconscious to bring about psychic order. Its applicability reaches, therefore, mainly into the area of pedagogical methodology. If and how far this methodology can also help determine the questions of goals is not easy to decide. This task reaches far beyond the area of psychology and, therefore, also beyond the area of psychoanalysis.[69]

This first programmatic paper, "The Area of Application of Psychoanalysis for Pedagogics," carried the early enthusiasm which was bringing psychoanalytic insights to the field of education, but it also bore the seeds of theoretical and practical dilemmas. It opened a new field and confronted us with the new questions arising out of these first experiments.

Schneider and many of the early authors, who published in the *Zeitschrift für Psychoanalytische Pädagogik*, tried to differentiate between psychoanalysis and pedagogy. They saw in the one a therapeutic procedure and in the other a technique for education. At the same time, and this was the trend of the time, both procedures were somehow fused. Both were thought to be educational, and no clear boundary lines between them were established. Analysis was seen as post-education, and much of pedagogy was seen as a form of therapy. But because there were many serious attempts at clarification of this issue, this first phase, in which education and therapy were undifferentiated, is better described as phase-dominance than phase-exclusiveness.

The mainstream of interest concerning the application of psychoanalysis in the life of the child was expressed in the late twenties by teachers. Many of them, originally kindergarten or elementary-school teachers, became the first child analysts. Psychoanalytic pedagogy and child analysis, sociologically speaking, derived from the same social matrix, the teaching profession. At that time, much of what was taught to the teachers centered around the early maturation of the child.

We think, for example, of Anna Freud's famous *"Introduction to Psychoanalysis for Teachers"* (1931), her four lectures originally published in 1930 and given to the teachers at the Children's Centers in Vienna. These lectures deal with infantile amnesia and the oedipus complex; the infantile instinct life; the latency period; and the relation between psychoanalysis and pedagogy. She discusses the "definite danger arising from education" and the nature of the restrictions imposed upon the child. She speaks of the psychoanalyst as one "who is engaged in therapeutic work of resolving such inhibitions and disturbances in the development" and who, thus, learns "to know education from its worst side." But she also warns against the exaggeration of this impression. She struggles with and argues against the one-sidedness of such views, trying to take a second look at the positive aspects of education. She describes the work of Aichhorn in his *Wayward Youth*, and tries to outline an educational task which keeps a balance between the danger of the "injurious effect of too great repression" and the equal danger of "the lack of all restraint." She suggests that "the task of a pedagogy based on analytic data is to find a via media between these extremes— that is to say, to allow to each stage in the child's life the right proportion of instinct gratification and instinct restriction." This is a far cry from the previously quoted viewpoint of Wittels in his *Liberation of the Child* in which he seems to indicate that the adults, the teachers, should abdicate their role. Anna Freud suggests that there is not yet analytical pedagogy, but that there are individual educators who are interested in this work.

She sees the main application of analysis to education—we believe that this is also true in the American scene today—as experimental and as a hopeful indication for the future. But she also maintains "that even today psychoanalysis does three things for pedagogics." She refers to the criticism of existing educational methods; the increase of the teacher's knowledge of human beings, including an understanding of the relations between the child and the educator; and, finally, his knowledge of the use of analysis as a therapeutic method for those children who have suffered injuries "which are inflicted . . . during the process of education."

It can be seen now that the temper of the times from the twenties to the thirties changed the psychoanalytically oriented educator. He was no longer stressing almost exclusively the liberation of the instincts and the crusade against the faults of parents and educators. Instead, he was beginning to stress the creation of an optimum situation in which his orientation was to help the child grow toward maturity on a middle road which avoided the pathological traumata of too much strictness as well as unlimited indulgence. This new trend is reflected also in Anna Freud's discussion of the concept of the rejecting mother (1955).[33]

The first application of psychoanalysis to the field of education, as we note in the new efforts following the First World War, was an expression of protest, a demand for the new. The second step was one in which specific techniques were evaluated through actual application.

Burlingham described this new phase of psychoanalytic pedagogy in 1937 when commenting on "the problem of the psychoanalytic teacher":

> In recent years the number of those called by us "psychoanalytic pedagogues" has steadily increased. All these pedagogues have gone through their own analysis; they have been introduced to psychoanalytic theory through theoretical courses; and they have participated in seminars where they could report difficult cases from their children's groups and where they could try together with an analyst to apply the fundamental principles of analysis to their practical work. The pedagogues work in this way on the slow development of psychoanalytic pedagogy.[14]

In her paper in the training course for psychoanalytic pedagogues (*Lehrgang für Psychoanalytische Pädagogen*), Burlingham describes her accumulated experience in training educators. The first difficulty which she reported stemmed from the original, initial phase of application of psychoanalysis to education—the counterpressure against outmoded repressive educational techniques. The second difficulty was one which had to do with the misconception of the function of the pedagogue; he identified with his own therapist and saw himself as a child analyst rather than as an educator. Interpretation was the only reliable tool for him, and the role of education was seen as a therapeutic one. The third misconception which Miss Burlingham discussed could be called the "parent-blaming doctrine." According to this doctrine every educational problem would be resolved, not through the educational techniques of the teacher, but through analysis of the parent and manipulation of the environment.

The discussions in the next few years attempted to examine these three issues and to offer suggestions for the necessary differentiation.

We mention papers such as Steff Bornstein's on "*Misunderstandings in the Application of Psychoanalysis to Pedagogy*" (1937), and Editha Sterba's on "*School and Educational Guidance*" (1936). These attempt to tackle the problem concerning the means by which the educator may draw knowledge from the field of psychoanalysis but not apply himself as a child analyst. Sterba's paper summarized the situation with:

> It must not be stressed that in comparison to child analysis these interpretations (in education) are altogether incomplete and too much related to the situation. But the dynamic changes, which developed in consequence of these interpretations, demonstrate that in terms of that which was to be achieved, they were effective and sufficient in spite of their incompleteness. For the goals of the teacher which were decisive for the cases discussed, these interpretations did suffice. We must guard ourselves, of course, against believing that children so educated could be called "analyzed." We have simply gained some insights into the actual symptomatic picture, nevertheless sufficient to make possible for the child to continue in school and to function in his home environment.
>
> The fruitfulness of such collective work between the analyzed educator and the child analyst cannot be doubted after what has been discussed.[71]

According to this differentiation, child analysts would make complete use of interpretation. The analytically oriented pedagogue would resort to interpretive means only in relation to the situational crisis, and then only as much as was necessary to help the child with the current educational task. Such differentiation, however, does not clearly explain the qualitative difference between the two fields. It refers more to problems of education as we encounter them in the kindergarten, nursery-school situation, the home or, perhaps, in the primary grades. It does not, therefore, help us to relate much of our psychoanalytic insights to problems of education in which there is a didactic task; in which the educator is primarily a teacher. It also continues to stress primarily the incidents in the life of the child in which there are symptomatic disturbances, the beginnings of pathological crises, rather than ordinary education.

During this period, then, psychoanalysis offered the educator inspiration, identification and an opportunity for the critique of available techniques. It facilitated the task of creating a new technique without yet having accomplished the job. This new demand for scientific techniques of education was well expressed by Erikson when, in 1930, he said:

> It is surely no coincidence that the desire for a science of education should appear on the scene at the moment when, in the form of psychoanalysis, the truth of the healing power of self-knowledge is again establishing itself in the world. And to this truth much has been added since the times of Socrates, namely, a method. If education earnestly seeks to rebuild on a new conscious basis of knowledge and intelligence, then it must demand radical progress to the point where clear vision results in human adjustment. Modern enlightenment can best achieve this through psychoanalysis.[25]

Many of the concepts of psychoanalysis were applied in individual remedial work with children as well as in the classroom situation. The papers of Zulliger (1926, 1930), Redl (1932, 1934) and Buxbaum (1931, 1936) apply analytic understanding to the classroom situation.

Anna Freud, has called to the attention of the authors a similar development in England. She wrote us in 1962 that "there are very few people who have actually applied psychoanalysis to classroom teaching. But there is one man here in London who has done so constantly all through his career. He began work as a university teacher of psychology and then taught for the London County Council where he became the inspector of elementary schools for a large London area. I met him soon after arrival in London in 1938; and I was amazed at his grasp of psychoanalytic principles and their usefulness for education."[34] She referred to J. C. Hill. Now a retired inspector of schools in London, Hill was actually the man who arranged Anna Freud's first public address to teachers in London in October, 1938. Some of his recent work is contained in this volume. We find that his approaches are very much influenced by the theory which was prevalent during the first

```
Admission No. 140

          LONDON  COUNTY  COUNCIL.

     Lectures and classes for teachers, 1938-39.

               ADMIT BEARER
      to the course of three lectures on

               PSYCHOLOGY
                   by
               MISS A. FREUD

                   at
   The Central School of Arts and Crafts, Southampton
                Row, W.C.1.
   THURSDAYS, at 6 p.m. beginning 27th OCTOBER, 1938.
```

phase which we are discussing, although the actual practical applications are very much in accord with our current interests. In order to understand fully the historical impact of this man, we want to quote from a 1926 publication of his:

Freud is sometimes spoken of by psychoanalysts as the "Darwin of the mind." The writer of this book is not a practising psychoanalyst; he has little experience of abnormal human beings, and on some of Freud's work he is not competent to express an opinion. But he has applied Freud's main hypotheses to the study of normal human conduct, and the results have been so illuminating that he has no hesitation in subscribing to the view that Freud's work is the greatest individual contribution that has ever been made to psychology, and a contribution with which parents and teachers should be acquainted at once.[38]

In 1935, when associated with the University of London in training teachers, he wrote:

The child should grow in knowledge as a tree grows, and not as a wall grows, with every brick well and truly laid. The student in training as a teacher should grow in knowledge in the same way. It is hoped that this book will give him some fresh views about education and will help him to gather together his own experiences and the experiences of his tutors and colleagues.[39]

He has told the present authors how difficult it was to carry on as a trainer of teachers, especially when he had to confront his own superiors with views often entirely different from theirs. This passionate struggle, of course, is not yet over, and Hill's words of 1935 might well have been written in 1969:

These are great claims to make for the new psychology and, of course, they have to be proved. Freud and his disciples have tried to prove them and have met in many quarters with derision. But since several English and American psychologists of high standing have investigated Freud's work and proclaimed the truth of, at least, a great part of it, the problem is receiving serious consideration from educated people. It is this more hopeful atmosphere which encourages the present writer to try to explain to parents and teachers some of the more important aspects of Freud's work. The bitter opposition which his work has aroused will not surprise those who have studied the history of any of the sciences. It is almost a general rule that the great scientific discoveries have been opposed for years just as Freud's work has been opposed. There is a special difficulty, however, about accepting Freud's work: It unmasks humbug in our daily lives. It shows up the skeletons in the cupboards, and proves that honesty is the best policy—truly an uncomfortable discovery for most of us. But eloquent protests will not save us. If Freud has equipped others with the means to see through the cupboard doors, the sooner we examine his work, the better.[39]

Hill, like many psychoanalysts and psychoanalytic educators, speaks out of a spirit of humanism, a spirit which pervades the climate of psychoanalysis. Psychoanalytic insights and theories are meant to be free of value judgments but that scientific standard cannot be used in the applications of these insights. Hill is a part of this humanistic spirit.

The Viennese group started to experiment with kindergarten systems, with elementary schools, as well as with infant observation. The occupation of Austria, part of the upheavals in Europe which finally led to the Second World War, destroyed much of this training work and opened our eyes more fully to the relationship of social systems to the problem of education and the applicability of psychoanalysis as a social force. Bernfeld's warnings in Sisyphus were now being understood as, later, the frightful prediction of Orwell's 1984 would be, but Bernfeld was not the only one to relate psychoanalysis, education and the social system.

Alice Balint's book, The Early Years of Life—a Psychoanalytic Study, originally published in Hungary in 1931, republished in England in 1953 and here in 1954, makes this point most eloquently. Her ending sums up this phase of the relationship between psychoanalysis and education:

In conclusion, a few words as to the relation between education and civilization. The study of various people shows that there can hardly be any method of education which is not practicable. From the greatest imaginable freedom to the most cruel tyranny, everything has been practiced and the children have borne it. It is only the particular civilizations themselves that cannot tolerate a deviant system of education. There is no absolute pedagogy, no absolute mental hygiene. Changes in a civilization must be underpinned by corresponding educational measures, if they are to last. It follows conversely that reforms in education necessarily bring about a change in the civilization, even when that was not the conscious intention. For every improvement affects the whole of a given situation. Hence pedagogics is the most revolutionary of all sciences. Perhaps the inconspicuous "improvements" in methods of education are the prime mover in cultural evolution, for every educational system has its defects and tends towards change.[3]

Such ideas which forced us to look at the "reality" of the child as part of a dynamic, ever-changing social reality have led to many studies. Perhaps the best-known exponent of the attempt to understand educational systems culturally as well as analytically has been Erikson. In *Childhood and Society* (1950), he examined educational systems of primitive tribes and reflected on the concept of identity in American, German and Russian society.

As far as publications are concerned, there was a comparative void between 1938 and 1945, the end of the Second World War. However, some of the early group undertook to understand the psychological elements of democratic and totalitarian education. One such was Ekstein (1939), who compared educational devices used in totalitarian systems with those applicable to a democratic society.

The comparative silence in these seven years is no indication that either the analysts or the analytically oriented educators had given up their work The European analytical organizations had been destroyed, and the attempt to build up equivalents in England and in the United States had been hampered, of course, by the war. Two volumes, published toward the end of the conflagration, are lasting testimonies to this effort. Both volumes, by Anna Freud and Dorothy Burlingham, describe the educational and research work in three war-time nurseries in England.

No sooner did the war end than we find, this time in the United States, a new publication, the heir, as it seems to us, of the *Zeitschrift für Psychoanalytische Pädagogik*. We refer to *The Psychoanalytic Study of the Child*. Perhaps even the change in name is important: the stress of the earlier journal was on application while the stress of this new annual is on study, on research. The early enthusiasm from the days of the "Psychoanalytic Movement (Psychoanalytische Bewegung)" was transformed into organized scientific work. Hoffer, one of the prime participants in the *Lehrgang* in Vienna, wrote on "Psychoanalysis and Education" in the first issue of the new annual (1945). His was essentially a descriptive study of those early days, and he, too, mentions that, beginning with the days of Hug-Hellmuth, the attempt was made to disentangle analytic and educational processes. He speaks of Melanie Klein's negative attitude toward education, and he writes of the "crying need for longitudinal research in personality development" in order to help the educator acquire more insight into the child.

The first issue contained a variety of papers by analysts who originally belonged to the central European group and who, now, participated in the development of psychoanalysis as well as its application to education in a new country. We think of Fenichel's paper, "Means of Education," and Editha Sterba's contribution, "Interpretation and Education," as well as Erikson's papers on two Indian tribes and Edith Buxbaum's on "Transference and Group Formation (all in 1945). A paper by Ruben (1945), "A Contribution to the Education of Parents," seems to have been the beginning of a lasting interest as reflected in some of her 1960 work.

This second phase seems to differ vastly from the first. We must remember the fact that the social scene for psychoanalysis is a different one. Analysts in Europe worked primarily in private practice; had few clinical facilities nor any social-agency structure; and did not work in close contact with general psychiatry. In the United States, psychoanalysts work hand-in-hand with psychiatrists, clinical psychologists and social workers. We find, therefore, that the relationship to the teaching profession and to school systems is a rather different one. Many of the original child analysts came from the teaching profession in Europe, while the American training system made no provisions for such opportunities.

The colleges for teachers' training had comparatively little use for psychoanalysis. This may well have much to do with the fact that progressive educational theory and philosophy were influenced in the United States by John Dewey, whose work was compared with that of Freud in a recent volume by Levitt (1960), *Freud and Dewey*. Oberndorf (1953), in his history of psychoanalysis in America, actually believes that we owe Dewey a great deal for his work which made the country ready for analysis:

> The third reason for the widespread acceptance of psychoanalysis is due to another philosopher whose theories affected education fundamentally and radically. In all psychotherapy the re-educative factor plays an important, perhaps an indispensable, part. Just at the time when the new psychotherapy, psychoanalysis, was slowly but surely affecting American psychiatry, a powerful figure advancing a new theory in the educational field was making his bid for recognition in New York City. In 1904 John Dewey became Professor of Philosophy at Columbia University, and for the next 25

years his ideas about education dominated the instruction of students at Columbia's Teachers' College. Dewey, greatly influenced by James' pragmatic philosophy, regarded James as a pioneer in his perception that experiences "an intimate union of emotion and knowledge." So Dewey in the theory of education insisted that learning is an experience of individual experimentation to be opened by those who participate in it. The basis for learning in a child should allow a maximum freedom of initiative rather than the absorption of facts from books or teachers.

The widely scattered alumni of Teachers' College have introduced this form of teaching through experimentation values through which childhood growth could be molded. The educators in schools, public and private, elementary and collegiate, were ready to welcome and to understand the psychoanalytic psychiatrist as an aid and co-worker in preparing students for adaptation in the democratic society. They found that interpretive psychiatry assisted in solving the problems of both normal and deviant cases.[52]

We do not quite share Oberndorf's optimism. Rather, we believe that the clinical application of psychoanalysis, the stress on its therapeutic application, has created a social problem which is different from the one in central Europe, and actually should be described as a second phase. In the first phase it was almost possible to think of analysis as post-education, as a kind of progressive pedagogy. But in the second phase, psychoanalysis has become so much a part of the medical psychiatric scene, that only the therapeutic application is stressed. It is almost forgotten during the training of the physician that there are many applications of psychoanalysis beyond the therapeutic one. We find, therefore, that the analyst, the psychiatrist, clinical psychologist and the social worker look at education, as well as at all other activities, in terms of therapy or prevention. Many of the teachers who become interested in analysis ask for help with their deviant problems. If they do identify with psychoanalytic science, it is as "educational therapists."

Only the first volume of The Psychoanalytic Study of the Child contains a group of papers under the sub-heading "Problems of Education." In the second volume (1946), this sub-heading changes to "Problems of Education and Sociology," and contains the contributions of Erikson and Peller, but later volumes have given up this sub-division. We read, rather, about therapeutic nursery schools, frequently attached to child guidance clinics, and most of the experiments with analytically oriented education are now basically seen as therapeutic ventures. Psychoanalytically oriented educators are now frequently attached to clinical institutions, such as child guidance clinics, therapeutic nurseries, residential treatment centers and children's hospitals. The contact with the ordinary school system is a comparatively peripheral one which serves, at best, as a bridge for the severely disturbed child for whom treatment is needed. The primary interest is the deviant child who needs treatment and the cry is for prevention. Thus a situation has arisen which seems to leave little room for the educator except as a frustrated, second-class therapist or as a seeker of training opportunities ultimately leading to the clinical field. A good example for the development of this point of view can be found in a comment by Alpert (1941) in her paper on "Education as Therapy":[2]

> Educational group therapy may be considered a period of intensification of an intelligent educational program, as it should be conducted from day to day. An intelligent educational program is one in which the subject matter and the approach to it are sufficiently challenging to the children to afford them ample opportunity for sublimation; one in which the teacher is as interested in the personality of the pupils as she is in the subject she is teaching; one in which group discussions are conducted informally and purposively. Such an educational program is as feasible in public schools as in private schools.
>
> While planning for mental health should be a requirement of all responsible education, the progressive type of school has a special responsibility in approximating this goal, because in it the personality of the child is encouraged to reveal itself more completely and is, therefore, more accessible to mental hygiene through education. Though most schools gravely acknowledge this responsibility, opportunities for mental hygiene inherent in education have scarcely been tapped. The mental hygiene program usually operates more indirectly through teacher-child relationship, disciplines, home-school relationship. *This paper will discuss a more direct and specialized use of the educational setting for the purpose of mental health.* (Italics ours.)

A similar stress on the mental health aspect was expressed in 1953 by Blos in a paper on "Aspects of Mental Health in Teaching and Learning," as well as in Berman's "Mental Hygiene for Educators" (1953) and Weinreb's "Report of an Experience in the Application of Dynamic Psychiatry in Education" (1963).

This attitude of helping some teachers to move toward psychoanalysis but ultimately leading to their identification with its therapeutic aspect, was also expressed by Pearson in his volume, *Psychoanalysis and the Education of the Child*, published in 1954. His recommendations remind one of the *Lehrgang für Psychoanalytische Pädagogen*. While one cannot help but identify with his essential purpose, the creation of a more permanent bridge between psychoanalysis and education, one also realizes that the original problem of differentiation is not yet resolved. He says:

> It would seem to me that all psychoanalytic institutes which give instruction in psychoanalysis of children and adolescents could increase their services to the community by carefully selecting certain students to be students in the institute. These teachers might be chosen partly from among instructors in schools of education and partly from those in the school system itself. They should be given exactly the same instruction as are the psychiatric students in the course of psychoanalysis of children. They should have the same preliminary personal analysis and the same theoretical instruction, and should attend the same clinical and technical seminars. They should conduct a supervised psychoanalysis of at least one adult and three or four children. In this way they would learn by theory and practice the principles of psychoanalysis. When a teacher had completed such a course, he can return to the school as a reputable consulting psychoanalyst. If after completing his course he should desire to devote himself entirely to psychoanalysis, as many pediatricians who have had psychoanalytic training have done, then the institute should demand that he limit his practice to the psychoanalysis of children in cases referred by a physician-psychoanalyst and under his supervision. If the personal psychoanalysis has been really successful—and no such student should be permitted to complete his training otherwise—the teacher's increased ability to adjust to reality will enable him to accept these necessary restrictions with good grace and in good faith. There are relatively more teachers than physicians who show an intuitive ability to understand and work with children, and so the practice of psychoanalysis of children would actually be benefited by this procedure. It would be hoped, however, that teachers with such intensive training would prefer to employ their knowledge of psychoanalysis in the field of education rather than in the practice of psychoanalytic therapy. As I said before, the procedure I have suggested would not lower but raise the standards of the American Psychoanalytic Association.[54]

This point of view favors utilizing the resources of people who are interested in children and who show intuitive talents to supply a gifted group of child therapists. In recent years such child psychotherapeutic training programs have been started. The best-known example is the Hampstead program for child psychotherapists, conducted so successfully and creatively by Anna Freud and her collaborators. In addition, there are some beginnings in the United States, such as the program in Cleveland. Nevertheless, this does not solve the problem which we are now posing, the problem of strengthening education as a positive and creative force.

Tracing the history of psychoanalysis and education reveals, then, two essentially different phases. The first phase occurred in Europe. Its main characteristics were enthusiasm, protest, and the slow beginning of the application of psychoanalysis to the training of child analysts and pedagogues. This last-named characteristic was the basis of questioning the differences between education and child analysis. The first phase, then, was one in which psychoanalysis was considered an educational procedure.

The second phase, after the Second World War, was characterized by experimentation in Great Britain and, particularly, the United States. The psychoanalytic study of the child, no longer in need of the early protest movement, has become more fully a serious professional and scientific issue. Technical questions have been raised, but much of what has been developing in America and in England has been either in the field of therapeutic endeavors or in the field of prevention. Frequently the teacher sees himself, or is invited by us to see himself, as an educational therapist. The accent has changed from analysis as post-education to education as prevention of emotional illness, but some of the basic issues of differentiation still concern us.

Is it possible now to think of a third phase in the making, a phase in which there are two distinct fields, both benefiting from psychoanalysis as a scientific body of knowledge? Such future development was anticipated by Kris, when, as early as 1948, he wrote "On Psychoanalysis and Education." He envisioned "a process of communication between experts trained in different skills in which cross-fertilization of approaches is likely to occur."[48]

The influence of psychoanalysis on the school teacher and on modern education started, of course, with the deviant child. With the introduction of the school psychologist and with the focus on finding techniques which would be of service to the group of deviant children, psychoanalysis was a constant force on the educational scene. This concern for the deviant child has in recent years been quite well summarized in two volumes. The first of these, edited by Nelson B. Henry, called *Mental Health in Modern Education* (1955), is a volume in which there are many friendly comments on the contribution of psychoanalysis. One of its contributors, Olson, Dean of the School of Education at the University of Michigan, had already expressed himself on the psychoanalytic contribution to education. He wrote, "Originally designed for work with children who are ill, dynamic conceptions have proliferated so as to dominate or influence many modern approaches to the understanding and education of children in general.[53] His book (1949) makes much use of basic psychoanalytic knowledge, but its focus is on the achievement of mental health.

Another contribution, *Professional School Psychology*, was edited by Monroe G. and Gloria B. Gottsegen (1960).[36] This volume is primarily concerned with the role of the school psychologist, and has a strong bias, of course, in the direction of psychotherapy and diagnostic testing. Its articles deal with different illnesses of children in addition to the adjustment problems of the major deviant groups of children.

A recent volume of Krugman (1958), *Orthopsychiatry and the School*, expresses the same spirit and sees the psychoanalyst as a consultant in the school system, with the diagnostic ability to prescribe therapy when called for. He is not seen as a potential collaborator for educational problems with the average, the so-called normal child.

But there is a function beyond the issue of mental health that the school must fulfill. Peller's discussion (1956) brings us nearer to a clarification of this task. She says that:

> good education is not characterized by its degree of permissiveness or strictness . . . The pendulum may swing all the way back from over-indulgence to strict discipline and still miss the essential. A school may be very permissive, take a very lenient attitude toward some of the child's instinctual needs, and consider academic work a necessary evil, something that children naturally dislike. In consequence, it will postpone academic learning, reduce the study load, and for the ineducable rest impose passive acceptance upon the child.[56]

She speaks about the need to cathect activities and interests and she describes the process of sublimation. She discusses the libidinal charge on activities, be they collective activities or solitary pursuit. She thus includes, beyond the problem of the interpersonal relationships, the learning task of the school and leads us to techniques to help the children meet this task. Education is not only seen in terms of mental health and the prevention of ill health, but in the didactic terms of growth, enrichment and meeting tasks of life. The educational problem moves, then, out of the area of mental health or ill health toward the problem of learning, the acquisition of knowledge and skills. It seems to us that the new dimension which is thus created must lead to a new task in the rapprochement between psychoanalysis and education.

Lili A. Peller's professional life covered all the phases in the relationship between psychoanalysis and education.[24] She originally came from the field of education and was one of the pioneers of those exciting days of psychoanalytic ferment and courageous experimentation. Anna Freud suggested this in a letter to Ekstein:

> The first meetings of my colleagues and myself with Lili Peller were most exciting ones. This was in Vienna, in the 1930's, i.e., when we

were intent on forging links between psychoanalysis and education. At that time Lili Peller had already built up a model nursery school which combined the best elements of the Montessori method with the application of the most important principles of psychoanalytic child psychology. Her work in that setting was admirable and acted as an inspiration. We formed contacts then which continued on a different level after she had become a psychoanalyst herself, and which did not cease to exist until her death.

It is important to stress that Peller's contributions were not restricted to offering psychoanalytic understanding of and to educators. They also went in the other direction and helped psychoanalysts learn much about education. One of her first papers was published in a 1932 special issue of *Zeitschrift für Psychoanalytische Pädagogik*. It was on "Playing and Games" and was concerned with the most important theories of play— pre-analytic attempts to understand the phenomenon of play, based largely on the work of Groot. Peller understood these theories within the context of nineteenth-century psychology, which explained all human play activities as being based on reason and utility. It did not encompass the view that play was in the service of instinctual forces or of unconscious conflict. However, as she subsequently identified with the psychoanalytic viewpoint, she integrated with it the best ideas from educational philosophy, as well as Montessori's findings. She thus created a synthesis between the most progressive educational thinking and the discoveries of psychoanalysis. Some of her valuable contributions add much to our understanding of the nature of play and the nature of language.

Influenced by Buhler in Vienna, and collaborator of such renowned teachers as Waelder, Erikson, the Sterbas, Anna Freud and many others, Peller directed a teacher's training school and worked in Vienna, Jerusalem and New York. Her paper published in this volume (chapter 25) was authored in a Reiss-Davis training institute in Los Angeles. All she left us of her impressive talk is the basic outline which does not fully communicate her warmth, her polished writing, her careful work as a scientific investigator. She had promised to prepare an article for publication, but death intervened. This, then, is an unfinished paper, to inspire those of us who take up her work in order to continue it.

In work done in 1955 but published later, Gerhart and Maria Piers speak about learning theories and the psychoanalytic process. They discuss different kinds of learning and submit that analytic insights and constructs, combined with what we can learn from the learning theories, offer us three basic models of learning: "Learning by repetition; by insight, and learning through identification."[60] Actually, all three forms of learning can be observed in the therapeutic process, and will find their equivalent in the kind of learning that goes on in education.

This theoretical contribution is followed by a practical book, *Growing Up with Children* (1966). For parents and educators, this work discusses major problems of child rearing as understood by the modern psychoanalytic educator. A similar volume, written for teachers and administrators, has been contributed by Barman (1968). Entitled *Mental Health in Classroom and Corridor*, it would seem to be connected with the second phase in the relationship between psychoanalysis and education. The contents, however, are in the direction of the future in trying to apply analytic understanding to the school setting; the focus of the book is on education, positive education, rather than simply on preventive techniques.

The question as to how one is to combine existing capacities for learning at different age levels with existing techniques of teaching seems to be the issue for him who wishes to develop insights into processes of learning and teaching. The authors' hope, of course, is that the contribution contained in the other chapters of this volume will give strong support to the development of that third phase in which there is a more sophisticated consideration of the difference between education and psychotherapy, and in which the stress is on developing collaborative methods. Earlier, we mentioned books by Barman and Piers which go in that direction. And it seems to us that Bettelheim's volumes, *Dialogues with Mothers* (1962) and *The Informed Heart* (1960), are also written in that vein. They stem from personal human suffering and from work not only with very sick children and their parents but from experimentation in normal child care and education. In addition, there is Redl's book, *When We Deal with Children* (1966), which consolidates his work of many years, and which goes far beyond his earlier volume with Wattenberg (1951) and its emphasis on mental hygiene. The newer book deals with experimentation and research in teaching techniques as applied to both the normal and the abnormal child. Redl's first publications date back to the early thirties and he is one of the few contributors in the field who has both lived through as well as pushed the historical development which we have been describing.

The psychoanalyst may then well be the resource person for the educator. The analyst can help the teacher use psychoanalytic insights and constructs in order to apply them to a process which is not therapeutic in nature but has as its purpose, training and education, the acquisition of knowledge, skills and social attitudes. The task of the educator is not to resolve unconscious conflicts, nor to cure the symptom of the deviant child, but rather to utilize analytic insights toward the teaching process.

So far, most of our experiences in collaboration with teachers and therapists have concerned children who were in both processes at the same time. Buxbaum, in Seattle, is engaged in such a collaborative study with co-workers in the teaching profession. Many schools for children whose problems do not permit them to use the public-school system work with analysts and clinicians on a similar level. We are concerned with the question of whether a third phase could be developed. In this phase, the collaboration between teacher and psychoanalyst could lead to the development of positive teaching techniques, rather than merely the avoidance of mental health risks or the fostering of good mental health.

It was in 1909 that Freud published the first analysis of a child. The study of Little Hans is the beginning of a powerful scientific and social influence on modern education. Freud's discussion of this case leads to:

> Hitherto education has only set itself the task of controlling or, it would often be more proper to say, of suppressing the instincts. The results have been by no means gratifying, and where the process has succeeded it has only been to the advantage of a small number of favored individuals, who have not been required to suppress their instincts. Nor has anyone inquired by what means and at what cost the suppression of the inconvenient instinct has been achieved. Supposing now that we substitute another task for this one, and aim instead at making the individual capable of becoming a civilized and useful member of society with the least possible sacrifice of his own activity; in that case the information gained by psychoanalysis, upon the origin of pathogenic complexes and upon the nucleus of every nervous affection, can claim with justice that it deserves to be regarded by educators as an invaluable guide in their conduct toward children. What practical conclusions may follow from this, and how far experience may justify the application of those conclusions within our present social system, are matters which I leave to the examination and decision of others.[35]

The third phase that we talk about is the envisioned collaboration between teachers and analysts, deriving applied principles from the same generic body of psychoanalytic knowledge. Whether it may actually lead to the development of new techniques; to new forms of collaboration; to a concept which includes, not only therapy and prevention, but also techniques which will more fully "enable the individual to take part in culture and to achieve this with the smallest loss of original energy" remains an open question. Since the Second World War, we have seen that in many places in Europe much of the original achievements described in the first part of this paper has disappeared. We must realize, consequently, that this third phase will depend, in part, on the strength and the interest of analysts who will encourage such development and participate in it.

One of the present authors has indicated in "Reflections on Parallels in the Therapeutic and the Social Process" how the applicability of discoveries and, sometimes, the very discoveries themselves, seem to be related to the Zeitgeist, to the ups and downs of history. We have seen educational techniques more readily influenced by psychoanalysis and by psychological considerations whenever society is, relatively, relaxed. In such periods there may be social experimentation, including attempts to discover better means of education. In times of acute stress, we pay less attention to the individual; we speak of crash programs, in which education of the individual child is subordinated to goals which are frequently far beyond the interest of the individual child. Thus, this may not be a good time to attempt to predict the third phase.

Moreover, it is well to remember that whenever one describes historical trends for an open or an implied purpose, one must learn to cope with the danger of interpreting the past in the shadow of one's wishes for the future rather than in the light of actual reality. But even remembering this, one must acknowledge that seemingly impossible, almost Utopian tasks are sometimes made feasible through the inspiration of leaders.

BIBLIOGRAPHY

1. Aichhorn, August. *Wayward Youth*. Leipzig, Vienna, Zurich: International Psychoanalytic Publishers, 1925.
2. Alpert, Augusta. "Education as Therapy." *Psychoanalytic Quarterly*, 1941, 10:468.
3. Balint, Alice. *The Early Years of Life—A Psychoanalytic Study*. New York: Basic Books, Inc., 1954.
4. Barman, Alicerose S. *Mental Health in Classroom and Corridor*. Racine, Wisconsin: Western Publishing Co., Inc., 1968.
5. Berman, L. "Mental Hygiene for Educators: Report on an Experiment Using a Combined Seminar and Group Psychotherapy Approach." *Psychoanalytic Review*, 1953, 40:319.
6. Bernfeld, Siegfried. *Kinderheim Baumgarten* (The Baumgarten Children's Home—A Report on a Serious Experiment in Modern Education). Berlin: Judische Verlag, 1921.
7. ———. *The Psychology of the Infant*. Vienna: Springer, 1925.
8. ———. *Sisyphos oder die Grenzen der Erziehung* (Sisyphus or the Boundaries of Education). Leipzig, Vienna: Internationaler Psychoanalytischer Verlag, 1925.
9. Bettelheim, Bruno. *The Informed Heart—Autonomy in a Mass Age*. Glencoe, Illinois: Free Press, 1960.
10. ———. *Dialogues with Mothers*. New York: Free Press of Glencoe, 1962.

11. Blos, Peter. "Aspects of Mental Health in Teaching and Learning." *Mental Hygiene*, 1953, 37:555.
12. Bornstein, Steff. "Misunderstandings in the Application of Psychoanalysis to Pedagogy." *Zeitschrift für Psychoanalytische Pädagogik*, 1937, 11:81.
13. Bruner, Jerome S. *The Process of Education*. Cambridge, Mass.: Harvard University Press, 1961.
14. Burlingham, Dorothy. "Problem of the Psychoanalytic Educator." *Zeitschrift für Psychoanalytische Pädagogik*, 1937, 11:91.
15. Buxbaum, Edith. "Question Periods in a Class." *Zeitschrift für Psychoanalytische Pädagogik*, 1931, 5:263.
16. ————. Problems of Group Psychology in the Schoolroom." *Zeitschrift für Psychoanalytische Pädagogik*, 1936, 10:215.
17. ————. *Your Child Makes Sense*. New York: International Universities Press, 1949.
18. Ekstein, Rudolf. "A Refugee Teacher Looks on Democratic and Fascist Education." *Education*, October, 1939: 101.
19. ————. "Reflections on Parallels in the Therapeutic and the Social Process." *Values in Psychotherapy*. Charlotte Buhler, editor. New York: Free Press of Glencoe, 1962, p. 181.
20. ————. "The Boundary Line between Education and Psychotherapy." *Annual Report*, Los Angeles: Reiss-Davis Clinic for Child Guidance, 1960-61, p. 14.
21. ————. "Siegfried Bernfeld—1892-1953: Sisyphus or the Boundaries of Education." In *Psychoanalytic Pioneers*. Franz Alexander, Samuel Eisenstein and Martin Grotjahn, editors. New York: Basic Books, Inc., 1966, p. 415.
22. ————. "J. C. Hill's Psychoanalytic Contributions to Teaching." *Reiss-Davis Clinic Bulletin*, 1966, 1:14.
23. ————. "Willi Hoffer's Contribution to Teaching and Education." *Reiss-Davis Clinic Bulletin*, 1968, 1:4.
24. ————. "Lili E. Peller's Psychoanalytic Contributions to Teaching." *Reiss-Davis Clinic Bulletin*, 1967, 1:6.
25. Erikson, Erik H. "Psychoanalysis and the Future of Education." *Psychoanalytic Quarterly*, 1935, 4:50.
26. ————. "Ego Development and Historical Change." *Psychoanalytic Study of the Child*, 1946, 2:359.
27. ————. *Childhood and Society*. New York: Norton and Co., 1950.
28. Federn, Paul. "On the Psychology of Revolution; the Fatherless Society." *Der Aufsteig, Neue Zeit-und Streitschriften*, 1919, 12-13, Vienna: Anzengruber, 29 pp.
29. Fenichel, Otto. "Means of Education." *Psychoanalytic Study of the Child*, 1945, 1:281.
30. Freud, Anna. *Introduction to Psychoanalysis for Teachers*. London: Allen and Unwin, 1931.
31. ———— and Dorothy Burlingham. *War and Children*. New York: Medical War Books, 1943.
32. ———— and Dorothy Burlingham. *Infants without Families*. London: Allen and Unwin, 1943.
33. ————. *An Inquiry into the Concept of the Rejecting Mother*. New York: Child Welfare League of America, February, 1955.
34. ————. *Personal Communication*, 1962.
35. Freud, Sigmund. "The Analysis of a Phobia in a Five-Year-Old Boy." *Collected Works*. Standard Edition, 10, London: Hogarth Press, 1955.

36. Gottsegen, Monroe G. and Gloria B., editors. *Professional School Psychology*. New York: Grune and Stratton, 1960.
37. Henry, Nelson B. *Mental Health in Modern Education*. Chicago: University of Chicago Press, 1955.
38. Hill, J. C. *Dreams and Education*. London: Methuen and Co., 1926.
39. ———. *The Teacher in Training*. London: Allen and Unwin, 1935.
40. ———. "A New Technique of Teaching." Presidential Address, National Association of Inspectors of Schools and Educational Organizers. Annual Conference, London, 6th, 7th and 8th October, 1938.
41. ———. "Freud's Influence on Education." Presidential Address, Annual Conference of National Association of Inspectors of Schools and Educational Organizers. Annual Conference, London, 8th October, 1949.
42. Hoffer, Willi. "Psychoanalytic Education." *Psychoanalytic Study of the Child*, 1945, 1:293.
43. ———. "Siegfried Bernfeld and 'Jerubbaal.'" *Year Book X of the Leo Baeck Institute, London*, 1965, p. 150.
44. Hug-Hellmuth, Hermine von. "Analysis of a Dream of a 5 1/2-Year-Old Boy" (Analyse eines Traumes eines funfeinhalbjahrigen). *Zentralblatt für Psychoanalyse und Psychotherapie*, 1912, 2:122.
45. ———. *A Study of the Mental Life of the Child*. James J. Putnam and Mabel Stevens, translators. Washington: Nervous and Mental Diseases Publishing Co., 1919.
46. ———. "On the Technique of Child-Analysis." *International Journal of Psychoanalysis* (Rosalie Gabler and Barbara Low, translators), 1921, 2:287.
47. ———. *A Young Girl's Diary*. Eden and Cedar Paul, translators. London: Allen and Unwin; New York: Thomas Seltzer, 1921.
48. Kris, Ernst. "On Psychoanalysis and Education." *American Journal of Orthopsychiatry*, 1948, 18:622.
49. Krugman, M. *Orthopsychiatry and the School*. New York: American Orthopsychiatric Association, 1958.
50. Levitt, Morton. *Freud and Dewey*. New York: Philosophical Library, Inc., 1960.
51. Mayer, Martin. *The Schools*. New York: Harper & Brothers, 1961.
52. Oberndorf, C. P. *A History of Psychoanalysis in America*. New York: Grune and Stratton, 1953.
53. Olson, Willard C. *Child Development*. Boston: Heath & Co., 1949.
54. Pearson, Gerald. *Psychoanalysis and the Education of the Child*. New York: Norton & Co., 1954.
55. Peller, Lili E. "Incentives to Development and Means of Early Education." *Psychoanalytic Study of the Child*, 1946, 2:397.
56. ———. "The School's Role in Promoting Sublimation." *Psychoanalytic Study of the Child*, 1956, 11:437.
57. Pfister, Oskar. "The Faults of Parents." *Zeitschrift für Psychoanalytische Pädagogik*, 1929, 3:172.
58. ———. *What Does Psychoanalysis Offer to the Educator?* Leipzig: Julius Klinkhardt, 1917.
59. Piers, Maria A. *Growing Up with Children*. Chicago: Quadrangle Books, 1966.
60. Piers, Gerhart, and Maria. "Modes of Learning and the Analytic Process." *Selected Lectures, Sixth International Congress of Psychotherapy, London, 1964*. Basel/New York: S. Karger, 1965.
61. Redl, Fritz. "The Educational Duties of a Homeroom Teacher." *Die Wiener Schule*, 1932: 12.

62. ———. "We Teachers and Examination Anxiety." *Zeitschrift für Psychoanalytische Pädagogik*, 1933, 7:378.
63. ———. "The Concept of 'Learning Disturbance.'" *Zeitschrift für Psychoanalytische Pädagogik*, 1934, 8:155.
64. ———. *When We Deal with Children*. New York: Free Press, 1966.
65. ——— and W. W. Wattenberg. *Mental Hygiene in Teaching*. New York: Harcourt and Brace and Co., 1951.
66. Ruben, Margarete. "A Contribution to the Education of Parents." *Psychoanalytic Study of the Child*, 1945, 1:247.
67. ———. *Parent Guidance in the Nursery School*. New York: International Universities Press, Inc., 1960.
68. Schmidt, Vera. *Psychoanalytic Education in Soviet Russia—Report on the Experimental Children's Home in Moscow*. Vienna: Internationaler Psychoanalytischer Verlag, 1924.
69. Schneider, Ernst. "The Area of Application of Psychoanalysis for Pedagogy." *Zeitschrift für Psychoanalytische Pädagogik*, October, 1926, 1:2.
70. Smolen, Elwyn M., and Carolyn E. Jensen. "Educational Director in a Child Guidance Clinic: Report of a Pilot Project." Presented at Annual Meeting of the American Orthopsychiatric Association, Chicago, February 26, 1960.
71. Sterba, Editha. "School and Educational Guidance" (Schule und Erziehungsberatung). *Zeitschrift für Psychoanalytische Pädagogik*, 1936, 10:141.
72. ———. "Interpretation and Education." *Psychoanalytic Study of the Child*, 1945, 1:309.
73. Weinreb, Joseph. "Report of an Experience in the Application of Dynamic Psychiatry in Education." *Mental Hygiene*, April, 1953, 2:283.
74. Wittels, Fritz. *Die Befreiung des Kindes* (The Liberation of the Child). Stuttgart, Berlin, Zurich: Hippokrates-Verlag, 1927.
75. Zulliger, Hans. *Psychoanalytic Pedagogics. A Report on Mass Education and Individual Education*. Zurich: Orell Füssli, 1926.
76. ———. *Loosened Chains. Psychoanalysis in School Education*. Dresden: Alvin Hinkle, 1926.
77. ———. "Psychoanalysis and Leadership in School." *Imago*, 1930, 16:39.
78. ———. "Failures in School." *Zeitschrift für Psychoanalytische Pädagogik*, 1930, 4:431.

CHAPTER 2

Three Great Psychoanalytic
Educators

EDITH BUXBAUM

SIGMUND FREUD'S EMPHASIS upon the experiences and libidinal development of early childhood made educators aware of the importance of
psychoanalytic theory for education. Between 1925 and 1930 three
books on psychoanalytic education were published: Siegfried Bernfeld's book *Sisyphus or the Limits of Education*,[3] August Aichhorn's
Wayward Youth[1] and Anna Freud's *Psychoanalysis for Teachers and
Parents.*[6] It is significant that these major works of psychoanalytically
oriented educators came out just at this time. I assume that the stimulus
came from Freud's two new books, *Group Psychology and the Analysis
of the Ego*, published in 1921,[10] and *The Ego and the Id* in 1923.[8]

These two books reach beyond the psychoanalysis of individuals
into problems of society and its influence upon individuals. In *The Ego
and Id*, Freud dealt with the development of superego and ego-ideal.
He pointed out that both are derived from the parents who represent
society. In *Group Psychology and the Analysis of the Ego*, he discussed
the relations between the leader and group as well as the leader's and
the group members' influences upon each other. He discovered one of
the most important factors for the formation of a homogeneous group
is the identification of the members with the leader.

I had the good fortune of being acquainted with and learning from
Bernfeld, Aichhorn and Anna Freud. I might add that knowing them
had a decisive influence on my choice of career.

Siegfried Bernfeld was a socialist who, in his capacity as a social
worker, was working with all kinds of youth groups: in institutions, in
the socialistic youth movement, as well as with teachers and students
in the promotion of the revolutionary and controversial students' self-
government. He was, as he advocated in his writings, "a charismatic
leader": a fascinating person who cast a spell on adult audiences in the

28

same way in which he was the undisputed leader of youth whenever he chose to be. He had studied biology and psychology before turning to psychoanalysis. Bernfeld's particular strength lay in his brilliant, inescapable logic.

The analytic approach, his natural way of thinking, was what attracted him to Marx as well as to Freud. He maintained that reading the works of these two great men sufficed for everybody. The time when I met Bernfeld was a period of social revolution with great political interest for all. He was a Socialist, but a skeptical one. He questioned the ideas and hopes of socialism as much as he questioned those of any other system or ideology. His views on education in a socialistic regime were expressed in Sisyphus or the Limits of Education.

In this book he showed not only the limitations of a socialist education but also the limitation of any education by society, of which the educators are a part and by which they are employed. He viewed education as a function of society, and analyzed society's goals and means of reaching them as manifested in its educational system. He maintained that the important point of all education up to this time is the socio-economic class of the children the educator educates. The method by which they are being educated, he said, was not of importance. One part of Sisyphus was written as a fictitious speech given by Machiavelli, in a secret meeting, to the top administrators of the department of education. He exhorts the administrators to keep a firm hand on the organization of education, since the methods are inconsequential. Education, he says, serves the purpose of perpetuating the status quo in society; the children of the ruling class have to be kept in their position of superiority. Their parents wish to keep them there through their position or money by which they allow them to enjoy the institutions of higher learning.

Bernfeld's book was published in 1925. His views were in bitter contrast to those of the Socialists of Germany and Austria, who were optimistically assuming that the world is getting closer to the realization of their ideal of equality and equal educational opportunities for all. Living in Germany he saw the development of National Socialism and perhaps foresaw that approach to education. The Hitler youth fulfilled his Machiavellian speech to a T; nobody who was not a member of the master race was allowed to partake of the benefits of education. Of course, this now seems a minor issue in view of the total destruction to which non-Nazis were condemned. Yet it is interesting to see that National Socialism used education as a means to accept one part of the population and to reject the rest. Education was used as a tool of power. Whatever changes developed in the Nazi educational methods or in its system were consequences of their regime and its philosophy.

Bernfeld conceived of every education as "being conservatively organized in relation to the society who educates," and saw "changes in educational systems always as consequences of political happenings."

Erikson[4] expressed similar views when he described the impact of early training upon the formation of the individual. The practices of child rearing are a social tradition which is never questioned; it automatically prepares the child to become like other members of the society to which he belongs. Through these traditions he is being adapted to it. To use Bernfeld-Machiavelli's words, Erikson, too, saw the function of education in the "conversation of the biopsychological, socioeconomic and cultural-spiritual structure of society."

As much as educators may want to play a part in shaping the future society through their disciples, they are products of that society themselves, unable to rid themselves and their students of the limitations which society puts upon them. This pessimistic view was counterbalanced in Bernfeld by the hope which he derived from the possibility of educational methods based upon scientific investigation of childhood development which psychoanalysis makes possible. For a society in which high value is placed on the functioning of the individual and scientific understanding, he suggested investigating human functions. By so doing it could be determined under what conditions they develop best and what conditions inhibit, disturb or perhaps destroy them. The method for such investigation is psychoanalysis. A precondition to such an undertaking is the analysis of educators, who then would be able, like psychoanalysts, scientifically to understand the working of mind and body without being swayed like weathervanes by political, and other, ideologies and the prejudices of society. Or, rather, one should say that educators should at least be aware of their own frailties and the societal influences under which they work and be able not to be entirely swayed by them.

This scientific approach to child development is the important departure from the moralistic approach which prevailed up to that time. It is a break with the idea that a child has to obey the rules of society, to be a "good" child, whatever it may cost in loss of abilities and creativity; it opens the way to permit the best possible realization of human functioning. The educator's role is projected not so much as a conservator of society, but as a scientist who promotes human development, which in turn may point towards a changing society. There is kinship between these ideas and Freud's thinking, as expressed in *Future of an Illusion*[9] and in *Civilization and Its Discontents*.[7] Bernfeld was aware that it was impossible to put education on a scientific basis before the science of child development was developed. Some of his work was concerned directly with such scientific efforts. He wrote the first psychoanalytically-oriented *Psychology of the Infant*[2] as well as a number of books on adolescence. Other publications by him are concerned with questions of methodology, which he considered a necessary theoretical preliminary to establishing a science.

After emigrating from Germany, Bernfeld left the field of education entirely. It was impossible for him to continue with his work in Germany under Hitler, and when he came to America he was disillusioned with socialism. Apparently he felt that there was no reward at the time in attempting to influence youth or education. Perhaps he agreed with Freud, who said that "the three impossible professions are teaching, healing and governing." Like Freud, he felt that in doing clinical and theoretical work, he was doing all he could in serving education of the future.

August Aichhorn was quite the opposite of Bernfeld, the disappointed idealist. Aichhorn was an educator who remained one throughout his life, despite all political upheaval and changes. He was a realist who accepted society as it was, good and bad, and made the best of it for himself. He looked upon education as a means to adapt a child to the existing society. In his introduction to *Wayward Youth*, he said, "Life forces man to conform to reality; education enables him to achieve culture." The forms and institutions of society are part of its culture which man has to accept in order to live in it. Aichhorn looked upon educational work as "an art, in which intuition is of primary importance."

A personal friend of Freud, a partner in his *Tarockpartie*—the card game Freud liked so well—he valued psychoanalysis most highly. He considered a personal analysis indispensable for remedial educators. When I talked to him about my intention to work with disturbed children, his response was just to this point: "Well then, you just have to get yourself an analysis first, and then I'll talk to you again." Yet Aichhorn was aware of the dangers of undue emphasis and warned educators not to "overvalue the significance of psychology for remedial training. For well-rounded work he must take into consideration many other factors, psychiatric, sociological and cultural."

He also thought that educators must start with a capacity for this work. Although they may "learn a great deal through observation, experience and earnest study of the problems, . . . (one) cannot make an educator out of every personality." He said, somewhat impatiently perhaps, "I can give you no general directions how to proceed, every educator must work out the details of his own techniques." In his introduction to Aichhorn's book, Freud agreed: "Psychoanalysis could teach him little that was new to him in a practical way, but offered him a clear theoretical insight into the justification of his treatment and enabled him to explain his method to others in this field."

Aichhorn's book originated in a series of lectures. He was an excellent lecturer who spellbound his audience. He talked about the way he dealt with parents, children, educators; he described them with a few words so vividly that his listeners could see and hear them. He explained why he had proceeded the way he had—justifying with theoretical, analytical insight his procedures—but, as he said, he could not teach anyone how to do it in another case, because no two cases were the same.

The way he worked was an art, and as such it was unteachable. He did many things that were anathema for correct analytic procedure at one time and eventually became fashionable at another. He used all the tricks and manipulations which are now honored by the term "parameter"—which does not mean that they have become altogether teachable. He saw his patients alone or with their families; he visited them in their homes or met them on the street. He saw them at the appointed time or deliberately kept them waiting; he saw them for one hour or for five minutes. He gave presents and accepted presents. Sometimes it seems it just happened that he did this or that, yet he was able to put to use all that occurred.

He considered it most important to assess a patient and a situation in the first interview and to proceed accordingly. It is only rarely true that one can consciously consider all the factors in such a short time—psychiatric, sociological, cultural; I know that I cannot do it. In a situation where time is of the essence, as it is with delinquents, one can only work with one's unconscious, which is what intuition really is, but it is not teachable. I don't think any student of Aichhorn's was able to work as he did. He remains a unique phenomenon among educators. He worked with his personality—which is what everybody in this field does more or less—but his was more effective than most. He said, "Specific educational methods are far less important than an attitude which brings the child in contact with reality." To get such an attitude, to be able to make use of what intuition one had, was his reason for thinking educators should be analyzed. With analysis, they would know themselves, be aware of the impulses, good and bad, acceptable and forbidden and understand empathically the other person. He had this understanding without analysis. Being acquainted with Freud personally, hearing him talk about his ideas and getting some on-the-spot analytic advice and interpretations influenced and impressed him and confirmed what he already knew and was.

Where Bernfeld impressed with dazzling brilliance and intellect, and Aichhorn with his magic personality, Anna Freud impressed with her clarity of thinking and lucid simplicity, a simplicity which, however, is most deceptive. Her early book, *Psychoanalysis for Teachers and Parents*, shows this characteristic as much as her latest book, *Normality and Pathology in Childhood*.[5] It delighted and captivated her audiences in lectures and discussions in the past as much as it does today. Her personal impression and appearance are very much in keeping with her way of talking. One of the most striking features is her voice, which is as sweetly musical today as it was when I first met her over forty years ago. It is easy to imagine how children react to her: they immediately feel that here is a friend who understands, in whom they can confide. This was not so with Bernfeld or Aichhorn. With Bernfeld the adolescents felt a certain distance and awe; only gradually was this superseded by the feeling that the beloved leader was very much interested in their lives and experiences, that he wanted to know; only when they felt this, could they talk. Aichhorn, on the other hand, seemed so completely the authority, the parental figure, that the children were completely thrown off balance and guard when this impressive big man burst out with his quite unexpected insight and empathy into their most hidden and secret feelings. With Anna Freud, it is only natural that she should understand and that one could trust her. Everything followed from there.

The reader or listener is in a situation somewhat similar to that of the child patient. It is easy to follow her thinking, it sounds as if one had known it all along anyway. Her presentation reminds one somehow of Freud's writing; there is the easy contact with the reader, the imagined dialogue, the anticipation of objections and resistances. When she finally comes out with her conclusions they are so well prepared that they are accepted without reservations. And if, at this point, the reader or listener feels a bit overwhelmed, it is too late; he has lost his objections along the way by reading or listening.

In her lectures to teachers and parents in 1930, Anna Freud said, "The universal aim of education is always to make out of the child a grown-up person who shall not be very different from the grown-up world around him. It regards as childlike behavior everything in which the child differs from the adult—education struggles with the nature of the child, i.e., with his naughtiness." Anna Freud began by assuring the readers or listeners that she, like them, is against childish behavior and naughtiness. She continued by subtly leading her audience first to accept naughtiness as "normal links in a pre-determined chain of development," then to recognize certain traits whose origin are in the past but which are still with them as adults in only slightly changed forms—like greediness and love of sweets; and, finally, to appreciate

naughtiness as the possible beginnings of valuable activities, i.e., paint-
ing and sculpture. In the third lecture she summarized the theoretical
knowledge which she had imparted to her listeners during the first
two lectures: "You have become acquainted with a number of the
most important fundamental ideas of psychoanalysis and with its
customary terminology. You have met with the idea of the unconscious,
repression, reaction formation, sublimation, transference, the Oedipus
complex and the castration complex, the libido, and the theory of
infantile sexuality."

This is indeed a great deal to have given in two lectures to a rather
unsophisticated audience, who took it in easily without realizing that
they were being introduced to rather complicated analytic theory.
However, the reader-listener is never left in doubt that he really has
just been given a taste of knowledge, enough to whet his appetite for
more without satisfying him.

Anna Freud, like Bernfeld, thought that it was necessary to arrange
systematically the phenomena facing the educator and to trace them
to their original source. She has done just that in her book, *Normality and Pathology in Childhood*. She has collected and classified a
tremendous catalogue of human behavior and put it at the disposal
of educators, researchers and psychoanalysts. Years ago, however, she
warned, "Such classification requires special knowledge." She says now
that "without exploration during analysis, these forms of behavior remain
(therefore) inconclusive."

She has stressed repeatedly that observers need to be analytically
trained. In 1930 she maintained that "psychoanalysis is well qualified to
offer criticism of educational methods," but that "no analytical pedagogy
exists . . . it will be a long time before theory and practice are complete
and can be recommended for general use." In 1965 she described certain
areas within which psychoanalytic theories can be applied profitably to
preventive work. Preventive work in psychiatry is generally considered
mental hygiene; insofar as it concerns children it is an area close to
education. Although Anna Freud does not offer an educational system,
she considers herself an educator, particularly an educator of educators.
What she has to teach is a catalogue of forms of human behavior and a
method of understanding and influencing it.

Aichhorn who worked mainly with his intuition left rather stranded
the educator who was less gifted in that way. Anna Freud's book, *Normality and Pathology*, gives the educator a large amount of material
which he may store within himself, so that he may draw on memory
rather than intuition for his understanding and reactions. However, only
the analyzed educator will be able to learn from this book, to forget

it and to remember it at the appropriate place and time. And I should like to add, intuition so far is not superfluous.

Ekstein and Motto (Chapter 1) distinguished between two phases in the history of psychoanalysis and education. In the first one they say psychoanalysis was considered an educational procedure; what they refer to is the concept of psychoanalysis as post-education. In the second phase, they show that the emphasis is on prevention of emotional illness. Both phases share the focal point of emotional illness: either in regard to correction of faulty development or in prevention of faulty development. This is easily understandable since psychoanalysis as a therapy is primarily concerned with the residues and results of development which were manifest in maladaptations. Child analysis is concerned with post-education in the sense of correction of faulty development. We call it preventive when we deal with beginning disturbances which are noticeable on the surface, in order to prevent them from becoming permanent and spreading to other areas. When Freud published *The Ego and the Id* and *Group Psychology and the Analysis of the Ego*, psychoanalytically oriented education came into its own.

The emphasis was shifted to systems of the ego and superego. These are important for the adaptation to reality and society for the control of instinctual drives and the ability to tolerate frustration, a condition which is indispensable for the ability to learn and sublimate. Bernfeld, Aichhorn and Anna Freud were the first ones to realize that Freud had given them the tools for education in addition to those of therapy. This is why I think these three educators were able to write their pioneering books.

BIBLIOGRAPHY

1. Aichhorn, A. *Wayward Youth*. Vienna: International Psychoanalytic Press, 1925.
2. Bernfeld, S. *Psychology of the Infant*. Vienna: Springer, 1925.
3. ————. *Sisyphus or the Limits of Education*. Vienna: International Psychoanalytic Press, 1925.
4. Erikson, E. *Childhood and Society*. New York: Norton, 1950.
5. Freud, A. *Normality and Pathology in Childhood*. New York: International Universities Press, 1965.
6. ————. *Psychoanalysis for Teachers and Parents* (Einfuhrungin die Psychoanalyze für Pädagogen, vier Vortage). Stuttgart: Hippocrates Press, 1930.
7. Freud, S. *Civilization and Its Discontents*. London: Hogarth, 1930.
8. ————. *The Ego and the Id*. Vienna: International Psychoanalytic Press, 1923.
9. ————. *Future of an Illusion*. Vienna: International Psychoanalytic Press, 1927.
10. ————. *Group Psychology and the Analysis of the Ego*. Vienna: International Psychoanalytic Press, 1921.

CHAPTER 3

A Translation of and Comments on Bernfeld's "On Sexual Enlightenment"

RUDOLF EKSTEIN

THE READER MAY WELL benefit from an historical overview to serve as background for Bernfeld's classic essay. It belongs to those early collaborative efforts between psychoanalysis and education. Although coming from half a world away and two score years past, we find that Bernfeld's contribution is remarkably appropriate to our place and time.

Bernfeld contributed this paper to the very first volume of the *Zeitschrift für psychoanalytische Pädagogik*, published in 1926 and 1927. The place of this journal in the history of psychoanalytic pedagogy was discussed in chapter 1. Issues 7, 8, and 9 of that very first volume appeared as a special edition dedicated to Freud on the occasion of his 71st birthday in 1927. Most of the material published in that edition concerned the problem of sexual enlightenment; in German, *sexuelle Aufklärung*, derived perhaps from the *Periode der Aufklärung*, the age of reason.

In chapter 1, there were several references to Bernfeld. He contributed the lead article in the special edition and his work was followed by similar contributions from Friedjung, Hitschmann, Landauer, Liertz, Meng, Pfister, Reich and a good many others. Bernfeld's lead article which I have translated for this occasion, offers me an opportunity to say more about his influence, his specific techniques and his insights. My comments, I hope, suggest meaningful connections between the late twenties and the late sixties, between the problems of Central Europe and events in the current American scene.

Bernfeld, a youth leader, deeply immersed in progressive political youth movements, a Zionist and Socialist, was also strongly committed to modern pedagogy and psychoanalysis. He joined Freud at a time which might be considered historically as the era of *die psychoanalytische Bewegung*, the psychoanalytic movement. He gave a vivid picture of his relationship to Freud, the state of affairs of early psychoanalytic training, and his own struggle as he moved towards becoming a psychoanalyst, in his contribution "On Psychoanalytic Training,"[3] published posthumously in 1962. He speaks of the deep commitment of the early pioneers, a commitment that was also characteristic of the earlier political and youth movements which motivated him to create a variety of pedagogical experiments, which have been discussed in other chapters of this volume and elsewhere.[4,6]

Many of us who joined psychoanalysis between then and 1938 brought with us the enthusiasm of *die neue Erziehung*, a new kind of psychoanalytic pedagogy, which was an attempt to bring science to education, to our work. Bernfeld's paper well represents the debate then taking place. His position was against certain earlier liberal and progressive illusions which must have been his own viewpoints not too long before. As he invents his opponents, I have the feeling that he is conducting a debate with himself in order to bring his own viewpoints concerning modern pedagogy to a higher level of sophistication and effectiveness.

Let us then follow the dilemma, the hopes, the techniques and the knowledge available at that time, as reflected in Bernfeld's account:

Whether one should offer children candid information on sexual facts, at what time one should offer such information, and just how one ought to convey these facts are questions over which, in recent years, a remarkable change in our point of view has taken place. Regardless of how different the reasons that individual pedagogues offer to justify candor, regardless how greatly the methods of various enlighteners vary, all modern educators essentially agree that the fairy tale of the stork must be abolished. One reason for such a change is obvious. Within the last few years, the sexuality of the child—and this, indeed, is the great merit of the contribution of Freud and his school—has been explored and recognized without prejudice.

This sexuality, of course, was always known. The very fact that there is a tale about the stork proves what has always been observed: children, even at a very early age, manifest an interest in questions of sexual content. This does not occur by chance and cannot be considered accidental, since it could never be squelched through such answers as, "When you are bigger, you will understand these matters." Children insistently demanded an answer, and, for this reason, the stork tale was invented.

Allegedly, adults did not want to convey the truth because children, so it was reasoned, would not understand it. But nobody ever tested this assumption. If children would not understand the truth, adults could indeed tell them about it without worry, since then they themselves would realize that here was a problem they could not solve until they, too, became adults. The truth was withheld because it was realized children would, in fact, understand, and that was exactly what everyone tried to prevent.

Modern educators no longer want such concealment to exist. This is so, I believe, for two reasons. First of all, they realize such concealment is not only damaging but also impossible to maintain. Secondly, the essential nature of new pedagogy may be characterized as truthfulness vis-à-vis both oneself and the child. I believe they are entirely correct in assuming such a position. But, as so often seems to be the case with all human affairs, a good many of these modern educators believe that with sexual enlightenment they have introduced—God only knows what important new trend through which they hope to bring about enormous benefits. Some of them even believe this question touches upon the center of all pedagogic problems, and that the answer to this question will enable us to establish a new generation of human beings.

These convictions of educators influenced by psychoanalysis were derived from early case histories, the place of the sexual trauma and repression in its theoretical assumptions and in its views concerning the etiology of neurosis, particularly hysterical conditions. These views must be connected with the first theoretical assumptions characterized by the topographic model of personality, and the technical view of treatment summed up by Freud as "making the unconscious conscious." The pedagogical equivalent of all this was, of course, the idea of enlightenment, of sexual education, of not witholding information from children, etc.

But it must also be remembered that this was a time when established authority had been overthrown in favor of the social reforms which followed the end of the first World War. Much of that postwar period sought freedom from all the old dogmas, and education was understood, in the phrase of Wittels, as the liberation of the child. Social enthusiasm and scientific zeal had united to produce a rich, if small, experiment, the new psychoanalytic pedagogy. Bernfeld himself had been fighting the old authorities, and Hoffer[6] describes well Bernfeld's political struggle against the "establishment" of his time. The Kinderheim Baumgarten, as Bernfeld's book reveals,[1] was one of the early experiments in modern education partially based on the kind of sexual enlightenment that Bernfeld is now attacking:

> May I be permitted to indicate shortly why I do not follow such belief, and how such belief is not without danger for pedagogy.
> Occasionally, one has the astonishing experience of discovering during the analysis of both children and adolescents that they have acquired neurosis or neurotic trends or asocial attitudes, even though

they have been enlightened by their parents in a seemingly correct way, very early and very skillfully. This, of course, is no more than an indication that sexual enlightenment alone cannot prevent infantile developmental disturbances. No reasonable person will ever overestimate enlightenment that greatly. But, and this is what is strange, these fully enlightened children often behave both in life and in their analytic treatment as if that enlightenment had never taken place. In no way have they taken cognizance of these explanations.

In two cases, I had the opportunity to determine that the rejection of enlightenment did not take place instantly, but rather, occurred a few months later. In one case, I recognized a motivation for such rejection. This child, a girl, in answer to her questions at the age of three, received all the necessary information from Mother. At that time, the child understood well the information. When the mother said, "Your sibling grows in my tummy," the little girl responded in a lively manner, "Please, Mommy, in my tummy." Several times she indicated through her remarks that she understood the facts completely. But a year later all that was forgotten. When she was offered the sexual explanations once more, she ignored them. Later on, she did not want to hear anything about them, and behaved quite prudishly. Actually, she had been bitterly disappointed because her request had not been fulfilled: the little sister did not grow in her tummy. Moreover, she had another traumatic experience, surgery with anaesthetics. While space does not permit me to describe this case in detail, the insight must suffice: sexual enlightenment can also be repressed.

And most probably, in a certain sense, this is always the case. Freud taught us that at an early age children develop their own theories about the differences between the sexes and about the origin of babies. Possibly the development of their views is also influenced by hereditary dispositions. Thus, they more or less conduct their own and very important exploratory work. They start with the facts experience offers, and draw their own conclusions with their own infantile logic. As greatly as their own personal experiences differ, so, too, are their own theories diverse.

Children lack certain suppositions in this exploratory work; therefore, in certain characteristic points, their conclusions do not always agree with the facts. For example, children generally lack the notion of the vagina. Regardless of how correctly one enlightens them, they cannot accept this fact, but keep the theories they had accepted earlier: the baby comes out of the mouth, the rectum, the navel, etc. They draw such conclusions with infantile logic. But this infantile logic is completely ruled by the infantile wishes from which they have not yet freed themselves, as is the case with adults. Therefore, these children often reject a piece of enlightenment, since that fact corresponds less with their wishes than do their own theories. Thus, one frequently finds boys who absolutely do not want to accept the fact that only women can have children.

What conclusion are we to draw from this? Something very simple and matter of fact, something the educator himself does not like to admit and cannot easily accept as true. The fact is that enlightenment, like any other educational measure, rarely achieves its aims; at best, a compromise takes place between the tendencies of the educator and the instincts of children. Of course, in the majority of cases, children are well brought up; they do not so much as dare not to believe us. They believe us when we tell them the tale of the stork. They believe us with their conscious minds when we tell them the truth in a medically correct way. But unconsciously, they do not believe either version; they believe exclusively in their own experiences and wishes.

Children usually form these theories during the third and fourth years of their lives; this is also the time when they usually start to ask questions. It would seem self-evident that enlightenment, if it is to have any meaning, must start early. Still one must say that sexual enlightenment always comes too late. The child starts asking questions with vigor and true interest only when he has formed a theory of his own, when he encounters a new difficulty or when he looks for confirmation. It is a very basic and well-founded pedagogical assumption that one must wait for the child's interest to develop. One cannot spare the child the great intellectual problems, the development of curiosity or the desire to explore, as expressed through sexual questioning. What one can spare him is the disregard for his intellect. One can spare the child from being forced to believe fairy tales brought to him by adult authority. This is particularly important since the tales are brought to him just when the child, through independent exploration, has already brought himself closer to the truth; just at the time when these fairy tales may force him to push his knowledge into the unconscious.

Much of what Bernfeld suggests was written before the advent of ego psychology, although The Ego and the Id[5] had appeared some four years earlier, in 1923. That Bernfeld's contribution was not written against the background of Freud's structural theories of 1923 becomes readily apparent when Bernfeld speaks of "compromise between the tendencies of the educator and the instincts of the child." But it is not difficult to translate the issues of infantile logic into our present ideas of primary- and secondary-process dominance, our present emphasis on object- and self-constancy, and our present, more sophisticated knowledge of the different states of learning readiness. The new concepts of ego psychology are but implied in Bernfeld's description of the kinds of theories that children form during different stages of their growing up. But his examples show that he was aware that these theories are not only functions of psychosexual development or the vicissitudes of the instincts, but also have to do with the development of the child's logic, emotional differentiation and other intellectual capacities. That the movement of the processes towards emotional growth and a true capacity to cope with sexual problems is often derailed creates a specific task for the educator. In the next section, Bernfeld deals with the nature of the expectations of the educator as he faces the educational task:

The reduction of intellectual conflict that enlightenment brings, though useful in itself, is not the solution to all conflict connected with the sexual theme. We see the child all too much as an intellectual being and not as what he really is, an instinctual and sensual being. The child's original interest is not to know, but to see and to act. His question of where babies come from is often the result of his past, unsuccessful efforts to have children. This wish remains on an instinctual level and unsatisfied even if the wish to know is intellectually satisfied. Then the child also wants to see all that has been explained to him. If one were to fulfill this wish out of a misunderstanding of child psychology, the child would still remain unsatisfied and would then want to perform the sexual act himself. In any case, a great many of his instinctual demands must be left unsatisfied. And it is out of such compulsion that these conflicts, necessary for development, prepare difficulties we cannot predict, difficulties which sometimes lead to derailments.

Two forms of such derailments are neurosis and asociality. The child's impulse to act must in part be satisfied through mere knowledge. This does not always succeed; we have no method to enforce it. Sexual enlightenment certainly does not offer such a method. But sexual enlightenment at least does not forcefully prevent the transformation of the instinct, its sublimation into the wish to know.

Other reflections could be considered. This or that experience could be utilized. Yet, one could demonstrate again and again how a scientific examination of sexual enlightenment shows the limitation of its importance and effectiveness, and, in fact, shows itself to be much less profitable than the pedagogues believe. To offer a side remark, I believe that the most important function of science and pedagogy seems to be to redirect the pedagogues' wishes and hopes, which always go far beyond what experience proves. In fact, the actual value of enlightenment most likely is a negative one: sexual enlightenment is not harmful, while lying to children frequently is. Beyond that, sexual enlightenment is a rather negligible factor in the solution of problems of education.

I do not want to be misunderstood. Yes, children, as early as they wish, should hear the truth from their parents and educators. But having told the truth, the elders should not think they have done something unbelievably important and special. After all, one tries not to lie to anybody and should not feel entitled to special praise for not lying, especially where children are involved. Relationships with them are difficult enough. In no way can one justify destroying the atmosphere through lying, thus removing possibilities for further educational effectiveness. Yet he who is not dogmatic must admit that situations may arise where there is no room for candor with children. But one would need to judge such situations with extreme care before deciding that the necessity for leaving the truth is beyond doubt.

Children's questions about "from where" and "how" babies come do not belong in this category. Sexual enlightenment is not a special trick, nor is it a special method of its own with its own beneficial consequences and hopes. On the contrary, it is merely and exclusively a small part of the generally useful principle requiring all of us to respect the child. It is from this principle that the demand for our truthfulness is derived.

Only in such a context does sexual enlightenment have that limited value one can assign to it on the basis of the present state of scientific experience. One often finds in current pedagogical literature enthusiastic commendation of such enlightenment. One hears, at the same time, that this highly lauded procedure should be applied during the fourteenth year of life and should be accompanied by earnest exhortations about the ethical importance of sexual questions and by warnings against excesses and venereal disease. It is then that one begins to understand the nature of the exaggerated enthusiasm for sexual enlightenment. After all, how and when one ought to give children information about sexual processes seem to be questions that should be dealt with in a matter-of-fact way. So much in this area is a question of experience, the weighing of pros and cons, that it is very hard to grasp why such debate should be accompanied by fanfare. Fanfare, of course, seems to draw attention away from the main point. But this seems to be exactly the intention. Inasmuch as one heartily favors sexual enlightenment and promises humanity a thousand beneficial consequences from it, one has done enough, one believes, towards promoting the fashionable trends of our time. One can now leave everything just as it is.

Everything else—one's own position with regard to sexuality, the "complexes" of one's own unconscious and the total sexual education—need not be revised or worked on through psychic labor. "Sexual enlightenment" relieves us of this work. That is why we are so enthusiastic about it.

Perhaps something similar can be observed when pedagogy

combats or defends a particular method with passionate enthusiasm, and makes great promises about the advantages of its position. In such cases, we should be suspicious, since education is a most difficult, objective task. Our hopes must always be accompanied by an earnest examination of what we have learned via experience. Such procedure alone deserves the name of scientific education.

Instinctual development was very much in the foreground then, and characteristic of much psychoanalytic discussion. Even in an essay[2] published almost ten years later, in 1935, Bernfeld described puberty primarily in terms of the solution of these sexual conflicts. The ideas of ego psychology, of the apparatuses of defense and adaptation, and of identity conflicts and intimacy conflicts, are all contained in that particular paper as they are in this paper. But they were only descriptive notions, since his basic principles made use of the concepts of metapsychology which had been developed by Freud before 1920.

But Bernfeld's great skill as a teacher is forcefully illustrated by his ability to indicate how any issue in the forefront of our attention is there because of the background elements involved. Sexual enlightenment seems to be the focus of his discussion, and frequently is seen as one of the basic contributions that psychoanalysis has made to the upbringing of children. But there is more behind the selection of that problem than the problem itself. Sexual enlightenment is not the core problem of education; rather, it points to a core problem. Bernfeld's beautiful way of discussing the issue leads us to the core problem and to the creation of an educational philosophy and technique that is based on psychoanalytic insights.

It may be that our own current ways of formulating psychological problems tempt me to read more into Bernfeld's essay than is warranted. But I understand him to tell us that we are not to take the issue of sexual enlightenment merely in a concrete way. Of course, there are always issues of when to offer information honestly, and to whom; of establishing the readiness of the child for such information, as well as the readiness of the teacher. But I think he says we must go beyond the facade of the specific issue, so I see his essay as a condensed simile about the total educational process. It seems to me he is telling us that sexual enlightenment is a two-way street. We shall be able to offer enlightenment to our children if we will allow ourselves to be enlightened by them.

Sexual enlightenment can be compared to the ball that makes the soccer game possible; it is the issue around which much goes on between the adult and the child. It is the issue around which external and internal organizers are formed so that the child can grow towards mature object relations, the capacity to love and to work. Bernfeld pleads for an attitude that will enable us to tame our premature enthusiasm and our exaggerated expectations. With such an attitude, love can be guided by wisdom, educational goals can be reached through rational techniques, and educators can be made aware of the child's inner world, as well as their own.

BIBLIOGRAPHY

1. Bernfeld, Siegfried. *Kinderheim Baumgarten* (The Baumgarten Children's Home—A Report on a Serious Experiment in Modern Education). Berlin: Judische Verlag, 1921.
2. ———. "Uber die einfache männliche Pubertät" (On Simple Male Puberty). *Zeitschrift für Psychoanalytische Pädagogik*, 1935, 9(5/6):360.
3. ———. "On Psychoanalytic Training." *Psychoanalytic Quarterly*, 1962, 31:453.
4. Ekstein, Rudolf. "Siegfried Bernfeld—1892-1953: Sisyphus or the Boundaries of Education." In *Psychoanalytic Pioneers*, Franz Alexander, Samuel Eisenstein and Martin Grotjahn, eds. New York: Basic Books, Inc., 1966, 415.
5. Freud, Sigmund. *The Ego and the Id* (1923). *Standard Edition*, XIX. London: Hogarth, 1961.
6. Hoffer, Willi. "Siegfried Bernfeld and 'Jerubbaal.'" *Year Book X of the Leo Baeck Institute*, London, 1965, 150.

PART II: Issues of Curriculum, Methods of Teaching and Modes of Learning

It is possible of course to abuse the office, and to force the activity of the young into channels which express the teacher's purpose rather than that of the pupils. But the way to avoid this danger is not for the adult to withdraw entirely. The way is first, for the teacher to be intelligently aware of the capacities, needs, and past experiences of those under instruction, and, secondly, to allow the suggestion made to develop into a plan and project by means of the further suggestions contributed and organized into a whole by the members of the group. The plan, in other words, is a co-operative enterprise, not a dictation. The teacher's suggestion is not a mold for a cast-iron result but is a starting point to be developed into a plan through contributions from the experience of all engaged in the learning process. The development occurs through reciprocal give-and-take, the teacher taking but not being afraid also to give. The essential point is that the purpose grow and take shape through the process of social intelligence.

—JOHN DEWEY

CHAPTER 4

Psychoanalytic Notes on the Function of the Curriculum

RUDOLF EKSTEIN

ACCORDING TO FREUD'S BON MOT, there are three impossible tasks: to heal, to teach, and to govern. I can add a fourth one equally impossible: to develop and to administer a sound curriculum. As I attempt to arouse interest in this issue, I recall how some of the teachers on the program committee for a teachers' institute believed that the topic "Psychoanalysis Looks at the Curriculum" would not draw many teachers. Teachers, they thought, would be interested only in psychoanalysis and not in curriculum questions. This was their everyday concern and one from which they sought surcease. Yet it turned out that they were sufficiently interested to attend in large numbers. I wish to consider the curriculum in order possibly to gain a new perspective. Rather than looking at the curriculum as something external, an outline, a text to be followed, a course of study, a sequence of tasks to be covered, I want to look behind its facade and into its psychological nature.

Kant was said to have started his lectures on philosophy with the announcement—a task-setting injunction to himself—that he had come not to teach philosophy but how to philosophize. I surmise, he wanted to encourage in his students the action of thinking, to develop the capacity to think, and he did not want merely to transmit to the students the product of his thoughts. He thus seems to have thought that the good teacher, when following a curriculum, would not merely make the students absorb a body of knowledge, as advocated by the teaching philosophy of the Nuernberger Trichter—pouring knowledge into the empty mind via a funnel. The good teacher, rather, would bring about an active process of thinking, of learning and of mastering. Certainly, Kant never fully succeeded with the task he set for himself. Many of his students who came to study philosophy did not learn how to philosophize but merely to repeat the master's words and fulfill mechanically the external requirements of the Rigorosum, the final exams which are used as evidence that the requirements of the curriculum have been met.

Kant described the intense struggle between those who insisted on a strict and demanding curriculum and those who believed in a free atmosphere of inquiry. His famous treatise, "The Strife of the Faculties,"[6] reads much like modern discussions of curriculum questions and teaching methods.

The dictionary tells us that "curriculum" is to be understood as a course of study. This definition fails to emphasize that this entails more than a body of knowledge to be transmitted, more than a lecture outline, a textbook, a Hundred Great Books. The original root of the word goes back to the Roman chariot races over a pre-defined course. The Latin verb curriculare refers to running over a fixed course. However, we do not merely offer the student the structure of a fixed course but an opportunity to function by moving forward in it. The concept of curriculum does not simply contain the thought of the goal to be reached at the end of the school term but also conveys the idea of a process leading to it. The means-and-end discussions, the subject-versus-method controversies, focus on but two inseparable sides of the same coin. However the usual, and frequently violent, swings in teachers' colleges, boards of education, public sentiments and political-action committees make it difficult for the educators, caught in the middle of these administrative and political storms, to synthesize these two aspects. All too often they are forced to reach an unhappy compromise between "progressive" and "conservative" factions in this modern strife between faculties.

Psychoanalysis has then to look at the curriculum issue as a dynamic struggle in which fixed outline and structure are one aspect, while the other is the competitive course, the process of change. The curriculum builders, comparable to institutionalizers, stress the stable structure and add to it requirement after requirement. The method people try to make room for growth, for change and adaptation, for inner process. The former stress the school and the subject matter, while the latter emphasize method and teachers, the personal equation. More sophisticated builders of curricula, of course, think not only in terms of subject matter to be taught but also process and method.

The child needs both the school and the teacher, the subject and the process, and has but few ways to influence the struggle we engage in at his expense. Siegfried Bernfeld discusses these two boundaries of education which confront the teacher in his famous Sisyphus.[2] He saw these boundaries as obstacles and limitations, but we should like to consider whether his ideas might not lead us towards new technical insights concerning the utilization of the curriculum.

A Stanford professor, Wayne Benjamin, has said all this in his delightful story, *The Saber-Tooth Curriculum*,[1] which projects the modern political struggle onto an imaginary primitive tribe in order to make the issues more acceptable to us. I shall follow his lead and use a metaphor of my own to bring out the inner dynamics of the struggle which is normally seen as an external or political conflict.

I suggest that the first curriculum struggle ever developed does not take place in school but rather ensues between mother and infant as she is nursing her baby. The full breast is the first curriculum the baby must empty and digest in order to meet the goal and requirement of satiation. Unfortunately, some mothers, as well as some teachers, do not have much of a curriculum to offer. As the child pre-empts that original curriculum and meets his task, he is called a good eater, i.e., a good learner since he takes it all in. The mother who teaches him to acquire this forerunner of wisdom, must be—if she is a good mother, a good teacher—concerned as much with the process of eating as she is with its results. That first teacher-student relationship, that trust- or distrust-producing situation, will contain both elements: the task (milk to be incorporated) and method (scanning, holding on, sucking, refusing, trying and searching). The full breast, the curriculum, is an external feature that creates a task for both mother and child. She wants to give to the child what she has available. She may get impatient or angry at times, use forced feeding or insist on an exact time schedule: set "institutionalized" demands. And she may not be able to help the child to develop good eating techniques. Sometimes she may turn to that first curriculum expert, the pediatrician, who will—according to his training or temperament—prescribe, frequently against her very nature, in which way she is to feed, how often and what. She may thus become the first problem teacher who unconsciously fights the curriculum expert. Or, as the other extreme, he may suggest to her a self-demand schedule. A conservative or a progressive curriculum may thus be imposed on a natural situation. The mother-child relationship, as steered by the pediatrician, turns into the forerunner of the oedipal triad, another way of saying that behind every mother-child situation is the father, the third corner of the triangle.

The mother is rather ambivalent and anxious about that curriculum and she often weighs the baby to see whether he has taken in enough, her way of grading him and comparing him with the grade averages of other students. The infant, that prototype of all later students, must scan, suck in, let go and work by the sweat of his brow, i.e., must learn, and is thus confronted with his first learning and working experience, his first teacher and his first core curriculum. The usual anxiety of mothers as well as of later teachers, the main concern of pediatricians and later school administrators, is always shown by stress on results. The gains in weight are noted rather than the changes in taking things in, the changes in the methods of acquisition, or the subtle development occurring in the infant. He, in his encounter with the breast, that core curriculum, discovers that there is not only an empty stomach, a need, a supply of milk, but also a mother who has a way of feeding, often opposed to his way of eating. And this is true even when the substance of milk is exchanged slowly for solids, the new curriculum, after the breast or the bottle has been given up. The curriculum is then a more solid one. How complex the discoveries are in this first dialogue,[7] this first mutual task of giving and taking, can be measured through the different and differing

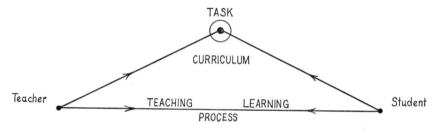

Figure I.

outcomes of this mutuality of interests and conflicts. It is they which will decide to what degree the baby will love to eat or eat to love and be loved. But from now on, learning will be within an interpersonal context even if the ever-increasing automation of the school industry will try to disguise this as the work of teaching machines. It is in this interpersonal context that intrapsychic learning goes on.

The core curriculum, like the breast or the full bottle between mother and infant, has to be understood as the external link which unites the student and the teacher at the common task, the common struggle. This mutuality of goal and conflict is what makes teaching possible as a process. In the graphic model of this mutuality, there is a triangle, the end-points of which are teacher, students and curriculum or task. See Figure 1.

The curriculum is imposed on both teacher and student by the school administration—the professional representation of the community—as the full breast, the empty stomach, the need to offer and the need to take in are imposed by nature on mother and child. The curriculum initiates the process, the interchange, the struggle, the mutual satisfaction, the failures and successes of teaching and learning. The biological "must" of the draining of the full breast versus the social "must" of the "training" of the school curriculum point up, of course, the short-comings of this metaphor.

Teachers and students alike stress only the end, the goal, the examination to be passed, the grade average for college entrance rather than the process, the pleasure of functioning, of achieving. In the original learning situation between mother and infant, the "curriculum" is a kind of private property between the two of them, disturbed at best by outside advice concerning the way the milk is to move from one to the

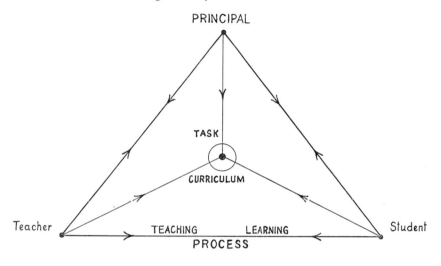

Figure 2.

other. In school, the learning situation becomes a much more complex social structure. The original issue of maturing is replaced by the one of developing. The next graphic model, Figure 2, pictures the curriculum, the task, as the center of gravity within a triangle; the end points of which refer to the different positions and functions of teacher, school child and school administrator.

The complexity of this figure is to insure the processes of learning and teaching, the base line of the triangle, as the basic connection between teacher and student body. The curriculum, the task, is given to them from the outside. The teacher's task is to identify himself with the goal of the school administration and the learning problems of the child. He must look at his tasks in terms of goal and process towards that goal. The ways of teaching a curriculum and acquiring a curriculum have to be synthesized.

In the third model, Figure 3, the triangle of teacher, student, school administrator is complemented with one that has teacher, student, parents as end-points. Actually, the second triangle is a mirror image of the first one. Its center of gravity is the measure of achievement, the grades, that is, the visible, external indicator that an internal process has taken place, that the external requirement has been internalized and fully met.

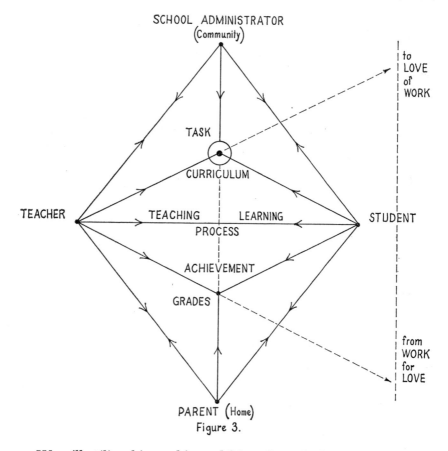

Figure 3.

We will utilize this graphic model in order to look at the curriculum task primarily from the viewpoint of the teacher and the child, and will offer only random observations concerning the position of the school principal and the parent. It will become clear though, during this discussion, that the model can be utilized in order to elaborate on the inner functions of each of these participants in the learning and teaching process.

I suggested earlier that the teacher's problem is to identify with the curriculum, the external task which it imposes, as well as the internal situation which it brings about and which initiates the process of change. The same holds true for the child who will oppose the external task as well as want to meet it, as he struggles towards his own autonomy and against external controls which he still needs. In other words, we have now set up natural enemies, though, hopefully, enemies with an underlying wish of surviving and succeeding together. There can be no teaching without creating, at times, natural hostility. The teacher cannot expect that his children will love him primarily. They may well love him dominantly but in part they must also dislike or even hate him because he imposes structure on them. The child must meet these external requirements, the core curriculum, in order to get grades, that institutionalized form of love, which he needs just as he needs acceptance, love and praise from his parents when he has done well. (While there are many successful experiments of schools without grades, they have equivalent forms of recognition and acceptance. It is only the form of the struggle about recognition which is concluded and experienced differently.) The model indicates that these grades are not only the student's link to the teacher but to the parents and the community as well. Thus, the child works for love, for reward. One might add that the teacher, too, teaches for rewards and for love. He is confronted not only with the student whom he is to help but with the school administration, the community, the generation of parents whose praise, whose admiration and rewards he, too, needs, regardless how mature he may be. (See chapter 8.)

Within the model as described up to now, one could very well describe the curriculum as a task imposed upon the child which he meets as he is confronted with methods of positive and negative reinforcement. Every positive solution will be met with reward and every negative failure will be met with punishment. Skinner's teaching machines, as he once suggested, may yet be better than any available teacher. But much more happens than such learning theorists consider; human learners are more complex than Skinner pigeons.

Just as that early dialogue between mother and child brings about more than the acquisition of milk and correct sucking activities, so the teaching and learning process around the core curriculum brings about more than the acquisition of mechanical skills. The curriculum is the guarantor, the link between the child and the teacher, the creator of an interpersonal situation and interpersonal need. The need for satiation turns also into a need for love and affection, for understanding and for guidance. The need for skill, the mere greed for "quiz-kid" knowledge turns into a search for insight, an internalization of the requirement for work and study. It creates, by means of identification with the aggressor, a love of work and productivity, a desire for creativity and goal-setting, far beyond the community's insistence on having to meet the requirements of that core curriculum.

Some school systems are overcrowded, confronted with many children who are not as yet ready for a normal learning situation, inadequately staffed, pressured by outside social goals like the desire to compete with Sputnik. Such systems will not make the fullest use of the structure described. For them, the structure will be a straitjacket of conformity, and they will fall victim to every mechanical shortcut that will get them through the next political election.

Let us return to Figure 3. The three corners of the triangle refer to three essential and different functions: the teaching; the learning in the school situation; and the administration of this process through the head teacher or school principal. If Bernfeld had developed a graphic model for his view of the teaching task in *Sisyphus*, he would have put the teacher in the middle of a straight line. At one end of that line there would have been the pressure of society, and on the other end, the pressure of the child. He thought, then, in terms of reality pressure—the demands of society—and the pressure from the instinctual need system of the child. The model of personality which Bernfeld would have used then would have been the topographic model as exemplified by Freud in *The Interpretation of Dreams*.[3] The structure indicated in the present model of the teaching and learning process could not well be fitted into the topographic model without losing some of the gains made with Freud's tripartite model of personality as described in *The Ego and the Id*.[4] We speak about the id in terms of its instinctual needs for gratification and the avoidance of danger and pain. We speak about the ego in terms of its executive functions, its capacities for delay, for mastery, for solutions, for defense and adaptation. We speak about the superego as having brought about the creation of ideal goals. This complex intrapsychic system is in constant interchange with external reality, which alters with the demands of society that fluctuate and change, progress and regress, as documented, for example, by the vicissitudes of curriculum demands on child and teacher.

Our graphic model constitutes an analogue to Freud's tripartite model. The teaching function is related to the function of the ego in terms of mastery. The learning function, the struggle against learning and requirement, is to be related to the psychic organization characterized as id. The administration function which sets the task of the core curriculum is to be related to superego formation. Our school system is then a kind of social replica of the tripartite model and expresses, I suggest, an insight into the intrapsychic and interpsychic nature of learning and teaching. This functional division requires differing skills at each end-point of the triangle, respectively, and at each end-point of the mirror image of the triangle. Consequently, this requires of those engaged in the teaching field a more sophisticated knowledge of what goes on in teachers when they teach; in children when they learn; in administrators when they administer systems within a given community, which is never entirely free of social change and social pressure. The curriculum is the common task, the external "bottle of milk" which unites them and about which they struggle with each other just as they must work for each other. The teacher will identify with the task set by the administration just as he will from time to time rebel against it. Sometimes he will overidentify with the administration and victimize the child. He must acquire the skill to maintain equal distance from administration and child, from child and parent, and he must be identified with the process of education rather than with any of the participants. That is his task. The way he teaches and enforces the requirements or adapts them for a special situation; the way he rewards and punishes; the way he loves his subject; the way that he, nevertheless, holds on to his purpose, his task, will sometimes influence the child as powerfully as, even at times more powerfully than, what he is teaching and what he offers as reward or punishment.

The child, on the other hand, will identify not only with the teacher's love of knowledge, mastery of subject, but his way of searching, of allowing difference of opinion, of allowing insight learning in addition to repetition learning. Even his ways of examining will influence what the child will draw out of the school system. The child will sense the teacher's reactions to authority, to parents, to the school administration, to political pressure. He will absorb all these things just as much as, if not more than, the text prescribed by the curriculum. The passivity and activity of the learner; the struggle for autonomy of learning; the capacity for acceptance of outer controls when necessary; the whole issue of initiative in learning and trust in teachers will be influenced by the teacher's awareness of the psychological impact of the curriculum and his skill in making use of that awareness.

But what holds true for teacher and student is also true for the administrator of the school system. Freud's theory of personality, after all, is not only applicable to the child and to the teacher but to the administrator as well. Does he leave room for the autonomy and the initiative of the teacher? Does he see the teacher merely as the blind executive organ of external tasks for which he is responsible? Does he help the teacher with the task of teaching, or is supervision for him an authoritarian function merely instead of an authoritative privilege? Is the administrator used by the teacher solely as a kind of external superego agent, a police officer to whom to send the child when he, the teacher, cannot handle him? Or, can a relationship develop between the principal and the teacher which is an equivalent of learning and teaching although on a higher level? How does the principal react to outside pressures?

I suggested that the child who enters the school system works at first for love, identifies with the idealized teacher and his ways of teaching, and learns, thus, to love the work. We have indicated this process of internalization in Figure 3 by extending the lines from teacher function through the curriculum center of gravity and through the mirror-image achievement center of gravity. The extension of the latter line leads to the notion of work for love while the extension of the former leads to the one of the love of work. Neither will ever be indispensable. There will be an ingredient of each aspect in the most adaptable person. But what holds true for the child is also true for the other participants in the process of education. There are mothers who do not feed primarily out of love but in order to get rid of the task as quickly as possible. In the same way, there are teachers and school administrators who have developed little in themselves which can be characterized as the love of educational work. Perhaps this has to do with the impossible tasks I mentioned in the beginning. Society's pressures and demands on educators have always been enormous while actual rewards and recognition have remained far behind.

The original overidealization of the teaching profession, so much a part of teachers' training and so much an inner expectation of the young teacher, leads to the confrontation with psychic and social reality. This process frequently ends with both disillusioned teachers and administrators and is often accompanied by outside ridicule. The teacher's professional skill is constantly beset by social unrest—revolutions and counter-revolutions, wars and fitful peace—while it is to remain the steady link for an adult generation full of uncertainties. The world has not learned all it needs in its struggle for adaptation and cannot really teach all that it ought to teach the young in preparation for future, often unpredictable, tasks. The teachers get the impossible task of transmitting knowledge, skills, attitudes of life to the young in such a way that the generation of children can be the fulfillment of the overt and covert hopes of the older generation.

I cannot see how that process can be maintained with courage and optimism unless the teacher, the educators, the teachers of teachers remain identified not only with the task of teaching but also with the task of learning. George Bernard Shaw offered the cynicism that "he who can does, and he who cannot teaches." May I suggest that he who wants to teach must learn, that he who learns and continues to learn can teach. Wordsworth's insight that the child is the father of the man teaches us that the learner is the father of the teacher—and the curriculum, that external organizer which facilitates the learning process, is the bridge between the teacher and the learner.

BIBLIOGRAPHY

1. Benjamin, Wayne (J. Abner Peddiwell, pseud.) *The Saber-Tooth Curriculum*, New York: McGraw Hill, 1939.
2. Bernfeld, Siegfried. Sisyphus or the Boundaries of Education (Sisyphus oder die Grenzen der Erziehung) Leipzig, Vienna: International Psychoanalytic Press, 1925.
3. Freud, Sigmund. *Interpretation of Dreams* (1900). Standard Edition. London: Hogarth Press, 1953, IV,V.
4. ————. *The Ego and the Id* (1923). Standard Edition. London: Hogarth Press, 1961, XIX.
5. ————. Foreword to: *Wayward Youth.* August Aichhorn. Leipzig, Vienna, Zurich: International Psychoanalytic Press, 1925.
6. Kant, Immanuel. *The Strife of the Faculties* (Der Streit der Fakultaeten). Koenigsberg, 1798.
7. Spitz, René A., in collaboration with W. Godfrey Cobliner. *The First Year of Life: a Psychoanalytic Study of Normal and Deviant Development.* New York: International Universities Press, 1965.

CHAPTER 5

The Influence of the Curriculum and Teaching
on the Development of Creativity

RALPH TYLER

"CREATIVITY," AS GENERALLY USED among educators to refer to an important educational aim, represents an emphasis upon the whole development of children, the effort to help children achieve a significant degree of self-actualization, of initiative; their own involvement in their work and their self-discipline. And, it also emphasizes helping them to develop the ability to deal in new and novel ways—at least for them—with the various aspects of life they encounter. Although it has become a kind of slogan or cliché to many people, the emphasis on creativity can have real meaning. It is used in contrast to an educational emphasis upon mastery of outside things to which the youngster responds merely by doing what is expected of him but without adding anything of his own, nor feeling himself deeply involved.

The interpretation of this emphasis for the curriculum and for the instructional program has been greatly influenced by the ideas of development arising from psychoanalysis. These ideas are not static for they are affected by the changes taking place in education. These, in turn, are closely related to the changes that are taking place in society, especially those changes that have been brought about through the postwar application of technology to many areas of life which had not been directly affected before. What is most relevant to education in this is the rapid shifts taking place in the nature of the opportunities for employment and the kinds of education that are consequently stressed.

When I was born at the turn of the century, 38% of the population was engaged in farming; now only 7% is so engaged. Another 23% was engaged in other forms of unskilled labor. According to recent Bureau of Labor statistics, only 5.6% is so occupied at present. Semi-skilled labor represented about 12% of the population then, and now represents only 3% or 4%. Skilled labor has remained about constant, near 10%.

What this means, of course, is a great reduction in employment opportunities for people who have little education, though there has been a great expansion in other areas. I shall return to the latter point shortly, but first want to note that the reduction in employment opportunities for unskilled labor has immediate implications for universal public education in this country, in Western Europe and even in Japan. About 15% to 20% of all school children in industrialized countries come from backgrounds where there is little educational opportunity in the home and not much educational emphasis nor educational experiences. About 15% to 20% of all school children do not now reach a level of literacy usually required for employment beyond unskilled labor.

This did not represent a serious economic problem to the United States as long as we had more than 60% of persons employed working largely in unskilled occupations. But now that only 5.6% are employed in relatively unskilled occupations, the fact that approximately 15% to 20% of our children reach a low level of literacy means that a considerable percentage must go on relief. Unable to find employment in unskilled labor, unable to attempt any skilled labor, they—and we—become increasingly involved in the "poverty complex" of our society.

This means that we now recognize a new task for American schools and schools in all modern industrial societies. It is to reach that sector of children who have had very limited opportunity in their previous background for learning and are not able to cope with the learning situations in schools that were established for five-year-olds who come from middle-class homes where much initial preparation for school learning has taken place.

A second kind of problem facing all rapidly industrializing countries is that most of the new occupations require more education, rather than less; that, in general, many of them require more than high-school education. There has, for example, been an increase in the proportion of people engaged in the whole range of health services, medicine, nursing and all the other related areas—a five-fold increase since the end of the Second World War. There has also been a great increase in the education field. More people are employed in teaching and other aspects of education because of the population increase combined with the demand for more education. There are great increases in the number of persons that are needed in social work. There are great increases in the number that are being employed in recreational areas. There has been a great increase, although it was never high, in the demand for scientists and engineers, and for persons in administration and accounting.

All of the occupations, therefore, which now offer opportunities for young people require more education than the occupations they have displaced. This creates the task of encouraging many young people, who come from homes where nobody went to college, to go on beyond the high school, and the task of learning how to educate them. In the past the people who went beyond high school, through college and graduate school, were well adapted to that kind of education because they came from educated families or had parents who aspired to more education. As long as our society needed only a small percentage of highly educated people, we got along very well. But now that we need a much larger percentage of people to work in education and the health services and other such areas, we must learn how to help the learning efforts of young people who come from backgrounds that have not included college.

A third consequence of present-day technology for education is the emergence of new educational objectives. For example, the "knowledge explosion" makes unrealistic an aim for students to acquire all significant knowledge. The current realization that research can provide information of very immediate usefulness for many purposes, ranging from medicine to industry to defense and to other areas, has increased our efforts to find knowledge. According to Jerome Wiesner, President Kennedy's science advisor, scientific knowledge is doubling every ten or twelve years, so that it is no longer possible to think of a person being educated in the sense that having finished high school or college, he has a good grasp of all knowledge. It's obvious that fifteen years after his graduation, there will have been much new specific knowledge accumulated since he started school. Hence, schools are now recognizing the need to develop students who like to learn, know how to learn and will be lifelong learners.

Another reaction to the "knowledge explosion" by our schools and colleges has been a re-examination of the role of education. Of course, the enduring role of education is always the same—if the generalization is made at a high enough level. It is always the effort to help children and youth learn those things that enable them to participate constructively in society and to gain personal satisfaction and self-realization. What this means in any particular time, what is required in order to gain such personal self-realization and to become a constructive member of society, can vary widely. It depends both on the nature of the society and its work and problems and on the discovery of that which can contribute to the individual's self-realization of his own talents and abilities.

Throughout the history of education, one problem has been that of maintaining some kind of unity between what is important for being a constructive member of society and what is important for realizing one's own capacities to their fullest. Very often, to children, the objectives of the school have largely seemed to be conditioning. The children have felt forced to acquire certain things that do not have any meaning or significance to them but have been imposed to satisfy society. In the degree that this was true, schooling was viewed as indoctrination in whatever were the values society considered important. In that sense, the school developed rote memorization in order to pass on our forefathers' picture of the world. And in that sense, specific skills could be required of the student which often conflicted, rather than harmonized, with the development of his self-realization.

In today's extremely dynamic society, it becomes clear, for example, that our children who are now in school will be living as adults in a world which is different from the present one in ways which we cannot now predict. This has meant that leaders in education and other aspects of social development have been compelled to re-examine the nature of the curriculum and learning. The new views of the curriculum that are emerging have a potential for making it easier to meet both the demands of society and the desire for self-realization in the individual. They have a potential but, because they are changing so rapidly, they may evoke a teacher reaction that may make education even more constraining and deepen the conflict between its two roles. Curriculum development is at present the focus of much interest in this country. Private foundations, public schools and many colleges are devoting a great deal of effort to building new courses and new parts to the curriculum in almost every field. The efforts began in the fields of science and mathematics, and the Federal Government spent $17,000,000 in curriculum development in 1965-66 and nearly $19,000,000 in 1966-67 on these tasks.

Several aspects of the new curriculum offer opportunity for greater creativity. In the first place, the selection of content is based upon the view that the curriculum is to help the student learn things that will enable him to understand the world. It will enable him to do things that are significant and possible in his life. It would enable him to enhance his own emotional reactions and satisfactions and learn to discipline and control them in areas where the emphasis is upon emotional development and appreciation, e.g., the fine arts. In another area, the field of science, the new high-school physics course attempted very directly to present a few basic concepts that can help a youngster more easily understand physical phenomena around him. The rationale was that everybody wants to understand, is curious about the world—not that he's got to learn physics because some physicist said so. That course is built around thirty-four basic concepts that can be used again and again to explain things the student observes. In terms of laboratory work, the student starts out with questions about the phenomena that he observes when he carries out some experiment. The emphasis is upon "insightful learning" which is called "discovery learning" by the Physical

Science Study Committee. The student's effort is directed to the discovery of relationships among these things and to the formulation of explanatory concepts as he works with the phenomena involved.

This, of course, is not new. It has been an emphasis in progressive teaching for a long time. But course after course is now being developed with the emphasis upon content that is not viewed as something out there which must be mastered because society requires it, but content that represents ways of helping the young student understand phenomena around him.

Correspondingly, in connection with courses requiring skills, the emphasis is on building up those skills that the child will find immediately helpful in his own living, in the things he wants to do. Content in each is selected on the basis of what is of most importance and most use to him in his effort to do things.

That's one direction of curriculum development. Another involves the restatement of the epistemology of knowledge. This is directly related to creativity. Many of us as teachers have the notion that knowledge is—out there. It exists in books or in something else, and the teacher's duty is to remember it and pass it on to the students. The new epistemology is based on the notion that knowledge is not something that just exists out there, but is man's effort to create understanding; to figure out ways to make sense of his experience; to organize observations from chaotic confusion into a form which can make sense and can be related to other observations. This is hard-won knowledge in itself: knowledge is man-made and is always being built. So many of these new curricular efforts for the student put him in a position to begin to build his knowledge and in so doing he discovers there are alternative explanations. He learns there isn't just a single set of ways, for example, in the new mathematics, but many kinds of number systems that he can learn to use. He learns that they are all man-made. There's nothing magic about any of them, nothing immutable. Knowledge is man's effort continually to understand and explain in ever more encompassing or more economical terms; it is not one thing that alone is right. The student learns that knowledge consists of approximations that are being built up.

This approach is difficult for some of us to accept. In the study of language, we must realize that grammar wasn't made out there any more than any other kind of knowledge. Human beings developed patterns of communication and speech and human beings can examine and describe them in many ways. One way arose from those who examined Latin and came up with classifications called Latin grammar. In our earlier worship of Latin, this grammar was applied to English and German and French, and we were brought up with the view that the right grammar was Latin grammar. Sometimes English is like Latin and sometimes it is not. Modern linguistics seeks to describe the language as it exists, that is, the reality of the language, and then seeks to explain it. Our grammar, any grammar, like any other form of language explanation, is man-made. The student studying linguistics doesn't have the feeling that language is immutable and he must learn it in its majestic immutability and entirety. Instead, he gets the enjoyment of looking at language and trying to figure out ways of making sense of it.

The examples I have used are to illustrate that as far as the curriculum is concerned, the new materials, the new ways of organizing the content and the objectives are in harmony with the effort to free the child to have a sense of accomplishment. How essential this is was brought home in the massive study of equality of educational opportunity in the United States conducted by James Coleman, of Johns Hopkins, and Ernest Campbell, of Vanderbilt, at the direction of Congress. They reported that the thing that distinguished most sharply the students who were achieving in school from those who were not was their answer when asked if they had any ability to control their own destiny or environment. The kind who, in effect, said, "No—everything is out there, I can only submit or rebel, those are the only alternatives," rarely achieved much in school. Those who replied that they could do things for themselves were generally superior achievers in school.

This is in harmony with our concern about creativity and initiative and self-direction developed by children. They are helped by seeing that learning is a tool. With learning, they become more able to do things, to be part of a world which is not simply forcing them to live in accordance with dictates from outside themselves. Through learning they can acquire the tools for increasing their own self-realization and, at the same time—in a society which can't use many unskilled laborers— a way of becoming a more constructive member of a society that needs more teachers, more persons in the health services, more persons in the social services, more in engineering and in science. We have a great opportunity to make use of technology rather than to have it destroy us.

In 1960, the study of the distribution of the labor force indicated that for the first time in the history of any nation, less than half of our people were being used in our economy to produce and distribute material goods. This trend is continuing so that it is anticipated that in another five years only 40% of our population will be required to produce our food, clothing, shelter and the like. About 50% will be available to meet our innumerable needs for health, for education, for various kinds of recreation, for aid in social services. To meet this need, we need to help develop many more youngsters into human beings capable of the kind of initiative and creativity required for these kinds of personal, spiritual services as contrasted with what may be required to run a lathe or work on an assembly line.

There is a great opportunity in the new curriculum and its emphasis upon discovery, or insightful learning, for the further development of creativity. But we must solve the problem of really educating our disadvantaged children, many of whom are not able to attain a constructive place in society. We need research and development centers seeking to find out more adequately about human learning and how it may more effectively take place. We also need to use what we find out, for despite all the experiments and current innovations, it appears that only a small fraction of the total number of teachers and schools are incorporating new ideas in their work and contributing to educational improvement through their own creative efforts. A considerable fraction simply take on new slogans and, instead of using "discovery learning," they still emphasize rote learning. They are responding to pressures from the outside rather than using the opportunity to be creative from within. There is the danger that we will make frantic efforts to deal with the rapidly mounting problems of education, as often happens when we feel insecure. Then we may respond to the sense of public pressures by becoming tough with children rather than by seeking to solve the problems so as to increase creativity. The challenge we face is to develop and use more understanding of children and of the processes of learning so that we can help to develop many more creative youngsters.

CHAPTER 6

The Child, the Teacher and Learning

RUDOLF EKSTEIN

ONLY HE WHO CAN REMAIN a student forever will be a good teacher forever. It is fitting, therefore, for a teacher occasionally to recall his own student days and reconstruct his state of mind at that time.

When I was a high-school student, I was very much intrigued with the heroes of antiquity. At that time, I thought it was because they challenged their fathers—the gods, the rulers—with their defiance, and wanted a new and better world. Now, many years later, as I look back at the heroes that I chose, it seems to me that the longing for heroism and the adolescent rebellion contain more than just the blind struggle against parental authority which is described and accepted as adolescent turmoil. I feel this way because one of my heroes was Sisyphus.

Mythology describes him as a very cunning and defiant man, who could teach things that other people did not know. The authorities, the gods of old, grew very angry at his defiance. Finally, they punished this very wise man. They ordered that he be forced to roll a huge rock to the top of a mountain. Whenever he had almost accomplished this task, the rock would crash down again, and the tired man had to start his labor all over again.

Another hero of my high-school days, again a very wise man, Prometheus, taught man how to use fire. Since he was an excellent and very successful teacher, who brought culture to man—for without fire there would be no civilization—the gods were said to have punished him by condemning him to physical agony forever. Even so, they never crushed the spirit of Prometheus, that guardian of the flame.

Another hero who inspired youths in the days when I went to high school was not mythological but the historical Hannibal. We were intrigued with the courage and genius and strength which enabled him to lead his army from Carthage in Africa across Spain and all the mountain chains to Italy, to fight heroic battles in enemy territory, and to threaten Rome in epic competition. While he never conquered Rome, his menace at her gates was remembered with alarm throughout Rome's hegemony.

As cited in earlier chapters, Siegfried Bernfeld chose Sisyphus as the hero who would symbolize the theme of one of his most important books. Sisyphus was the one who tried over and over again, and who was finally defeated. One might say of him that he was condemned to repeat over and over again and never to succeed, but one might also say of him that he chose this way. It was his character, his commitment, that drove him to choose a task which would make it necessary for him continually to start all over again, to try over and over again. Even though, perhaps, he knew himself that he might never succeed, he remained faithful to his commitment.

Sigmund Freud chose as *his* hero in high-school days the Hannibal who never yielded even though he must have known that he would never conquer. Of course, we know that the work of Freud, the work of psychoanalysis or, for that matter, the work of any scientist is an eternal task that is never quite fully accomplished; but of psychoanalysis it is especially true, as it was for Hannibal, that it always arouses resistance, that it always creates opponents who seem to lose in the field but who never give up and who cannot yield.

What has all this to do with the task of the teacher? I am speaking of the fact that Siegfried Bernfeld, as he wrote about Sisyphus, had in mind the teachers—the educators—who have to start over and over again. They are committed to a never-ending task as they dismiss class after class at the end of each year, always wondering whether they have succeeded; always exposed to pressures, against which no one could stand up with lasting success, and frequently losing; sometimes standing—like Hannibal—before the "gates of Rome"; yet always, like Prometheus, bringing knowledge to the child and fire to man; always being punished, but nevertheless standing up to the challenge again and again.

Bernfeld offered the following definition of education: "Education is the reaction of society to the facts of development."[1] As he describes that reaction of society, he suggests that the teacher has undertaken a task which is extremely difficult because he stands between that society —that generation of parents, that generation of politicians, of government leaders, who create the educational system that the teacher must use—and the facts of development, namely, the pressures that come from the growing child (see chapters 1 and 2). The teacher must try, over and over again, to mediate between the child and society in order to create a system of checks and balances. He tries to help the child grow up and learn in and through that society; and as he attempts this, he moves back and forth between two impossible tasks.

Let me try to describe these two tasks of the teacher, but in modern terms, in terms of a dynamic psychology of conflict, rather than through the imagery of Greek mythology or the simile from Roman history.

We as educators have recently been exposed to two major pressures, two major reactions of society in its battle for the mind of the child, and in its battle to direct the educational system, a goal of which is preparing the child to become part of the adult world. The first pressure rises from a response of American society to the outer pressure, the struggle between East and West, the struggle between the developed and the undeveloped nations. Concerning this vital competition, we feel that we do not want to surrender; and we do not want another Oswald Spengler to write once more *The Decline of the West.*

Pressure is then put on us in the educational field by a society that wants to compete with those who created Sputnik. We are told that we ought to get to the moon first, that we must reach outer space first. We are suddenly told that a strict, scientific and demanding curriculum should be put back into the elementary school, the kindergarten and perhaps even the nursery school. The school should put less stress on personality development and more on the development of skills in physics, chemistry and all the hardware sciences. The first response of the educators, of course, was to see whether this pressure of society— society's reaction to the facts of external developments and external competition—could be met and translated into educational philosophy and educational practice.

We found ourselves facing a task which we had not chosen ourselves, but which had been imposed upon us. The curriculum is not simply developed by teachers, but rather is decided upon by the administrators. The administrators are appointed and paid by the community, and the community frequently reacts to the administrators in terms of its adult problems. The community does not always react to the young in terms of the needs of the developing child, but rather reacts to the child in terms of the needs of society. The current anxieties, the panicky reaction that we sometimes face as we think of atomic fallout, the hydrogen bomb or political and military urgencies, make us exert pressure on the educational system.

Everybody in our profession—kindergarten teacher, nursery school teacher, grammar school teacher, administrator or instructor of teachers—knows what I am talking about, whether he comes from the allied sciences that help us erect a more perfect educational system, or whether he is directly rooted in teaching practice. There is hardly a day when the funds that come from government agencies for our educational systems and our training are not clearly recognized as being dictated by the political affairs of man. The vicissitudes of political issues directly and indirectly exert their vast pressures on the educational system and on us, the educators. While these are all external pressures, resulting from the international situation in a schizophrenic world divided into East and West, I also want to discuss internal pressure.

We deal today not only with the fear of atomic explosion, that threat from the outside, but we also face the fear of explosion within our country: we are confronted with the population explosion, the racial explosion and the explosion that comes from the wish to end poverty forever. We discover then that teachers have to deal with pressures that come not only from the outside because of the nation's wish to compete successfully with other systems, but which come from the country's internal conflicts as well. That pressure exerts itself in the plan to develop an educational movement like Head Start. The result is that many semi-trained and untrained people are put into short training programs so that they can be mobilized for the great masses of children who are considered to be culturally deprived and who deserve a head start in order to catch up with the rest of the children. We find ourselves suddenly exposed to enormous pressures created by the challenge of mass programs which undermine the careful and conventional plans for teacher training, and which would make it necessary for us to use short-cut methods in order to meet the broad tasks of the day.

I am speaking of the fact that many such programs, while allegedly serving the needs of the child, are actually inspired by our own anxieties which are of a social nature. I do not want to attack freedom and motherhood, nor do I want to overlook our responsibilities in improving the educational system, nor in meeting the needs of many children who do not get educational opportunities as they should be made available in a free society. But I do want to say that some of the current emergency measures, the mass programs and the shortcuts, seem to me primarily a short-sighted response to domestic political pressure and to social anxiety. If they are not to turn out to be a mere political expediency, a waste of public funds and, later, a terrible disappointment, they must be converted into professional opportunities. They must be carefully thought out to conform with what we know about the developing child, rather than remain on the level of naive mass programs which will drown out the effectiveness of the well-trained educator.

Under these circumstances, can we become an effective professional force, or must we fail like Sisyphus? Can we be effective in view of the fact that we are not only facing the gods of Sisyphus: the government, the communities, the boards of education, the research designers, the fund givers; but also, and most important, the child himself. If we are successful and, if out of these different and often conflicting aspirations of society, we do forge an educational program of reason, will we be able to bring that reason to the child, that very child who brings to us his unreason? He brings to us his unconscious urges, his impulsive and emotional life. He brings to us his fantasies and imagination. He brings to us all his growing-up problems in a world that is pressing upon him. We mediate between his internal pressures and the external pressures of an anxious world around him.

The other day I read one of England's educational journals, *The London Head Teacher*, and there I found a few paragraphs, written some 40 years after Bernfeld had written his *Sisyphus*. These paragraphs, contributed by Sir Alexander Clegg, were also entitled "Sisyphus," Clegg's synonym for teacher:

> The school must curb and contain and sublimate the sexual urges of the young while adult commercial interests exploit sex in striptease and other dubious joints.
> The schools must establish humane and unselfish relationships in their communities while both sides of industry recriminate against each other with charges and countercharges, strikes and lockouts.
> The schools must instill a love of good literature and good music while money-making interests flood the bookstalls with literary trash or beat up the pop music racket to extract every penny from the teenager.[2]

I was interested to see that educators everywhere realize that the task that society has vested in us is an impossible task, a Sisyphean task. It is about this task that I wish to discourse and, obviously, I do not use the adjective "impossible" in order to be discouraging. I say "impossible" because I think that a man or woman can do no better than to find a life's task or function that would permit total commitment forever and ever. What is there even in building a house, as important as that is, knowing that in three months it can be completed, and then proceeding to build another house? I would much rather have us build on something that can never be finished, an impossible task.

The educator's enormous task, then, is to try to bring together that society which I have described, and that child about whom I will say more. And they must be brought together so that the child will truly be ready to learn and the teacher will truly be ready to teach.

I think that a society which is concerned with its adult worries, and which feels pressed to use the child in order to rescue this society's system, is not truly ready to teach. One is not truly ready to teach when one has large sums of money rolling in for mass programs that, in six summer weeks, are to resolve problems of cultural deprivation which would need intensive years of careful work with the children concerned.

I think that one is ready to teach only when one fully knows what the teaching task implies, what it takes to make a teacher, when one knows what it really takes to repair the damaged learning ability of a child rather than hoping that an expedient crash program can wipe out the guilt or mend political fences.

The kind of development that is fostered in the nursery school and in kindergarten is learning, although it must be considered different from the formal kind of learning. I suggest that it may be looked upon as preparatory learning by means of which the child gets ready, when he becomes five or six, to go into that part of our educational system in which more formal teaching procedures are possible. It is in that later part in which the goal of learning and teaching is more oriented towards teaching subject matter, imparting knowledge and developing skills.

Nursery school and kindergarten teachers stand in the middle, between the formal education which starts in the elementary schools and the very first educational effort which was started when the child was still in the cradle. As a matter of fact, when the child is entrusted to a nursery school at the age of two-and-a-half or three, his teacher takes on a function which looks almost like an inheritance problem. He inherits the product of an educational process started by the mother, the first teacher of the child.

I have suggested elsewhere (chapter 4), half in jest and half seriously, that the first curriculum developed is the full breast. The first successful course is mastered if the baby can develop the skill, that wisdom from the milk, which will allow him later, when he becomes a formal pupil, to acquire also the milk that comes from wisdom. What I am saying is that when this young child comes to the nursery school he, perhaps, has already acquired the right amount of inheritance called basic trust, trust in himself and trust in others.

Erikson[4] beautifully discusses the psychosocial development of the small child which grows out of the struggle between the nursing baby's need for instant gratification and the mother's requirement that he learn to postpone. Out of the original child-mother unit will grow a sense of differentiation between the child's self and the mother-object. The child will not only develop a sense of self but also acquire the capacity to delay; and he will attain a sense of basic trust, in himself and the world around him, if the task inherent in this first developmental crisis is successfully mastered.

As this child comes to the nursery teacher, he must learn to live with what he inherited from that past developmental phase, a credit or debit accumulated by the child and his mother during his early days of education. Children who have not passed through a successful early experience which makes for the availability of basic trust, and who bring to nursery school the negative ingredients of distrust, low self-esteem and feelings of inferiority, can only be helped in years of careful work, if they are to get a genuine head start. They cannot be helped in a four- or six-week course in summer.

The outcome of the oral phase of development—with its inherent conflict and struggle characterized by the rhythm of frustration and mastery, of fusion and separation—will color all future object relations and all future self-experience. It will define the amount and quality of one of the basic ingredients of learning readiness available to the child and the teacher. Can the teacher nurture basic trust in that young being, can he strengthen and correct it so that the next in line, the teacher in the elementary school, will inherit a workable task; or can he perhaps do no more than predict that this young being, under-developed and weak as it is, will become the future dropout?

In the early days of psychoanalysis we stressed primarily those parts of education which imposed too much frustration and restriction upon the child. Psychoanalysis then advanced the idea that the child should be liberated from measures too oppressive, too forbidding. Freedom of play was advocated, and the cathartic function of play was stressed. Emphasis was placed on a certain degree of instinctual freedom, and it was advocated that these first impulses should be tamed slowly, rather than suppressed through strict punishment and violent threat. This, perhaps, was a justified reaction to the state of affairs at the time, but in the meantime we have learned, and we know now, that we must look at both sides of the coin. (See chapter 1.)

There is not only the necessity for gratification, but there is also the requirement of limitation. It is between gratification and limitation, between need fulfillment and the acquisition of the capacity for delay, that a child learns to acquire basic trust. This trust not only makes him feel that the world is essentially a good place, but also teaches him trust in himself so that he can utilize the world. He can then make use of his teachers and the school, his peers, his parents and siblings at home, and can see something positive in this world. That early reality was viewed previously by us as primarily a frustrating reality, but we know now that it also offers the nutriment for growth, maturation and development.

These first two basic ingredients—trust in himself, the beginning of self-esteem; and trust in others, the beginning of love and respect—are now part of our educational concern. It is true that at the time the child comes to the nursery-school teachers, much has already been accomplished or destroyed; but usually the situation is not so fixed that it cannot be repaired, maintained and improved through educational means.

We must recall that every mental and emotional achievement has nonpermanence attached to it. These internal accomplishments are labile, comparable, for example, to the freedom in our country for which we must always fight and which can never be taken for granted. The issue of trust, regardless of how excellent the first two years of life were for the child and mother, is one that will come up over and over again. Even the most trusting personalities can be exposed to conditions in a social structure not deserving of that trust which will undermine their trust in the world and in themselves. It is during nursery-school years that teachers have an opportunity to fortify their pupils' capacity for trust.

The second phase of the child's development is very much a part of nursery-school life and perhaps more dominant than the phase discussed above. In this phase we find the child, having freed himself from blind distrust and trust, from the megalomania that he can do everything and from the feeling of total inferiority expressed in the notion that he can do nothing, is now challenged with a new inner task. This, too, has its growth conflict, the necessary inner crises that the child must live through in order to achieve a new synthesis of inner forces. This second phase of the child's development is concerned with the issue of control. I am describing the toilet-training period, and the necessity of controlling the child so that he cannot run wherever he wishes; so that he can control his bladder and sphincter function; so that he knows what is right; learns to be orderly; keeps himself clean; is willing to accept control by the mother and learns to share with his siblings.

This control should not be over-control that squashes but, rather, it should be the kind of control which, as Erikson has described it,[4] will permit him to go through this next growth crisis, with the help of his parents and his teachers in nursery school, in such a way that he acquires two new capacities.

The first one is the beginning of autonomy, a degree of self-autonomy, so that he can begin to govern himself and need not be ruled by others. But this self-autonomy has to have room for other people, so that it is not at the expense of other people. Thus, he must be able to accept the control of parents and of society whenever necessary and be willing to see where his capacity for autonomy ends and his need for control begins. During this period he learns to negotiate and to compromise, to mediate between these different forces, so that he can create a system of checks and balances between the wish for autonomy and the need for controls.

This development is described by Erikson in psychosocial terms as the phase in which the balance between autonomy and control is achieved, and discussed by Freud in terms of psychosexual development as the "anal phase." It is a long struggle and is usually not ended at the time the child reaches nursery school. Mothers who believe that they must give their children all the autonomy that they want, create unknowingly the preconditions for a chaotic, selfish, impulsive psychopath who takes what he can get and mistakes it for freedom: such an individual has not acquired autonomy but license.

There also are mothers, at the other extreme, who believe that the control of their children is of utmost importance, and who cannot master their own inner anxiety, their own need to control, unless they always prevail. Because of their own insecurity, these mothers must gain their own ends to guarantee their own quasi-autonomy. Such mothers will react to their children by over-controlling them, so that there is no room left for these children to develop any form of autonomy. Between these two extremes, the irresponsible psychopath who takes what he can get, misjudges that attitude for freedom, and can never be truly happy; and the over-controlled, anxious child who has no freedom, no autonomy of his own and is completely governed by the mother, are the majority of children who define the field of activity for the educator.

The significance of Bernfeld's definition of education as the reaction of society to the facts of development should now be quite clear. As one thinks about these two extreme pictures of mothers, one might very well think of extreme pictures of two kinds of teachers, or probation officers, judges, police officers or voters who select the boards of education and determine the basic educational philosophy. We can begin to recognize them as forces who do not react to the child in terms of his needs, do not consider how to react to the child's inner conflicts so that the solution leads to internal growth. Rather, they are forces who react to the child in terms of their own needs, anxieties and feelings of helplessness.

We teachers and educators want to change this. We don't want to see education as a blind reaction to children; instead, we want to develop a rationale, an educational philosophy, backed by scientific data and scientific theories, which will permit us to respond to children in such a way that they can grow and resolve these conflicts instead of being crushed by them. It is in this area, then, that psychoanalysts and educators must get together in order to change blind reaction into a rational response, fed by the nutriment of science.

Before the influence of psychoanalysis was felt in the educational field, education was frequently seen as a process of molding. The educator fancied himself as someone who took a hunk of clay or a block of marble—sometimes unworkable clay and faulty marble, impervious to the chisel and the shaping hand—and tried to shape it into the form it should take. The psychoanalyst brought something new into consideration in the way he perceived the child. The child was seen now as possessing his own internal structure, his own inherent possibilities, and his own reaction to the influence of external force. Psychoanalysts have tried to add insight into the growth mechanisms of the child and into the reactions of the educators. For this reason, it has been recommended that individuals who are preparing themselves for a professional career of teaching would do well if they, too, would undergo analysis so that they could better understand themselves.

Many people who were trained in the early days of the psychoanalytic influence on education later became leaders of child analysis, although originally they all were active teachers. All wanted to develop the teaching profession in such a way that there would be a synthesis of scientific methodology and educational love (and sometimes hate, because that, too, is a part of our reaction to the child), developed into an applicable system. By using this system, it would prove possible to react to the learning child with a new kind of teaching readiness based on a thorough understanding of the child's learning readiness, his ever-changing capacity to make use of trust, autonomy, initiative and industry.

This leads me to the third phase of psychosexual development, Freud's "phallic" phase, described by Erikson as the one characterized through the struggle between initiative and guilt. As the instinctual needs slowly shift in their dominant expression from oral and anal expressions to genital interests, the growing child develops new expectations of and wishes towards the parents, the primary objects of his early years. During this time the child thrusts out into the world, develops initiative and curiosity, a wish to conquer and to initiate new types of relationships. This initiative was illustrated by Freud through the powerful image of the myth of Oedipus, who was driven by the wish to possess his mother and was enraged by the obstacle, the opposing father. That phase of the oedipal conflict characterizes the development of initiative which is, in part, fostered by the parents and society and, in part, must be squashed.

In the past, many of the child's instinctual expressions were stopped, too, but they were punished then because they were dangerous to him. The phase of initiative is one in which there slowly develops not only a sense of what is realistically dangerous or what can be pursued, but also a sense of moral and ethical values. The sense of shame and guilt which he now feels is different in quantity and quality from its forerunners which concerned earlier development. He is caught in a new conflict, the one between initiative and guilt. He experiences the desire to thrust out into the world, to be curious about his body and the nature of his origin, to experiment, to touch, to find new sensations, to discover physical joy. On the other hand, he fears that most of it, or some of it, will be forbidden. It depends on the structure and moral codes of society as to what kind of initiative will be approved and what kind will be limited, and what kind of sense of guilt will govern his life and make him into a more fully moral human being.

The myth of Oedipus projects into adulthood the conflicts which are part of the child's mental life. The myth tells us that Oedipus, as he moves against his father, whom he slays, and marries his mother, does so unwittingly. It is fate that drives him toward the catastrophe. Though driven by fate, he ends with a deep sense of guilt, reacts towards himself with severe self-punishment and has himself persecuted by the goddesses of vengeance.

Through that myth the Greeks of antiquity conveyed to us an important aspect of the child's mental development, his unconscious conflict in the oedipal triad. The outcome, if the conflict is mastered, Freud summed up in these epigrammatic words: "The superego is the heir of the Oedipus complex." That is, without that struggle between initiative and guilt—the wish to possess, to enjoy, to love, and the recognition that premature possession, forbidden initiative, must be restricted—the child could never develop a conscience, could never complete that psychic structure which Freud described through the concept of superego.

Equally true, without the mastery of that struggle, the child could never develop those functions which Freud has subsumed under the concept of "ego ideal." That is, the capacity to identify with other persons, his identity models, in such a way that he wants to be like them and can develop the initiative by means of which he will try to live up to positive examples and positive goals. He is now confronted not merely with primitive initiative, but with an initiative guided by rules of the game, by moral and religious examples of society, personified by idealized parents.

Each young Oedipus of our day—the growing preschool child—as he gives up his early strivings by postponing fulfillment and exchanging the goals of his aspirations, attempts to be like his father rather than trying to take his place. He hopes that someday, when he is like his father, he will possess someone modeled in part by that earliest love object, his mother. The little girl will go through a similar development. She will want to be like her mother, will identify with her, and her initiative will be dedicated to that attempt.

It is clear that this struggle between initiative and guilt will be resolved in the mind of the child in such a way that he will give up the early need for instant gratification, the early erotic and sexual urges. He will postpone not only because of external pressure, but because he will have acquired the capacity for delay. When he comes to kindergarten and elementary school, he will have acquired the capacity to look up to his teachers, and be ready to trust and respect them.

But if he has not resolved these early conflicts, or if his conflicts should reawaken, he will turn out to be hostile and reckless. He will be defiant, distrustful and untrustworthy. His initiative will be more a destructiveness than a constructive capacity to learn, his curiosity a primitive voyeurism instead of a thirst for knowledge. He will hardly be capable of the next phase of inner development in which he should acquire the capacity and desire for industry so that he can learn under the guidance of a teacher. Instead, his response will be one of apathy and indifference.

There are six internal achievements, brought about through educational pressure as well as through the resolution of inner conflict. They are the capacity for trust in others and self-trust; the capacity for autonomy as well as the capability of accepting control by others whenever necessary; the capacity to develop initiative and a working conscience which contains not only the interdictions, but also the aspirations. These six achievements are the basic ingredients that make for learning readiness in the young child. Nursery-school teachers add the decisive finishing touches to this phase of development, a phase of learning, a painful and, at the same time, inspiring solution of tasks.

As the child is father of the man so is the pupil the father of the teacher. And keeping the student state of mind makes the teacher better prepared for his own task; namely, to match that learning readiness not with the blind reaction of society—since blind reactions do not teach—but rather with teaching readiness. I suggest we develop a scheme, an evaluation procedure, to be repeated during training and later during staff development, which would permit us to see whether these teachers have achieved teaching readiness. Do they have trust in themselves as teachers? Do they trust the child? Have they achieved professional autonomy, or do they need to over-control the child? Are they capable of developing teaching initiative, and are they capable of stimulating learning initiative, encouraging curiosity in the child; or did they never accomplish this aspect of professional skill?

Many have never achieved these aspects of professional identity. Instead of being industrious teachers, they are beset by apathy and unhappiness. We may find them constantly complaining about the school board or the principal, about the children's parents, about the children themselves. They can only be critical of society and cannot stand social pressures. They will frequently get out of the field as quickly as possible; if they stay, they are embittered and have achieved but a labile professional identity.

Teachers' colleges stress, as they should, courses on child development. I would like to suggest that in order to round out teachers' training we should develop courses and workshops to further teaching readiness, the constant self-development of the teacher. It will then become clearer to the teacher that he recapitulates in his training, on a higher level, exactly what the child goes through during the first stages of his schooling. Therefore, learning readiness can be considered a simile for teaching readiness.

The contribution of psychoanalysis to education may be put in terms such as these: Psychoanalytic knowledge can help the teacher understand the psychic organization of the child, the phases of his growth and development, the task that the child must resolve in order to acquire learning capacity. Psychoanalysis can also help teachers understand themselves as teachers, as professional persons, and has much to contribute toward insight into the nature of the whole educational process.

The teacher committed to the task of mediating between the internal and external pressures on a child would find out very quickly that society is not necessarily helpful. Consequently, the teacher will find himself in the condition of Sisyphus when he tried to be wise and Prometheus when he brought fire to the world. The teacher's demand for such an ideal educational system will be met either by attack or by apathy. In the latter case, society will claim that there is not enough money for the right kind of facilities, teacher training and salaries, or for the use of other helping professions. In short, society will not be able to offer enough time and funds, enough patience and insight, to permit this Utopian development which I have suggested. Rather than meeting the demands for improving the status quo, society will even worsen it. Instead of powerful teacher-student relationships in which the individual counts, society will say that we need mass institutional instruction with television and teaching machines. Such emergency measures will be proposed as being better than doing nothing, and emergency conditions require emergency measures.

We live in an industrialized world where our educational facilities have developed into huge complexes that look more like factories than institutions which provide for individualized processes. One compelling need for a teacher in such a world is, reminiscent of the student emulating his model, to identify with those heroes who believe in individualism. And the heroes of antiquity—Sisyphus, Prometheus, Hannibal—are not so different from modern heroes like Goethe and Freud and Jefferson when it comes to the subject of individualism.

BIBLIOGRAPHY

1. Bernfeld, Siegfried. *Sisyphus oder die Grenzen der Erziehung* (Sisyphus or the Boundaries of Education), Vienna: International Psychoanalytic Press, 1925.
2. Clegg, Sir Alexander. "Sisyphus," *The London Head Teacher*, 1966, 305:246.
3. Ekstein, Rudolf. "Siegfried Bernfeld," *Psychoanalytic Pioneers*, F. Alexander, S. Eisenstein and M. Grotjahn, eds. New York: Basic Books, Inc., 1966.
4. Erikson, Erik H. *Childhood and Society*. New York: W. W. Norton & Co., Inc., 1950.

CHAPTER 7

The Unconscious Mind in Teaching

J. C. HILL

PSYCHOANALYSIS AND EDUCATION are related subjects if we are thinking in terms of the ideal, but if we are considering what an analyst does with one patient and what a teacher does with thirty or forty children, the relationship is not so obvious. Education as practiced by teachers often seems to analysts to be full of faults, but if the analyst cannot himself teach a class of forty children successfully, he does not know what the difficulties are, and his advice to teachers may be useless or even harmful. First-class teachers can use first-class methods, but if third-class teachers attempt to use first-class methods the results are usually disastrous. Few head teachers would put the proportion of first-class teachers as high as twenty per cent.

This is where Anna Freud has an advantage when she speaks as a psychoanalyst to teachers. She has been a successful teacher and knows the difficulties. She is in no hurry to tell them all about psychoanalysis. How much can they take? How much is really relevant to the work they are doing? Of Freud's many discoveries what are the two or three of most importance for these teachers to know now?

The hopeful thing is that third-class teachers may become second-class teachers, some of them even first-class teachers, if they have an enlightened headmaster to give them suitable classes to practice on, and to show them gradually how to use better methods. In our smaller schools in England, heads did most valuable work in this way. In the present-day reorganization of our schools, this factor is not allowed to come into play. The large comprehensive school makes it extremely difficult for a headmaster to improve the quality of the teachers. Mechanical sequence in teaching becomes more necessary, and psychological sequence seems to be lost.

Specialization in teacher training has also created difficulties. It used to be possible for a headmaster to give a young teacher a class of younger pupils who were fairly easy to manage. When he had acquired good discipline, and a large background of knowledge and technical skill, he would be given a class of older children, if he wanted such work. Now, the younger teacher trained for secondary work is given straight away a class of thirty older pupils—a task very few of them can manage successfully. In the struggle for existence the young teacher throws overboard all the good modern methods he learned in the training college, and he is soon working in the same way as the older teachers in the school.

Like all heads of schools, I have a great respect for orthodox teaching methods. They have been arrived at through the experience of generations of teachers, and an impressive background of books and apparatus has been built up to support these methods. Most teachers who leave this background and adopt any new method usually give it up before long, or have a nervous breakdown.

Yet the ten to twenty per cent of teachers who are first-class have always had the most striking success with their teaching. The children are happy, they learn an astonishing amount, and they leave the class interested in knowledge and in life. These teachers, like good mothers of young children, understand intuitively the unconscious mind, and adopt educational methods which make use of it. This is a gradual process, and the young teacher cannot begin where the first-class teacher finishes.

In this article, I am trying to explain how teachers can take advantage of freer educational methods, and how they can make use of the powerful unconscious minds of their pupils, but still keep the situation in hand. I want them to retain their power to change back when necessary to the more formal methods, so that they can cope with any of the awkward situations with which teachers have to deal.

While teaching techniques have changed somewhat since classes became smaller and more books and apparatus became available, human relationships do not change much in a hundred years. We have always had teachers who saw their fifty or sixty pupils as individual members of a large family, whom they educated with love and kindness; and we have had teachers, and still have teachers, who regard a class as a uniform block of humanity on which they try to stick certain bits of information. The former are the salt of the earth, the latter make a very small contribution to the good life, if indeed they do not make a negative contribution.

Most of these less effective teachers have within them the possibility of good teaching. I have seen teachers so bad, that some principals would not accept them even temporarily, and I have seen some of these transformed into good teachers when left for a time with a sympathetic principal who could evoke the good that was in them and help them with class management. So many young teachers begin with high ideals and

love of the pupils, and for lack of skill in handling the class, become
mechanical or aggressive teachers, with no joy in their work.

I attach the greatest importance for education to Freud's discoveries,
but I do not want a psychoanalyst on the training-college staff unless he
is a skilled teacher himself, and is prepared to demonstrate in the classroom how teaching should be done. Psychoanalysis is a huge subject, and
students in training as teachers cannot cope with it. Academic psychology, sociology, philosophy, the history of education, the results of
educational research are also huge subjects, and small doses of each of
these may only confuse students unless they are related to the handling
of children in the classroom.

One-subject teachers are not wanted. Children's minds don't develop
in grooves. In order to feed the interests of a five-year-old boy, a parent
must know a lot, and a good teacher should know more. I would rather
have teaching students helped with the subjects they will be likely to
teach, than with the more philosophical subjects, valuable as these could
be for teachers who are already experienced and successful. Few students
leaving the training college are really trained teachers. Let us concentrate
on equipping them better to handle efficiently the first class they take in
hand. This would help them make use of the unconscious mind in their
teaching.

I shall now try to relate the unconscious mind to some of the school
subjects. I am not, of course, presuming to tell the various experts how
to teach their own subjects; but the concept of the unconscious mind
could help in the teaching of every subject, and I may be able to explain
this more clearly if I deal with the subjects one at a time.

ART: If one visits an exhibition of children's art, one is surprised
by the very high standard of the work. It will be found that almost every
picture was painted from a visual image. In other words, with the intellect in abeyance, the unconscious mind (the dream mind) has produced
the picture which the child copies on to the paper. It will be found on
visiting the drawing class the children are concentrating intensely on
their work, and have great pleasure in doing it.

We are all visualizers, as we know from our dreams, but many adults
have lost the power in their waking life. Visual imagery can get in the
way of scientific or logical thinking, and many of us have repressed it
so successfully that we no longer realize that such a thing exists.

But most children visualize easily. If a child can form, and hold, a
visual image of anything, he has a perfect picture. The grouping cannot
be wrong, for the unconscious mind must integrate in order to hold. If
he sees his mother's face and paints it, he will paint his love of his
mother as well as her face. In other words, every child's vision is real art,

and even if the representation of the vision is inexpertly done, the picture will be effective.

It is not surprising therefore that some teachers who cannot themselves draw, can get beautiful pictures from the children, while other teachers, some with good art training, but who make no use of the unconscious mind, are unsuccessful.

The surprising influence of the dream mind will be seen in some of the pictures. A shy little boy may draw the adults much too big. He sees them like that, and the teacher would spoil the picture if he got the boy to correct the mistake. A too long arm may seem grasping after someone, an ear too big may mean listening, as the cartoonists draw sometimes. Emotions will be indicated by remarkable subtleties of gesture or expression.

The richness of our visual and dream images can only be realized by one who understands Freud's work. Tell your dream to a psychoanalyst and he will help you find out what some of the details mean. It is these deeper meanings which give the value of art. We are surrounded by beauty, but we don't see it. The artist chooses a bit of it, his dream mind eliminates the inessentials, and we then see the beauty which we had missed before.

Every good artist puts more into his paintings than he realizes, as every inspired poet, novelist or dramatist puts meanings into his work which he knows nothing about. "Was it really I who wrote that?" Voltaire once exclaimed as he watched his own play.

This method of art teaching has great importance: The unconscious has many unused "drives" which are calling for expression. It contains repressed material which is also calling for expression. All this material tends to take a visual form and often causes troublesome dreams. If we turn these visions into pictures, we have given the material a run in real life, as it were, and the outflow has relieved the tension.

MUSIC AND SPEECH: "The sensation and ideas thus excited in us by music, or expressed by the cadences of oratory, appear from their vagueness, yet depth, like mental reversions to the emotions and thoughts of a long ago past." . . . I wish I could quote the whole long passage from Darwin's *The Descent of Man*, for it explains many problems. Darwin traces music and impassioned speech back to the season of courtship of our animal ancestors. At that time animals of all kinds are excited not only by love, but by the strong passions of jealousy, rivalry and triumph. Darwin thought the musical intervals used to express these emotions have come down to us by inheritance, and been modified and complicated as evolution proceeded.

We are all aware of "sexy" themes and their effect on young people. The classical composers often make use of what we may call the "mother complex" theme, i.e., the intervals the baby uses in crying, and the intervals the mother uses in comforting a baby. The first ten bars of Brahms' "Variations on the St. Anthony Chorale," for example, suggest to me the infant's cry, and the next eight bars suggest the mother's comforting. Wagner and others make frequent use of aggressive themes, and songs of triumph are, of course, common.

Music is in the unconscious all right, but it has to be evoked. Children whose musical mothers sang to them tend to appreciate music. Children who have never had music associated with their emotions may have no interest in it. One cannot, of course, evoke and deal with all one's rich heritage, but if we are going to try to interest children in music we should begin in a simple way in order to get back to the unconscious mind.

An experienced teacher, engaged in the training of teachers, was asked by his students to show them how to take a singing lesson. As the pupils would be strange to him, and many would not be interested in singing, he prepared the approach carefully. He thought a sea shanty would be a good beginning. He went to the school to see if a picture of a big sailing ship could be obtained, and was lucky enough to find a model of one. He borrowed this, and also the rope used for tug-of-war games. In his lesson he first showed the pupils the model, told them about the tea clippers, their races for the markets, the many changes of sail necessary and the shanty man's songs to keep the sailors in time when, e.g., they were hoisting sail. Then getting some of the boys to act as the sailors pulling the rope, he sang to them "Blow the Man Down," while the boys pulled in time. This was good fun, it had taken only a little time, and now the boys all wanted to learn the song. A simple start of course, but then fast progress with future lessons because the unconscious minds were functioning.

Voice production is another striking example of inherited skill. Every normal baby is born with perfect voice production. Notice the way he makes use of his full lung power; listen to the resonance from the cavities above the mouth; look at the open throat. No wonder his voice can carry on for hours and penetrate brick walls.

Why does the child lose that voice? A succession of colds leaves mucus in the nasal cavities and this in time blocks them. Then "color," as the experts call it, is lost. He is told to speak softly, then the full lung power goes out of practice. He learns the rapid speech of our civilization, and the muscles of the lips, tongue and throat tire with so much movement, and some of these cease to function. It soon becomes increasingly difficult to use the full voice.

And what is the remedy? Let the children take part in plays, and speak clearly to the back of the hall. Give them opportunities to read aloud. Let them sing often. Voice training is difficult enough when a professor has one pupil, and a teacher can hardly cope with thirty or forty pupils at once, even if he knows a lot about the subject. But some of the original power can often be regained if opportunities are provided.

Tape recorders are very useful, both for letting the children hear good speech, and letting them realize how bad their own speech is. Children are good mimics. Let them become interested in speech, and hear good speech, and they will copy it.

GEOGRAPHY: When my youngest son was about five or six, I often put him to bed when I came home. "Tell me a story, Daddy." "What about?" "Whales." I told him. Next night it was elephants. I had spoken about the oceans of the world when dealing with whales: the Greenland whale, the sperm whales of the warmer seas, the killer whales which had knocked Captain Scott's ponies off the ice in the Antarctic, and I had reached for the globe, of course. In dealing with elephants I had explained about the tropical forest region of Africa. "These are quite useful geography lessons," I said to myself. "I'll do the tropical grasslands tomorrow."

"Shall I tell you a story about antelopes tonight?" I asked hopefully. "No, I don't want to know about antelopes," the boy replied, and my nice sequence fell to pieces."Well, what story shall I tell you tonight?" "What stories have you got?" "Oh, I could tell you about lions or tigers, bears, seals, monkeys, camels—" "What's a camel?" I did not expect that choice, but that night he learned something about the Sahara and other deserts.

This illustrates two aspects of what I consider a good lesson: I am apparently following the boy and doing what he wants; but he is also following me and doing what I want. I may appear to jump about from one subject to another, but I have in my own mind the symmetry of the climatic belts of Africa, for example, and I'll gradually teach that symmetry and the reasons for it as the boy can take it.

The tremendous advantage of following the boy's wishes is that a child who wants to know anything, need only to be told once. Repetition, question and answer, revision, are all unnecessary.

But let me define what I mean by wanting to know. A child may want to know things to please the teacher, or to pass an examination. I don't mean that kind of wanting. It is in the same category as the man who wants to give up smoking, and continues to smoke. It is the unconscious mind which must want to know, not the conscious mind.

Here is a lesson I took occasionally with junior pupils to demonstrate the method to the class teacher: I got a globe and a big map of the world, and said to the class, "I'm going to take a geography lesson with you, boys and girls. What would you like me to tell you about? Africa,

America, Australia, lions, tigers, elephants, kangaroos, or love birds? Any suggestions?" "Africa, Sir." I gave my best and most suitable talk on Africa for two or three minutes.
"What next?" "Greenland, Sir." Greenland for one or two minutes. "Tigers, Sir." I gave my best talk on India. "Budgerigars, Sir." Australia, and so on for fifteen or twenty minutes. Then I said, "Now could you write something about the lesson? Any part you like, but I can only give you five minutes. Put your name at the top of the sheet of paper, pencil will do, and don't worry about writing or spelling. I can read them all right. Off you go."

I would give them ten minutes if they were all writing fast, as they usually were, for I had already broken down many of their inhibitions. Then I asked them to bring their papers out to me. I read them out to the class praising every effort. They were usually surprisingly good, and some children had added information they had learned from other sources.

Some of the efforts would be poor, of course. Suppose a boy wrote "Elefants live in Greenland." I should say, "You are interested in elephants, John? Good. They don't live in Greenland, however, it's too cold there. They live here, in Africa, or here, in India," and the boy would soon make progress.

Teachers who are well informed on geography could make use of a few lessons of this type to get the children interested and free, and then get them settled down to study and write books.

Teachers who are not well enough informed to follow the children's requests could work through the class textbooks, giving a talk about the subject with a globe and a large map, then let the children read about the subject for ten or fifteen minutes, then write about it. In the silent half-hour the teacher could give some individual encouragement and a few hints or corrections. He should remember, however, that silence is essential and that he should walk slowly to where a nucleus of disorder was showing rather than bawl across the classroom at a troublesome pupil.

It will be appreciated that the best approach is to try to get the pupil to gather, write about and illustrate the geographical knowledge he wants. The influence of the teacher, the class and the books will keep him in a useful track.

I should like to see more scientific geography taught, even in the lower grades. A half-hour lesson on the movements of the earth would not be suitable for the lower grades, but an occasional demonstration with a globe and a lamp would soon lead to an understanding. Let a few pupils in succession carry the globe round the light until no one makes the mistake of moving the axis from the imaginary North Star.

It is quite wrong to think junior pupils can only take stories about children of other lands, or a few simple facts. For if their unconscious minds function freely, children are as clever as we are.

HISTORY: In a letter to James J. Putnam, Freud wrote, "So one could cite just my case as a proof for your assertion that the urge towards the ideal forms a considerable part of our inheritance."[5]

Freud arrived at this view from a ruthless, scientific investigation of his own life and conduct, undertaken for the purpose of proving his theory of dreams, but the view is held intuitively by most good citizens. We read history in the Bible because we find there men who were making use of this urge towards the ideal, and we hope to learn from them.

No historian can know all history, and his interest should guide him in making the selection. In the same way, we should allow the child's real interest to guide more in what we teach, instead of trying to stick "interest" on to what we prescribe for him. The weakness in our present system is that it is ineffective. Apart from the pupils who are taking history as an examination subject in grammar schools, very little history is known by school children.

Professor M. V. C. Jeffreys, now at Birmingham University, maintained many years ago that the history we try to teach the children is a "conglomerate," which they cannot understand. By dividing history into "periods" we cut the longitudinal strands of history, and school children can never find any real sequence in it. He thought we should begin with some of the longitudinal strands: the history of transport ships, sea battles, houses, clothes, and so on. In the Science Museum there are beautiful dioramas of the history of transport and lighting. There are models of the early railway engines, motor cars, motor bicycles, airplanes, sailing ships, warships and other interesting objects, and colored postcards or diagrams are available, which could be bought by the children to illustrate their original books. There are so many of these strands that one of them would surely interest the child.

To be the author of a book on history is a great encouragement to the children, and once the unconscious mind is engaged, progress is rapid. The boys would see themselves paddling the dug-out canoe, learning to use a sail, inventing the steam engine and the paddle wheels, and so on; such study would evoke and develop the inherited knowledge of what their ancestors did, and so enrich their own personalities.

If the more orthodox books are used, I think, teachers should try to give richer lessons than they usually do, and let the pupils select what they will write about. Talk for about a third of the time, let the children read about the subject for another third, then let them write about it. That would give a nearly silent half-hour, when the teacher could be giving some individual extra help in a quiet voice; the children's ears would be rested, and they would be ready for the next oral lesson.

A headmaster has an immediate check on what is going on with this free work in a class. He has only to look at a few of the children's books. If the written work is getting steadily better and more valuable, success is assured. If it is not, it should be stopped, and another attempt with better preparation made later.

Young teachers should not attempt too much original work of this kind at once. Children need time to develop their creative powers and their confidence, especially if they have been strictly controlled in earlier classes. Keep to one original book written by the pupils until that is going successfully before trying another.

SCIENCE: Science teaching is now so well organized, and schools so well equipped with expensive science laboratories, that what I have to say on the subject may sound elementary, untidy and out of date. It should give science teachers pause, however, when the top executives in our science industries describe some science graduates, even first-class honors graduates, as knowing no science at all. They have merely memorized some information.

It is interesting, too, that a real scientist like Einstein is equally critical of our methods of teaching. In his *Autobiography*, published in 1953, he wrote:

> I soon learned to scent out that which was able to lead to fundamentals and to turn aside from everything else, from the multitude of things which clutter up the mind and divert it from essentials. The hitch in this was, of course, the fact that one had to cram all this stuff into one's mind for the examinations, whether one liked it or not. This coercion had such a deteriorating effect that after I had passed the final examination I found the consideration of any scientific problems distasteful to me for a whole year. . . .

> It is, in fact, nothing short of a miracle that modern methods of instruction have not yet strangled the holy curiosity of enquiry; for this delicate little plant, aside from stimulation, stands mainly in need of freedom. Without this it goes to rack and ruin without fail.

No parent who understands science would think of buying his young son an expensive steam engine. He would buy the simplest one he could find so that the boy can take it to pieces and see how it works. My son developed a keen interest in chemistry from his long and deliberate play with red and green lucifer matches at the age of five. A few years later he called downstairs enthusiastically, "Daddy! I know what an electric fire is! It's a short!" He had shorted some of his electrical connections and got a hot wire.

We learned from the BBC broadcast on Einstein (April 27, 1965) that his first piece of scientific apparatus was a large compass needle on a pivot, and that he spent many hours wondering where the force came from. He greatly enjoyed his post as a clerk in the Swiss Patents Office, because it gave him plenty of time to wonder about, e.g., the unexpected result in the measurements of the speed of light by Michelson and Morley. He was still a clerk there when he published his first book on relativity.

All of which goes to show that mechanical, "brick-built" science, however elaborate, is not really effective. The scientists who make the discoveries work largely by the unconscious mind, in the same way as the creative artists do, and children should learn to do this from the beginning.

Experiments which could be included in the elementary science laboratory are:

1. Explosions. Punch a small hole in the top, and one in the bottom of a cocoa tin. Fill the tin with gas, place the tin on a match stick to let air in at the bottom, light the gas at the top, and wait for the bang to blow the lid off. This is a useful introduction to the internal combustion engine.
2. Air pressure. Buy or prepare a sealed tin with one outlet. Add a little water, boil out the air, close the exit, and pour cold water water over the tin. The collapse of the tin will give a useful introduction to information about air pressure, water pressure, divers, submarines, etc.
3. Latent heat. Cool warm water by a piece of ice, and then by the same weight of ice-cold water. Raise the temperature of water with boiling water, and then with an equal weight of steam.
4. The Principle of Archimedes. Let a boy face the class and hold a brick on a loop of string over his little finger, then lower it into a bucket of water, and note the sigh of relief. Weigh the brick in air and in water, by means of a spring balance. An iron ship floats because it is shaped to displace a much larger volume of water than the volume of the iron.
5. Lines of force. Provide bar and horseshoe magnets and iron filings, and let the children copy the lines of force into their books.
6. Reflection and refraction of light. Provide mirrors and prisms.
7. Blowing bulbs with glass tubing.

Science books will give many more examples, but in the early stages they should all be reasonably safe experiments. This would be real science for young children. They would be free to experiment and repeat the experiments. Their curiosity and wonder would grow. What child wants to blow a glass bulb for the first time and then go on to something else! He wants to blow a dozen bulbs in his efforts to get a really good one.

In our new schools the science laboratories are equipped with expensive apparatus and chemicals and they could be dangerous places for children who know no science. Any good science master would be inclined to keep the children strictly to what they were told to do. This tends to take the unconscious mind out of the subject and destroys the curiosity and wonder which are the basis of all good science work. It would be a great advantage if the children could begin their science at an early age, and in simple laboratories of the type we have described.

PHYSICAL EDUCATION AND HANDWORK: Physical exercises and games now form part of the work in most schools, and great improvements in the methods of teaching have taken place. One or two fundamental points may, however, be worth mentioning.

Children could get pleasure and valuable exercise from climbing a hill, but not from climbing a treadmill, although the movements are similar. Freud found that stimulation and inhibited response tends in time to cause hysteria, and that activity without stimulus tends to cause mental and physical exhaustion. This applies to all reflex and instinctive actions, and even to the more intellectual processes. Hence, play with balls, or skipping ropes or happy activities in the gymnasium tend to be more beneficial than physical exercises done to order.

Much physical damage is caused because many people do not yet understand the changes that take place when the body "goes on a war footing," as W. M. Cannon called it.[1] When danger threatens us we tend to feel the emotions of fear or rage, and for our animal and savage ancestors this situation usually meant fast running to escape or fierce fighting to survive. Either fear or rage immediately releases into the blood stream a small amount of adrenalin from the suprarenal glands. This chemical makes the body prepare for "war" and its "civilian" activities are shut down.

No harmful effects need occur when the "war" powers caused by the release of adrenalin take place for short periods. Human beings, however, often suffer sustained fear or anxiety, often from unconscious causes, and this prolongation of the "state of war" can have harmful results.

Here then is another reason for the freer, happy schooling which we advocate. A bullying teacher can put the normal bodily mechanisms of his more nervous pupils out of action, and possibly cause permanent injury to some of them.

An important part of physical education is handwork. When our primitive ancestors adopted the upright posture and released the hands, there was a rapid development of the mental powers, and there is still a close relationship between the development of the hands and mental development. I published some years ago[6] a case of a boy of six who could not talk at all, and was only learning to walk. On questioning the parents the astonishing fact came to light that the child had been tied hand and foot almost continually since he was six weeks old. He was a normal baby, who had been circumcised when he was six weeks old. On medical advice his hands were tied to stop him from touching the affected part. Then eczema developed, and the tying was continued to stop his scratching the eczema. The eczema continued and got worse, and the tying up was continued. The parents had done their best to develop speech, but it would not develop. We recommended the removal of all restrictions, and the child at last began to make progress.

This was an extreme case, of course, but it is a great mistake to keep the brighter pupils on intellectual work and omit handwork, as if it was an activity suitable only for the future "hewers of wood and drawers of water." There is more to human development than intellectual ability. We have too many children in our child guidance clinics who have a high intelligence quotient but no common sense. Handwork which interests children develops common sense and many other valuable qualities.

CREATIVE WRITING: There are still many teachers who think good writing has to be "built up." They teach pupils to write in short sentences and get the full stops right; then to write longer sentences, and hope ultimately to introduce similes and metaphors to ornament the writing. This is the intellectual approach.

But the unconscious mind can produce such wonderful writing that no writer of any repute would let his intellect interfere while creative work was in progress. He keeps his intellect as a critical faculty to be used when the creative work is finished.

Of course teachers are not dealing with forty poets or forty novelists, but they should recognize the fundamental necessity of letting the children write in peace. Teachers know they cannot themselves write a good report if they are interrupted every few minutes, yet so many destroy the peace of the classroom with their audible comments. When children write freely from interest, their language is usually remarkably good. There are mistakes in spelling, grammar and punctuation, of course, but these are easily remedied if hints are given without discouraging the children.

Young children often write long sentences with many "ands." One could explain that one needs a pause in reading, and suggest that a sentence a page long should be changed to two sentences of half a page each, i.e., work from the too large sentences to the correct size, not from the too small sentences. The large sentences will keep the "tune," the short sentence seldom has a tune, and combined short sentences will have the words all out of step. The unconscious mind will supply suitable rhythms, and all the similes and metaphors required. It tends, when feeling is strong, to run to poetry.

The following essay came from a class taught by a very skillful teacher. The child was 7½, and the home conditions can be judged from the essay. If the reader will mentally add a few full stops and commas for the little girl, it will be seen that the writing is beautifully balanced, the "tunes" are just right, and help to carry the message.

OUR HOUSE

When you go to brabazon Street look up at our house you will see white curtains and then look at the number if the number is 61 it is our house. we have only 2 rooms but we do not mind in the front room we have 2 beds and a sofa and a bed we sleep on the sofa dad mum and john sleep on the bed dad has to get up at 6 oclock in the morning and as soon as he gets the breakfast he begins to do his work he dod not leave his work until 5 oclock at night now I must tell you something sad about my house our baby had to go in Hospital and they sent her out too quick it was on a Fogy day she had to be back and she had to stay in and while she was there she rolled up when mummy found out she told us we were very sorry nearly all our aunts bought her a reiv altogether there were 10 rievs and as I came along our street I saw a funel come from our house.

This child is using the unconscious mind. She lets her thoughts flow freely, as the great writers do; but if a teacher marked every error in red ink she could not write like that again. I should praise her beautiful story and not spoil it with comments on details. There will be more suitable opportunities of helping her.

One word of warning: if a young teacher reading this carelessly thinks he has found a method of getting good compositions without the trouble of marking them, he is making a mistake. He will soon have compositions full of errors and getting steadily worse. If he is not going to give the same kindly attention to improving the child's work that a good headmaster would give to improving the young teacher's work, he will get nowhere with this method. The children will feel his indifference and lose interest in writing. Even if every care is taken he will have an occasional fluent writer whose contempt for spelling is too serious to ignore. He could say "I'm sorry, John, but I cannot understand your writing. Just write for five minutes today and I'll try to help you with your spelling." And if a young teacher's composition books from his pupils show steady deterioration instead of progress, he had better return to his red-ink correcting until he has more experience.

The subject of creative writing raises a great many interesting questions. When Shakespeare's "imagination bodies forth the forms of things unknown," he is writing from the unconscious, and that is why our conscious minds are sometimes puzzled. "Lear," for example, "is by common consent one of the supreme masterpieces of tragic drama," writes John Drinkwater, and then goes on to ask, "Why, at the beginning of the play, does Lear behave towards Cordelia like a crossgrained and unreasonable old fool?"[2]

But it was Shakespeare's unconscious mind which decided this, and in the unconscious the three women are, Freud, tells us, the Moirae of the Greeks, called the Parcae by the Romans, and translated by us as the Fates. The third one, "the Fate that cannot be avoided," is Death. In the unconscious, Cordelia, the silent one, is Death. Lear is not only an old man, he is a dying man. He still wants love, and drinks it up from Goneril and Regan, but Cornelia's silence frightens him. He tries to avoid her, but in the end, "Lear enters with Cordelia in his arms." This is the dream-mind inversion with which psychoanalysts are familiar, and means that Cordelia is carrying Lear away in her arms.

Freud's evidence for this view is given in his paper on "The Theme of the Three Caskets."[3] One needs some psychoanalytic knowledge to appreciate the evidence, but if we accept the underlying meaning that Lear is a dying man, and Cordelia represents Death, the play takes on a new and richer meaning.

Now this view of creative work has an important bearing on our class teaching. If children are to write well, they must write from the unconscious mind. Unless there is quietness and serenity in the classroom, the unconscious mind cannot function, for in uncertain situations the intellect takes control. The intellect can write, but it cannot write well.

A child who writes from the unconscious is an author, and must be treated as one. Red ink on his manuscript is an insult to him. Bold scribbled corrections are an insult, and if his work is treated in this way, the teacher will not see his creative work again.

First-class teachers have communed with noble minds, found their place in the world and know the beauty of it. They are cultured people who have found harmony between the conscious and unconscious minds. They want to help increase the number of cultured people in the world and decrease the number who live from hand to mouth and never realize the greatness that is in them.

Children who are brought up by good teachers in this kindly way, not only learn more, but they learn to take hold of the problems of life by the right handle, as it were. Think for example, how differently people conduct a discussion: one arouses antagonism immediately, and the discussion is fruitless. Another knows that there are two sides to most questions. He meets an extremist on what common ground there is. He holds his views quietly, and expresses them in phrases that sing of love and not of hate, and his opponent pays as much attention to the tune as to the words, and is grateful for it. The cultured man tries to speak to the other's meaning, not necessarily to the actual words used. Scoring a dialectic point does not interest him. He wants to understand, and help if he can.

There is a noticeable atmosphere in the classroom of a first-class teacher, which is explained by one of Freud's discoveries:

> It is very remarkable that the unconscious of one human being can react upon that of another, without the conscious mind being implicated at all.[4]

Good teachers seem to know this intuitively. They move about the classroom as if every step matters. Their silence is as eloquent as their speech. Psychoanalysts who do not get the right atmosphere with their patients have little success in curing them, and the most skillful teaching can fall on deaf ears if the unconscious minds of the teacher and the pupils have not met and flowed together.

Education is an unfolding. The whole history of mankind is in the unconscious minds of all of us.

> It is otherwise with the development of the mind. Here one can describe the state of affairs, which is quite a peculiar one, only by saying that in this case every earlier stage of development persists alongside the later stage which has developed it; . . . the primitive mind is, in the fullest meaning of the word, imperishable.[4]

We read good books and study art and music in order to evoke our own powers. We must not let books overrule us. We must not run to books or pictures or music to get away from the ugliness of life. If we are men we shall try to tidy up some of the ugliness.

The cultured man knows of our rich inheritance. If he does not see "the conscience, the better, the 'nobler' impulses" in another, he will think, with Freud, that they are in the unconscious and have not been evoked. If he can help to evoke them he will.

BIBLIOGRAPHY

1. Cannon, W. M. *Bodily Changes in Pain, Hunger, Fear and Rage*. New York and London: D. Appleton Co., 1920.

2. Drinkwater, John. *Shakespeare.* London: Duckworth and Co., 1933.
3. Freud, Sigmund. "The Theme of the Three Caskets," *Collected Papers, IV.* London: Hogarth, 1925, 244.
4. ———. "Thoughts for the Times on War and Death," *Collected Papers, IV.* London: Hogarth, 1924, 288.
5. ———. *Letters of Sigmund Freud.* New York: Basic Books, 1960, 307.
6. Hill, J. C. "A Case of Retarded Development Associated with Restricted Movements in Infancy," *British Journal of Medical Psychology,* 1930, 3:268.

CHAPTER 8

The Learning Process: from Learning for Love to Love of Learning

RUDOLF EKSTEIN

RECENT DEVELOPMENTS in the field of psychoanalysis permit us to envision a new relationship between education and psychoanalysis. In this relationship the teaching profession will gain not only mental-health principles, diagnostic understanding and information about the application of psychotherapy in the case of the emotionally labile child, but will benefit from analytic insights to improve the processes of teaching and learning. It seems to me that a new kind of collaboration between the fields of psychoanalysis and education is developing. If this is indeed the case, it may be based in part on the acceptance of a simple definition Freud once gave us of the nature of mental health, which he saw as "the capacity to love and to work."

At the age of five or six, the child becomes a part of the formal school system. The teachers meet a condition in the child of this age, prepared by his growth process in the family situation. This condition is characterized through his current capacity "to love and to work," which is a function of his state of development and maturation. The success of the teacher depends largely on the child's capacity for love and work.

We speak, of course, about age-appropriate capacities. We must constantly keep in mind what is meant in each phase of development of the child when we speak of his capacity or his lack of capacity to love and to work. What the child brings to the nursery school and to kindergarten frequently looks more like a capacity to play. We must always be aware, however, that the play of the small child is his way of working.

To the extent that the child brings these capacities into the school-room, the teacher is in a position to initiate a new process of learning. This new process goes through a demonstrable pattern, and repeats itself year after year, in class after class, and at different age levels. The repetition of this process will not, of course, be unvaried repetition.

95

Its variations will depend on the child's states of maturity and development, and also on the teacher's capacity to provide for the process itself. As a matter of fact, one must keep in mind that the capacity to teach—as well as the capacity to learn—is a function of the readiness "to love and to work."

As teacher and children meet in the beginning of the school year, they size each other up and attempt to establish a relationship. The teacher-student relationship establishes the requirements for a mutually satisfying work experience. The relationship is based on love in the broadest sense of the word, which includes natural antagonism and aspects of anger when the relationship proves unrewarding. The children quickly realize they must earn the love, the praise and the rewards of the teacher. It is because of this desire of the child to be accepted, to be recognized, to be rewarded, to be marked as a good student that he is willing to work.

Work at this stage, then, is usually based on the need for love. Of course, the teacher, too, needs to be basically accepted by the child. It is the teacher who must prepare the way for a relationship based on respect and affection, which will establish the conditions of the work situation. The child can then identify with the teacher, with his goals and needs; and in like manner, the teacher needs to identify with the child and his task. As this occurs, both teacher and child somehow participate in a process, the initial feature of which is that one must work in order to get the respect and the affection of the other.

For many people, this first phase of the process never stops. One may well say of such people, be they teachers or children, that they have not gone beyond the first step of a process which must be distinguished by additional characteristics, if it is to be a truly fruitful and positive one.

The problem of the teacher is to develop the process in such a way that he can reverse the phrase, "work for love," and help the child toward that stage at which he will primarily learn because of "love of work."

I suggest that the new collaboration between psychoanalysis and education, now pushing beyond the field of mental health, must be concerned with further investigations of the learning process to tell us how one can slowly change the psychological attitudes and capacities of the child from the stage of "work for love" to that of "love of work."

The nature of learning has been investigated by learning theorists and educational psychologists. Academic psychology has given us a great deal of valuable experimentation as well as models for learning. I borrow from a paper by Gerhart and Maria Piers in which reference is made to three aspects of learning considered by the learning theorists.[1] The first, as described, for example, by conditioning and reinforcement theories, sees in learning an accomplishment which is based on constant and endless repetition. This form of learning has always been underestimated by progressive education, since the progressive educator usually stresses aspects of learning which place a premium on curiosity, insight and discovery. However, even within a milieu which strongly relies on insight learning, there is the necessity to insure the development of skills and knowledge acquired through procedures based on repetition and conditioning.

The second model for learning is one which stresses the relationship between the teacher and the child. Love and hate, the positive and the negative features in this relationship, can be utilized for learning. Up to now, psychoanalysis has paid more attention to this model of learning than to the first mentioned, yet psychoanalytic theory and knowledge about personality organization provide ample opportunity for the study of the significance of repetitive processes, as in "working through."

We have already mentioned the learning theorists' third mode of learning, insight learning. The model for this type of learning is based on our knowledge of the nature of creativeness and inventiveness.

The learning theories have never fully succeeded in integrating these different aspects of learning. It seems to me that the present contribution of psychoanalysis to the field of education might be one in which we study the process of learning as it develops from one stage to the other. I suggest that we shall find that all three of these aspects of learning have their place in the total process, but each differs in importance in the various stages in which a child finds himself.

I suggested earlier that the first phase in the process of learning is that in which one works in order to get love. In this phase, much of learning might be mastery through repetition. During this repetition, identification with the teacher slowly grows. As identification develops, learning based upon the relationship becomes more and more dominant. With this identification with the teacher's ways of working and thinking, with his interests and curiosities, with his attitudes toward knowledge and skill, the identificatory processes themselves may lead to the third phase. Here, the reward and the punishment, the good and the bad mark, the love or the rejection of a teacher will not be the dominant feature, or the primary motivation for the child. These factors may give way to the child's learning to love the work itself, with its progress, discovery and mastery of skill and knowledge. Motivation for reward, for love, will be replaced by inner motivation, and the outer-directed child will have become an inner-directed one. If this is the sequence of learning events, we can see how deeply the modes of learning must influence the modes of character.

It is apparent that each change in the school situation—change of teacher or of subject—will shift the nature of the process. It is easy to prove that a child who has this capacity for inner direction with one specific teacher, this true and genuine interest in work and learning, might come to another teacher and have to start the whole process all over again. Acquired functions can be lost temporarily. In fact, to some extent the fluidity of this process will always exist.

I must also re-emphasize, of course, that these different phases of learning are not exclusive, but are, rather, different dominant phases. In each learning process, the others will be alive as well.

The best teacher would be one who is capable of integrating the principles of all the learning modes and using them in accordance with his understanding of where a child or a group of children may be at any given moment. Such a teacher is not committed to one specific tool of teaching but can shift these tools in accordance with the needs of the child. Indeed, the best teacher needs to have a mature capacity for love. If he has a primitive capacity, his teaching is a function only of his own need to be loved and admired by the child. Instead of developing a teaching process by which the child can use him for reaching the goal of learning, he brings about an aborted process.

The work of teachers and analysts together should be the investigation of this teaching process. We must see how we can free forces in the child to help him go through these three positions and thus make him truly capable of learning. The nature of work—learning—so frequently has stressed the pain and the repetition and the threats of a demanding society. Consequently, too often, there has been the tendency to overlook the pleasure in the acquisition of knowledge; the joy of discovery; the satisfaction from natural and worthwhile curiosity; the gratitude for skills and knowledge; the opening of new worlds. Perhaps this has occurred because our school systems so often seem to have been dominated by learning motivations based on acquiring good grades; on competing for a place in the sun; on going to a famous college. Such goals, however, are only characteristic of the initial phase of the process which leads us to greater rewards of joy and pleasure, of an expanding world, of a wish to contribute. And, for teachers, there is the additional reward that our own development can reach that phase which enables us successfully to permeate the teaching process with the love for work, the love of learning.

BIBLIOGRAPHY

1. Piers, Gerhart and Maria. "Modes of Learning and the Analytic Process." *Selected Lectures, Sixth International Congress of Psychotherapy*, London, 1964. Basel/New York: S. Karger, 1965.

CHAPTER 9

Play and Mastery

MARIA W. PIERS

ALL HUMAN BEINGS PLAY, but it is not a human prerogative to play. Many animals play—and we find it charming. It evokes maternal feelings in us because most animals play when they are children.[5] Human beings, however, play from cradle to grave. Some play way too much, though, and others not enough. There is a prototype for each extreme. One is the Playboy. The other is Jack of "All work and no play makes Jack a dull boy." Jack is the kind of guy no girl cares to date, even though her mother may urge her to do so, for he is perfectly safe. Playboy (also known as Casanova or Don Juan) is much sought after as a date, but is considered a poor marital risk.

They are both called "boy." This seems to indicate that one who only plays is not a fully developed man. Neither is the one who never plays. He, Jack, has learned to keep out of trouble and to make a living but he misses a great deal. His life is devoid of humor, wrath, a sense of tragedy or exhilaration. In the absence of the entire rich spectrum of emotions, Jack doesn't have what it takes to set the world (or a girl on a date) on fire. While Playboy has never learned to curb his appetite for play, it seems that our boy Jack has forgotten all about it.

At least a modicum of playful activity is essential to being a fully grown human being. So, once upon a time, even Jack must have known how to play. For if he hadn't played during his infancy, he would not be alive today—a baby cannot survive unless he learns to play. This may sound like a gross exaggeration, but it is literally true, as the "Hospitalism" study[6] amply demonstrates.

Some twenty years ago, a group of researchers headed by Dr. René Spitz inquired into the effect of institutional care for infants. They were originally intrigued by the extraordinarily high mortality rate among such infants (up to 100%, at the turn of the century). This did decrease markedly with the application of antisepsis and proper nutrition, but twenty years later, the situation was almost equally shocking. It became clear by then that children who had been placed in orphanages in their infancy almost invariably developed severe psychological disturbances, including psychosis, feeblemindedness and delinquency. Why? What was there in institutional upbringing that led to such severe pathology?

The researchers compared the inmates of two institutions, giving them the names Foundlings Home and Nursery, respectively. The team was first of all struck by the fact that the inmates of Nursery, by the end of their first year, had on the average developed steadily in keeping with their ages. Their D.Q. increased from 101.5 to 105. In contradistinction, the infants in Foundlings Home deteriorated under the very eyes of their caretakers, so that their D.Q. decreased from 124 to 72. By the end of the second year these inmates of Foundlings Home had gone as far down as 45, the mental age of ten-month-olds or imbeciles.

This means that the children of Foundlings Home could neither walk nor talk at the age of two years. Hardly any of them could eat alone, and they acted completely uninterested or even unhappy at the approach of any grownup person. Not a single child could control bowels and bladder at the age of two. Incidentally, they were all extremely susceptible to illness (during a measles epidemic, 23 out of 88 children died, compared with the usual ½%). Not so the inmates of Nursery. They acted roughly in accordance with their age and showed considerable appetite for food intake as well as for human contact, speech and motility. In fact, at the age of ten months, they presented a problem of "how to tame the healthy toddlers' curiosity and enterprise."[6]

At this point, one might logically raise the question whether the children of Foundlings Home were perhaps genetically inferior. Quite the opposite was true. It was the children of Nursery who had, genetically speaking, several strikes against them, for Nursery was a children's institution attached to a female penitentiary. The children's mothers were, without exception, young delinquent girls, prostitutes without license and, in many cases, of low mentality. Yet these children thrived. On the other hand, the steadily deteriorating babies of Foundlings Home came from an unselected variety of backgrounds, with a far better average heredity than the children in Nursery. This, incidentally, also explains their high original D.Q.

What were the reasons for the detrimental effects of Foundlings Home? A comparison of living conditions in both institutions showed only these differences:

(1) Foundlings Home offered no toys, whereas Nursery did.

(2) The visual radius of Foundlings Home children was sharply curtailed because each youngster lived in a small cubicle by himself; sheets hung over the sides of the crib left each child living in isolation. Nursery children shared a large room across which they were able to communicate with each other in their own preverbal way, and in and beyond which they saw furniture, household items, people going to and fro and trees and sky.

(3) Most importantly though, Nursery children had maternal care whereas Foundlings Home children did not. In Nursery, the mothers came from the penitentiary at regular intervals to feed and bathe and play with their own babies. In Foundlings Home, one nurse took care of eight infants. Understandably, time permitted her only to feed and bathe her charges but not the luxury of playing with them. It is this luxury, a mother's playing with her children during their first year of life, which, in a sense, seals the fate of the human being. Those who play will learn—and live. The others are fated to vegetate or die. This was indeed what happened to the inmates of Foundlings Home.

Documentary films of children in Nursery show clearly what all of us have observed many times; the infant's play, stimulated by his mother, involves his mouth, his eyes, his fingers and toes, his whole body surface, and yields an intense "erotic pleasure."[3]

Webster defines play as "to do something not as a task, not for profit, but for amusement; to act wantonly or thoughtlessly, to dally, to trifle. . . ." Mr. Webster notwithstanding, play is a necessary condition of life. Play is the means of waking up an infant's dormant sensory-motor apparatus without which none of us would be able to eat, walk, talk, love, think, drive a car, raise tomatoes or build skyscrapers. Play is, in fact, the bridge between the id and the ego. It is the beginning of all meaningful activity.

The body then (the infant's or his mother's—it matters not to the baby) can be considered the first toy. But, as soon as the child starts walking, he becomes intensely interested in an array of other possible toys. This presents a problem. "How," the toddler wonders, "can I follow the lure of the wide open spaces filled with luscious chairs, kitchen ranges, towels, ash trays and what not, and yet hang on to my soft, warm, protective mom?" The toddler solves this problem by taking to a cuddly blanket, thereby inventing the Portable Instant Mom. She is humanity's second toy. What does the toddler do with his Portable Instant Mom? He carries her around into the dangerous territory beyond the crib—and he loves her. His bleakest day is when Instant Mom disappears into the washing machine. At times he also tears her to shreds, for the blanket or the cuddly animal is a perfect target for both affection and anger. To the first one it yields, against the second it does not retaliate. As he walks farther and more securely, the child's horizon widens and he discovers pillows and towels and other things with the desirable properties, and he adopts a number of additional "Moms." A little later, hard-surfaced objects are included: fire engines, building blocks, pitchers, crayons.

Simultaneously, though, the small child's activity increases. It is no longer enough merely to finger and chew and smell a toy. The child discovers how to make blocks go through openings, to pull the fire engine on wheels, to fill and empty the pitcher, to scribble with a crayon on paper. He fills and pulls and fits and scribbles, and the fun is more and more in the doing. That a two-year-old's play, with its emphasis on action, its trials and errors, its repetition, is really learning, is self-evident. And, gradually, the child begins to enjoy what he has achieved. Not the filling, but the full pitcher. Not the fitting of the blocks into the opening, but the fact that they actually land on the bottom of the box; not the scribbling per se, but the finished page, adorned perhaps with three or four circular configurations.

By the time a child enters nursery school, the main fun lies clearly not in the doing anymore, but in the completed task. His actions are governed not so much by the primitive Funktionslust,[1] but to a much larger extent by the instinct to master.[7]

It isn't always easy for adults to keep up with a young child's developmental changes. The switch from bodily sensations to the doing, to the achieving, sometimes escapes our attention. Thus, some of us keep foisting finger paints, sand and clay on the preschool child, marveling at his gloriously free expression as he obligingly regresses.

Let it be said emphatically: The four-year-old who wallows in wet, wild, accidental blobs of reds and greens and dirty browns is not a budding Jackson Pollock, much less a Picasso. If it were not for those expressionistically inclined parents and teachers of his, he would probably much rather learn to master the painstaking outlines of a house, a dog, a letter A, the solution of a problem, the understanding of a puzzle and to finish what he has begun. The following little observation may stand for many. Larry, age four, draws rockets with great absorption. His mother calls from the kitchen that it's time for supper. Larry says, "But I'm not finished yet." Mother feels that her authority is being challenged and raises her voice. "Larry, what did I tell you? You better come right now!" No response. Larry is intently bent over his paper, tongue between lips, adds carefully one more dab of yellow, then heaves a sigh of satisfaction and completion, gets up and marches into the kitchen. Mother who, in the meantime, has come into the living-room to get Larry personally, looks at the paper in amazement.

She asks, "Is that all you had to add? You silly boy, why didn't you say so?" Larry doesn't answer.

Let it be said that such misunderstandings do not happen to the nursery school teacher. She's usually quite aware of the oedipal child's need for task completion and mastery. Parents, on the other hand, are often more aware than the teacher that the child is indeed in his oedipal phase. How could they help it? He has probably already informed them of his infatuation for his mother and his rivalrous feelings for his father. As one three-year-old I know put it when his father was proudly chauffeuring the family around in his new car, "Mommy, when I'm a big man, I'm gonna buy you a golden housecoat and a real T-Bird with white wheels, not just a Chevy." Every preschooler is under the sway of strong impulses of love and hate and is in conflict about both. Every preschooler is also filled with a drive toward mastery which, in the long run, accrues to actual coping. All the elements of future coping techniques seem to be present in the preschool child's play. All the modes of learning are clearly distinguishable and pure, not, as in later years, in an admixture. Take an episode such as occurs daily in any nursery school. The scene is the doll corner. The cast two four-year-olds, Rachel and Steve. Steve is an only child, Rachel has a sister Anne, age four months.

Rachel approaches the doll corner with big eyes and eager expression. Steve trails behind her, somewhat less decisively. Rachel examines the coffee pot, puts it down and turns to a doll buggy with Raggedy Ann Doll in it, starts wheeling the buggy around and around and around. Steve looks on, a bit bored. Suddenly Rachel turns to Steve and says with great urgency, "I'm the mommy, you can be the daddy." Without waiting for an answer she pushes the buggy into the corner, takes the doll out, seats the doll at the table and starts setting the table for three. She says speedily and urgently, "We gotta eat now. Time for dinner." She puts out three spoons, three plates, two cups —can't find a third one. She takes a plastic flower pot for a substitute. Steve, in the meantime, doesn't pay much attention to the domestic scene. He climbs into a box half filled with blocks, does some pretend chauffeuring with imaginary wheel. Suddenly he climbs out again, looks at the side of the box, frowns. "Darnit, got a flat. Gotta change the tire. Finky tire." With an air of importance, he goes through the motions of changing a tire, using a spoon for a tool. Rachel glances at him, "No, Stevie, you're supposed to eat now." She goes to the shelf, gets a piece of clay, fingers it, squashes it, pounds it and then cuts it. She puts a piece of clay on the doll's plate saying, "There. Eat your meat loaf." She then picks up the rag doll and starts scolding her angrily. "Wet again, she wet her pants again. And she spilled the coke.

I'm gonna throw you out the window. . . ." Rachel slaps the doll hard, then suddenly becomes sober again, clears away the dishes, puts the doll in the buggy, and says, "You got to go to bed, 'cause you were naughty." Steve approaches her with a tray full of blocks, says grocery-boy like, "Ma'am, here are your potatoes, Ma'am." But Rachel walks off and has lost all interest.

What is the meaning of such a play episode? There is still a lot of the pure sensual play of infancy, such as the fingering and squashing of the clay. This kind of sensualism has to a large extent outgrown its usefulness (awakening the sensory-motor apparatus). Nonetheless, it persists as a matter of fact and is of lifelong duration. The rag doll must be regarded as the transitory object, the Portable Instant Mom. But if she is the cuddly, comforting object, she is, at the same time, Rachel's pretend baby. Such an equation between one's mother and one's baby is easily made by the unconscious. The second stage of play activity, the toddler's enjoyment of doing, is also well represented in our episode. Rachel's wheeling the buggy around, the cutting of the clay, the laying out of the silver, each is pleasurable in and of itself.

There is evidence for mastery drive in the need to solve problems, such as the simple arithmetical one of setting three cups, three plates, three spoons, on the table. There is also the mastery of an adult role by practicing it right now. Steve, the would-be chauffeur and garage mechanic, is a case in point. The expression on his face, the bending down, the frowning, the entire air of seriousness and competence indicate his overwhelming urge to be in a man's shoes—we surmise, in his father's. But, carried on the wings of omnipotence, he becomes that man by sheer identification. He feels, "I envy my daddy. I want to be my daddy." And, presto, he is magically transported into a man's existence. But not for long and, as yet, superficially. He merely identifies with his father's stance. Two or three years hence, Steve will hardly be satisfied with identification pure and simple. He will have to fortify it with real understanding of his father's knowledge and skills. To wit: what makes a car run, how do you really drive it? How does one change a tire in real life? Once Steve has gained insight in the mechanics of, and practiced, tire-changing, a more profound (though merely partial) identification with his father will be possible. For the time being, he masters the tasks of becoming a man by practicing a man's way of talking, walking and working.

But more impressively, and more importantly, appears the mastery drive in Rachel as an attempt to come to grips with the world, while at the same time she keeps the id drive in check. Rachel feels as though she were in her mother's shoes. She is not only trying to master mother's stance by identification, but she also tries to master her own highly impractical impulse, the possessive love for her father and the rivalry with her mother. If she could, she would tell us, "I will be a wife, too. But I can't be my daddy's wife. I will have another husband, a boy. Perhaps Steve. I will be a mother, too. And if baby Annie can't be my baby but only my sister, I will have to accept another baby." Rachel also masters in an exemplary fashion her jealousy of her baby sister by punishing the rag doll.

Children who mistreat dolls and stuffed animals as well as engaging in direct "stick-'em-up" games, complete with guns and holsters, are often viewed with horror. "They will grow up to be gunmen or militarists" is the prediction of pessimistic educators. Others, more optimistically inclined, regard hostile games of three- and four-year-olds as cathartic "vents." They conjecture that it is a good idea to let the children "get it out of their system" and that the mistreatment of dolls insures the survival of baby brothers. Neither optimist nor pessimist is correct. Actually, hostile games serve, as clinical experience shows, the mastery of the inner reality. Rachel's behavior is a case in point. Like all preschool children, she gets frightened of her own anger and fears that it will kill or damage others. Perhaps her mother or baby sister will die as a result of her anger. The "as-if" character of the role play permits Rachel to let her anger come out in the open, and lo, it doesn't kill anybody. It doesn't even seriously damage the rag doll. What's more, Rachel can stop her outburst at will. She is capable of putting the doll back in the buggy and leaving the scene.

Sometime, when she is a few years older, Rachel will get angry again, but this time she will merely wish that she could hit someone over the head. She won't find it necessary to do so. She won't need a toy to let out her anger for, as children become older, thought processes become stronger and more independent of play-acting and props. For the time being, as we observe Rachel and Steve, the fantasy-cum-toy is the precursor of the pure thought process. Ekstein[2] has compared the physical object with "eternal crutches for the psychotic child" on which a delusion and hallucinatory ideation can be supported. Similarly, the normal child uses the toy until he has learned to play "merely with ideas." To play with ideas is what all grownup men are doing. All, except for Playboy and Jack, that is. Playboy got stuck on the level of play-acting out and never shifted to the mere thinking and fantasying. Jack dreads the confrontation with his own love and hatred so much that he distrusts the prop, the toy, that might bring his feelings irresistibly to the surface. Neither Jack nor Playboy is capable of fresh, original problem-solving and coping.

The repetition of a gratifying experience and the assimilation of anxiety are regarded by some experts as the central functions of play.[4]

In addition, we would venture to say that play can also be a pure mani-festation of the drive toward mastery. This seems particularly clear during the oedipal phase, when a child is usually in nursery school. As he plays, insight learning and identification each appear in unmixed purity leading toward mastery of the inner and the outer world. The behavior of the human race is not merely motivated by id impulse and defenses against them, but also by a strong urge toward mastery. Preschool play is its manifestation par excellence.

BIBLIOGRAPHY

1. Buhler, K. "Die Krise der Psychologie." 1. Aufl., Jena, 1927, 189f.
2. Ekstein, Rudolf, and Seymour Friedman. "On the Meaning of Play in Child-hood Psychoses." In Dynamic Psychopathology of Childhood, L. Jessner and E. Pavenstedt, editors. New York: Grune and Stratton, Inc., 1959.
3. Freud, Anna. "The Concept of Developmental Lines." Psychoanalytic Study of the Child, 1963, 18:245.
4. Peller, Lili E. "Libidinal Phases, Ego Development, and Play." Psychoanalytic Study of the Child, 1954, 9:178.
5. Schiller, Claire H., editor. Instinctive Behavior. The Development of a Modern Concept. New York: International Universities Press, 1957.
6. Spitz, René A. "Hospitalism." Psychoanalytic Study of the Child, 1954, 1:53.
7. Waelder, Robert. "The Psychoanalytic Theory of Play." Psychoanalytic Quarterly, 1933, 2:208.

CHAPTER 10

From Prevention of Emotional Disorders to Creative Learning and Teaching

RUDOLF EKSTEIN

TO DISCUSS CERTAIN ASPECTS of psychoanalysis and education, I find an eleventh century Normandy cathedral a most rewarding metaphor. Mont-Saint-Michel was erected on a mountain, and built as a fortress as well as a church. The water, even as it protects it, requires that worshippers must wait until the tide is out in order to be able to reach the church. Henry Adams wrote in *Mont-Saint-Michel and Chartres*:

> The church stands high on the summit of this granite rock, and on its west front is the platform. . . . From the edge of this platform, the eye plunges down, two hundred and thirty-five feet, to the wide sands or the wider ocean as the tides recede or advance, under an infinite sky, over a restless sea, which . . . we . . . can understand and feel without books or guides; but when we turn from the western view, and look at the church door, thirty or forty yards from the parapet where we stand, one needs to be eight centuries old to know what this mass of encrusted architecture meant to its builders, and even then one must still learn to feel it.[1]

To try to feel ourselves into the spirit and the meaning of that church, he thus insists, it is not enough that we travel in miles. We must also travel backward in time, for that church was standing before the Normans invaded England. At its top is the statue of Saint Michel, the patron saint of the Normans whose flaming sword points out to the raging sea and protects the faithful ones against invasion. Some 100 years later, the Normans built another church in Chartres, one dedicated to Mary. As we look at the holy angel with the flaming sword and at the Madonna we get the idealized version of perfection in medieval society—the Mother Church which tries to maintain and to perpetuate its system of life by actively protecting the necessary conditions for it

107

to carry out its function. By now I hope my allegory is clear. I am dealing with that function of the church that also unites teachers and psychoanalysts; I am referring to its educational function. In medieval days, education could be maintained only if the places of worship, which were the places of education and of reflection, were protected against enemy onslaught. At the same time, passion would run so high and the love for ideas was so great that one never knew whether the church was defending itself or whether the church—the ecclesia militans—was attacking.

Henry Adams tried to convey the spirit of the church this way:

> Of all the elaborate symbolism which has been suggested for the Gothic cathedral, the most vital and most perfect may be that the slender nervure, the springing motion of the broken arch, the leap downwards of the flying buttress—the visible effort to throw off a visible strain—never let us forget that Faith alone supports it, and that, if Faith fails, Heaven is lost. The equilibrium is visibly delicate beyond the line of safety; danger lurks in every stone. The peril of the heavy tower, of the restless vault, of the vagrant buttress; the uncertainty of logic, the inequalities of the syllogism, the irregularities of the mental mirror—all these haunting nightmares of the church are expressed as strongly by the Gothic cathedral as though it had been the cry of human suffering, and as no emotion had ever been expressed before or is likely to find expression again. The delight of its aspirations is flung up to the sky. The pathos of its self-distrust and anguish of doubt is buried in the earth as its last secret. You can read out of it whatever else pleases your youth and confidence; to me, this is all.

It seems to me that Henry Adams described here the spirit of a living society that must constantly defend itself against danger, a society that is never secure; something that is true of our society today as well as the medieval. For the tides come and go. Sometimes they are in and sometimes out. But during all this time we, the educators, stand in our church trying to maintain the spirit, trying to educate.

Sometimes, when the attacks on education are in the foreground, it seems that the tide is in and that we are surrounded by water so that those who should come join us cannot meet with us. We know then we must wait for that time when the tide is out.

While we wait, we must do something to strengthen the educational system, to strengthen that church of education that is not only a refuge, but a fortress under siege. Psychoanalysis can share in this. In the past, in particular, it has been identified with creating mental health, with prevention of illness, as a treatment of behavior problems.

The connection with education was a one-sided one. Psychoanalysts were accepted only as psychopathologists. Education functioned by itself, and psychoanalysis by itself. The two were separate islands, and much of what went on between educators, and psychoanalysts was very much like what I suggested about Mont-Saint-Michel. Most of the time the tide was in and we had no way of reaching each other. Sometimes, however, the tide is out and we can communicate.

In speaking about the place of psychoanalysis in education, it is beyond argument to say things have changed. We have gone a long way since psychoanalysis was seen only in terms of treatment and of early prevention; or in terms of attacking the traditional forces of education, that essentially defensive maneuver. Yet the idea of prevention in a society like ours can be turned into a positive one. It can contribute to an active program shaped by dynamic education and psychoanalysis. It is for this reason that we analysts now talk about growth and creativity. We are no longer concerned only with the prevention of ill health, but also with the active contribution of psychoanalytic understanding to learning. This entails the incorporation into educational theories of those preconscious forces which are the inner potential that enables man to be creative—and educators to be insightful and inventive. The defensive view of prevention belongs to an earlier phase in the relationship between psychoanalysis and education, one in which the topographic model of the mind, a kind of Pandora's Box, was prevalent. Children, it seems, had to be protected against evil inner forces, and this earlier model suggested that if we were to release these forces, which were locked up, new available psychic energy would free the child from the neurotic distortions which prevent learning. Kubie has suggested that this view of Pandora's Box has caused many educators to feel they do not dare to free preconscious forces in such a way that they can become part of learning. He has stated:

Whence then comes our creative function? To answer this, we have to stop for a moment to indicate what we mean by creativity. Clearly, by the creative process we mean the capacity to find new and unexpected connections, to voyage freely over the seas, to happen on America as we seek new routes to India, to find new relationships in time and space, and thus new meanings. Or, to put it in another way, it means working freely with conscious and preconscious metaphor, with slang, puns, overlapping meanings and figures of speech, with vague similarities, with the reminiscent recollections evoked by some minute ingredients of experience, establishing links to something else which in other respects may be quite different. It is free in the sense that it is not anchored either to the pedestrian realities of our conscious symbolic processes, or to the rigid symbolic relationships of the unconscious area of the personality.[4]

I have often wanted to take some of the ideas Kubie expressed in his book, based on the model of psychoanalysis Freud used in *The Interpretation of Dreams* of 1900, and retranslate them in terms of modern ego psychology, relating them to the structural model developed by Freud in 1923. But I think there is so much of value in Kubie's own technical language that this revision might only be necessary for those who wish to link up these early insights with the tasks modern ego psychology has set for itself.

Kubie also stated:

This is precisely why the free play of preconscious symbolic processes is vital for all creative productivity. Preconscious psychological functions stand on the fringes of consciousness. Here the meaning of the symbol is essentially analogic, yet relatively transparent, although it may be obfuscated in varying degrees for artistic purposes, as in the more obscure realms of modern art, modern verse and modern music. Yet preconscious processes involve much more than all of this. They are also the most important economizing device which implements our thinking operations.

And later he wrote:

The price we pay for traditional education methods is that they either tie our preconscious symbolic processes prematurely to precise realities, or leave them to the mercy of distorting influences which arise around areas of unresolved unconscious conflict.

These views of Kubie do not deny or underestimate the power of the intellect, or its importance in education, but rather try to put it in the right perspective, truly to free it, a notion beautifully defended by Murphy.[5] In addition, collaborators of psychoanalysis and education would assist in changing traditional educational methods so that the curriculum would not simply be considered an outside stereotype but would be related to learning readiness and the learning capacity of the child, a function enhanced or destroyed by his preconscious processes (see chapters 4 and 5.)

In the past, psychoanalysts were so over-occupied with the issues of neuroticism, pathology, dropouts, behavior problems, etc., that we did not get around to study the cognitive functions. Modern ego psychology is a more recent achievement. And it is only very recently that we have started to catch up with the work of Piaget and with Bruner and his research group at Harvard. So it is only recently that our professional concern goes beyond resolution of conflict to solution of task. Our interest in the mind now is not only in terms of trying to clarify the unconscious conflict which holds the child back, but to free the mental forces which make it possible to solve problems and, particularly, to study the nature of those cognitive functions which help us to contribute to the teaching of problem-solving.

I am, of course, talking about the growth of ego psychology. In *Studies in Cognitive Growth*, Bruner[3] refers to Leeper, as having written a brilliant and timely piece on the perceptual representation of emotions and motives. Leeper conceives of motives and emotions as making themselves felt through their participation in cognitive organization. In the past we saw motives and emotions as interesting only in terms of resolving the neurotic conflict. We did not see their adaptive strength as part of the cognitive organization. Bruner states it this way: "I believe that, where the emphasis of a technical society is on objects and acts in their abstract and linguistic connection, we may be missing the conditions for satisfying those human needs that are not related to objects, to instrumental acts, or to abstract hierarchies. Since we have often remarked . . . on the increased instrumental power that comes from 'forcing' a confrontation between the three systems of representing reality, it is a proper precaution to comment on the potential dangers of insisting that our acts and images should conform to the austere hierarchies of lexicon and grammar."

In developing the idea of instrumental conceptualism, Bruner has also said:

> It seems not unlikely that some of this axiomatic structure, in forming our models of reality, is already given in the innate nature of our three techniques for representing or 'modeling' reality: action, imagery and symbolism. That is, the physical requirements of adaptive action 'force' us to conceive of the world in a particular way, a way that is constrained by the nature of our neuromuscular system. So, too, are we constrained by the primitive properties of visual, auditory, and haptic space in our effort to represent our knowledge in terms of imagery. Finally, our representation of reality in terms of language or symbolism is similarly constrained by what again seems to be our native endowment for mastering particular symbolic systems, systems premised on rules of hierarchy, predication, causation, modification, etc.

He describes the growth of the mind from impulse to fantasy and acts, from imagery to thought and to logic. And he tells us that every educational system must combine all these sources in the child and cannot overstress the intellectual and the logical at the expense of all the others. For without the others, the preconscious forces will never be free or available.

Teachers, therefore, must be educated in such a way that they will have a new teaching readiness. They must not only study the changes in the child's learning readiness but also their own teaching readiness. As I have said before (chapter 6) while teachers' colleges stress, as they should, courses on child development, I suggest they should develop courses and workshops to further teaching readiness—the constant self-development of the teacher. It will then become clearer that the teacher recapitulates in his training, although on a higher level, exactly what the child goes through during the first stages of his learning.

Psychoanalysis can also help us to understand ourselves as teachers, and sharpen insight into the nature of the teacher-student relationship, as well as the learning and teaching processes.

Psychoanalysis thus contributes to the science of teaching while it continuously reminds us that education is never without art, never without skills, never without intuition and empathy. Psychoanalysis affirms the passion, the deep compassion, the constant search for insight, which characterize education.

The teacher who identifies with such a point of view would find out very quickly that the reaction of society is a reaction not only vis-à-vis the child but also vis-à-vis the teacher. That teacher would soon have to contend with society's lack of psychological and intellectual as well as financial support. Commonplace complaints would be: "I see no hope for the future of our people if they are dependent upon the frivolous youth of today, for certainly all youth are reckless beyond words. When I was a boy, we were taught to be discreet and respectful of our elders, but the present generation is exceedingly smart-alecky and impatient." The fact that this one was made eight centuries before Christ by Hesiod, the Greek poet, reminds us that not much has changed. The older generation has always been critical of the younger one, considering it immature. Yet the reaction of society to the facts of development[2] must be shaped into a science, a skill, a profession.

Our mass-production methods must not be applied to education. Because it is concerned with "inner man," Freud's science is a powerful bulwark to individualism, to freedom. When it is applied to education, it can prepare our children for a society dedicated to life, liberty and the pursuit of happiness. The profession of teachers must be a powerful and constructive counterforce to mass projections and thereby give meaning to the task of creating a great society.

In times of unrest, in times of anxiety, we feel often that we are on but a small island and that we are trying to defend the church on that island. It may seem at times as if we must retreat, but our effort will not be lost. The idea of individualism is old and everlasting. As Goethe expressed it, "The highest happiness, the highest goal of this earth's children is indeed the capacity for individuality." And this is the rock upon which the church of the psychoanalysts—and the educators—must stand.

BIBLIOGRAPHY

1. Adams, Henry. *Mont-Saint-Michel and Chartres.* Boston and New York: Houghton Mifflin Co., 1913.
2. Bernfeld, Siegfried. *Sisyphus oder die Grenzen der Erziehung* (Sisyphus or the Boundaries of Education). Vienna: International Psychoanalytic Press, 1925.
3. Bruner, Jerome S., Rose Olver and Patricia Greenfield. *Studies in Cognitive Growth. A Collaboration at the Center for Cognitive Studies.* New York: John Wiley & Sons, Inc., 1966.
4. Kubie, Lawrence S. *Neurotic Distortion of the Creative Process.* Lawrence, Kansas: University of Kansas Press, 1958.
5. Murphy, Gardner. *Freeing Intelligence through Teaching.* New York: Harper & Bros., 1961.

PART III: The Challenge of Discipline

Child rearing should never become an emotional activity; it must always remain a conscious endeavor aiming at the transformation of the child, an instinctual being, into a civilized person. Viewed superficially, education could therefore be conceived as a perpetual struggle against the child's instinctual wishes. The task of the educator would then consist in building a dam to hold back these impulses of the child. The success of such an upbringing would be measured by its ability to suppress the instinctual desires, at first through external coercion, and later on through the pressure of an inner power to be developed in the child himself. . . . Then it may become possible to lead the child eventually toward a position of self-control, where he should be able to restrict the fulfillment of his instinctual wishes. Instead of bringing about suppression of a wish, he would renounce an instinctual gratification, at least on its more primitive level; the instinctual urge would then become manageable, and could be diverted toward culturally more valuable aims.

—August Aichorn

Discipline is the gate to knowledge.

—Anne Sullivan Macy

CHAPTER 11

"It Hurts Me More Than It Hurts You"—
An Approach to Discipline as a Two-Way
Process

E. JAMES ANTHONY

IN DISCIPLINE, ACHIEVEMENT, AND MENTAL HEALTH[13] a determined effort was made to differentiate clearly between good and bad discipline, and to emphasize that good discipline was as desirable as bad discipline was unwarranted. The former was based on an understanding of the child and a knowledge of his strength and weakness. It improved the learning environment by unobtrusively, yet systematically, creating an atmosphere of encouragement, firmness, clearness and conscientiousness. Bad discipline, on the other hand, was characteristically unduly harsh and inappropriate to the occasion, and, by confusing education and correction, conduced to chronically negative attitudes and feelings.

In this presentation, I am taking for granted the good sides of discipline; there are good enough parents and good enough teachers who do an admirable job with good enough pupils most of the time. Consequently, I shall focus my attention on the disciplinary situation as it exists at its worst, either in the parent-child or teacher-child relationship. My reason for so doing is simply a matter of facility. As a psychiatrist and psychoanalyst, I am more at home with the pathological than with the normal. As a student of psychopathology, I have a strong though possibly misguided conviction that conditions of morbidity magnify, even while they caricature, the elements that are normal. The implicit assumption of psychoanalytic psychology is that there is a substratum of minimal pathology within the whole range of normal reactions, so that if you scratch a normal schoolmaster, you will find an attenuated Tartar.

To the general view of discipline as training, we can add the more psychological conception of it as a technique of influence. There are

117

gradients of influence operating in every area of life, running downward, gently or precipitously, from the subject to the object being influenced. In its mildest forms, the influence is so unobtrusive, so quietly persuasive and so discreetly suggestive that the object is hardly aware of his submission. This is the level at which the therapist often works. At an intermediate level, the pressure is more direct and pressing, and the modes of influence make use of induction, indoctrination and incentive. This is what often prevails in classrooms. At the other extreme, lie the coercive techniques which bring about their effects through compulsion, threats, punishment, seduction and enticement.

A great deal of work has been done on the consequences of exposure to these various disciplinary environments. In one of my studies, coercive and laissez-faire methods of toilet training were compared with cooperative ones. The former were shown to result in a greater incidence of bowel dysfunctions in later childhood, together with abnormal attitudes of disgust and fear towards the excremental products. In another study by Harris, Gough and Martin,[6] a comparison was made of authoritarian, permissive and integrated child-rearing attitudes elicited from parents by means of a questionnaire. It emerged that prejudice in children was associated with authoritarian handling of parental control, and that parental tolerance and good judgment fostered liberal and open-minded attitudes in the children. This finding bore out the previous work of Frenkel-Brunswik.[3] A third investigation, by Maccoby and Gibbs,[11] discovered significant differences between middle- and lower-class child-rearing practices. In toilet training, sex training, control of aggression and disciplinary techniques, the lower-class mothers tended to be severe, rigid and punitive, whilst the mothers that fell in the middle-class group were described as warm, tolerant, permissive and demonstrative. The lower-class parent tended to employ physical punishment and ridicule as techniques of controlling, whereas the middle-class ones used reasoning and praise more often, along with some forms of withdrawal of love. Baldwin's[1] research on the effects of home environment on nursery-school children again points to the advantages of democratic over non-democratic modes of management. Democratically handled children were shown to be more active, socially outgoing, creative, imaginative and constructive than the others. In their various studies of "climate," Lewin, Lippitt and White,[9] found that the democratic climate is the most conducive to socially integrated behavior in a group, leading to mutual acceptance and working together. Autocratic or laissez-faire groups, by contrast, provoke a considerable amount of domination and frustration with eventual group disruption. In each case, vicious circular reactions build up into intolerable tension states. The ensuing aggressiveness was often diverted from the leader of the group onto their fellow members. In the more general context of family life, this is supported by Sears's[15] findings that aggression breeds aggression, which breeds aggression, ad infinitum.

No one who has had to do with assessing ability and achievement in school children can fail to notice that they seem to function in various intellectual gears. The "average child" seems to run along smoothly in top, whereas there are children who persist in keeping to the bottom gears. In each class, there are always a few that appear to have got into overdrive. In an interesting study by Kent and Davis,[8] four types of disciplinary environments were described: normal, demanding, over-anxious and unconcerned. These were related to intelligence test scores obtained on the Binet and the WISC. It was found that children from "demanding" homes obtained relatively high scores on the Binet scales, higher than children from normal homes, but exhibited many more emotional problems. Children from over-anxious homes scored low on the WISC performance sub-tests, and the children from homes that were "unconcerned" did poorly on all tests. When the scene is shifted from the home and the classroom to a more primitive environment, similar findings were obtained. In their unique cross-cultural study, Whiting and Child[16] examined a worldwide sample of seventy-five societies. The three techniques of discipline discussed by the authors were the love techniques (punishment by denial of love, by threats of denial of reward and by threats of ostracism); fear techniques (physical punishment, threats of punishment and punishment by ridicule); and intermediate techniques (punishment by actual denial of reward and punishment by actual ostracism). They hypothesized that love-oriented techniques of discipline favored the development of guilt feelings because they threatened the child's attainment of the goal of parental love. Yet such techniques kept the childen oriented towards that goal and did not encourage avoidance of parents, as occurred with fear-oriented techniques. The careful examination of their data led them to conclude that guilt feelings were indeed related to the love-oriented techniques which offered greater opportunities for identification with the parents and, therefore, for obedience to the rules and resistance to temptation. Looked at developmentally, in the schema provided by Piaget,[14] the morality of constraint of necessity comes earlier and is absolute, rigid and external. The morality of co-operation is a product of the socialization forces at a later age of development and is flexible, relative and internal. As Piaget reasons, it would be inappropriate and anachronistic to apply techniques of constraint to the school child, since he has already put this mode of reaction behind him.

To summarize all these findings, it appears that what is needed from a disciplinary environment is not too much and not too little but something that is "just right." There is, however, a range to this via media, this golden mean, so that parents and teachers are not walking a tight-rope but a broad bridge which means that one has to be quite deviant to fall off one side or the other. Leaving too much decision to the child brings about excessive guilt, overconscientiousness, irritability and free-floating anxiety. In between, we have the reasonable child, as Aristotle might have called him, with whom it is a pleasure to deal, and whom we see in our own children and in the larger part of our class. He is alert, cheerful, patient, considerate, tolerant, inquisitive, industrious, con-structive, imaginative, courageous, realistic, sensible and, above all, rea-sonable. How does this sort of child come about, and if he is the "average child" of the average classroom or the average family, why isn't the world a better place to live in?

Two authorities have tried to give answers to these problems.

In one of her talks, Anna Freud[4] once raised the question: "Why do we teach children at all?" In psychoanalytic terms, she felt that we could not hope to influence the id which would remain its surging, pressing self no matter what we did; nor the superego, the internalized conscience, because we cannot lecture to children about good and bad. The gospel of sexual freedom, enlightenment and freedom of aggressive expression, culled out of context from psychoanalysis, had brought a little more honesty and directness into the world. But it also created a great many over-anxious and unlovable children in the process. We had, she concluded, to do something better with our psychoanalytic knowl-edge and insight. As adults, we learn to face danger and difficulty with the help of our egos, our reasonable selves. It is the ego which keeps us on a moderate course and acts as a mediator between the very unreason-able urges from the inside and the sometimes equally unreasonable de-mands from both our conscience and the outside. What is lacking in the small child is this reasonable self, and it is the only part that needs education. The mother's role is to help the immature ego of the child to find compromise between the very unreasonable inner world and the pressure of the environment and the superego. To do this, during the earlier years she must lend the child the strength of her own ego—her patience, her courage, her sensibility and above all, her knowledge of reality—until the child matures sufficiently so that he is able to take over the task himself with the help of his teachers and peers.

A. S. Neill[12] has had some hard things to say about discipline. At times he refers to it as the wrong kind of discipline, although it would appear that he is basically opposed to any kind of discipline. Why, he asks, should we demand obedience from a child? Only to satisfy our power lusts. At Summerhill there were two great commandments, the first of these, and the greatest (reminiscent of Aichorn), was: "Thou shalt always be on the child's side." The second commandment was that the child should be free to do what he liked, so long as he didn't interfere with the freedom of others.

In a diatribe against discipline, Neill condemns it as a weapon of hate, a projection of self-love. It aims at castration in the widest sense, the castration of life itself. A disciplined child becomes bad, insincere and a hater. His life is one long lie since he is never free and can never dare to be himself. Remaining a slave to established convention, he lives under the perpetual fear of censure and never becomes a free adult. The disciplined child, molded, conditioned and repressed, the unfree child, lives in every corner of the world (outside Summerhill). He sits at a dull desk in a dull school, and, later, at a duller desk in an office or at a factory bench. He is docile, prone to obey authority, fearful of criticism and almost fanatical in his desire to be normal, conventional and correct. He accepts what he has been taught without question, and he hands down all his fears and frustrations to his children. A good humanity cannot be created by treating it with hate, punishment and suppression. A loving environment, without discipline, would take care of most of the troubles of childhood. It is the self-disapproving parent, the parental failure, the parent who cannot love and who is afraid of life in its more spontaneous forms who resorts to discipline. Given self-regulation, self-government in the company of peers, self-respect from significant adults and the adults' belief in his personality, the end product is the Neillian child—the free child.

Anna Freud raised a very pertinent question for educators when she asked whether we could get a free child who was still lovable. Neill, like the child therapist, has had to do with pathologically suppressed and repressed children. His ideas and methods refer more appropriately perhaps to the clinic than to the school, and to the abnormal child than to the normal child. With abnormal children, therapists and analysts often feel that the major task is to undo the bad discipline of the past; to modify the archaic, primitive conscience that has resulted, and to substitute a more realistic and reasonable one.

George Bernard Shaw, in one of his more memorable aphorisms, pointed out that "to punish is to injure, to reform is to heal. You cannot mend a person by damaging him." To quote A. S. Neill again in the same context: "I haven't beaten a child for forty years. I never beat a child now, because I have become aware of the dangers in beating and of the hate behind the beating."

During the present century, there has been a marked shift along the disciplinary spectrum from the control of children by chastisement to the control by reward and positive encouragement. This has been part of a general change in public opinion from the strictly authoritarian to the more democratic forms of control.

Yet not so long ago Highfield and Pinset,[7] surveying corporal punishment in Britain, asked themselves why it persisted. Why did teachers continue to chastise and why did children continue to misbehave? Did the teachers do so because of their sadism, their love of domination? Was this their way of compensating for loss of self-esteem, their response to the arduous conditions of work, which were so often fatiguing, frustrating and exasperating? Or was it because they felt they had a moral obligation to achieve certain means that could only be obtained through this method? Did children misbehave because they were born depraved, corrupt and predisposed to evil; because they were well developed mentally and morally and only weakly in control of themselves; because they were pressured by various emotional factors such as insecurity, lack of affection and an abiding sense of inferiority? Or did they misbehave because their natural environment restricted their impulses and left them frustrated, exasperated or bored? Or were they simply reflecting an unhealthy home environment or a general cultural malaise?

The instrument of punishment used in British schools was a light, ordinary, flexible cane, coming in two sizes, and applied only to the palms of the hands and the buttocks. The canes had to be authorized, inspected and approved by local authorities. They were not to be kept in the teacher's hand whilst he was teaching, and on no account was he to use the cane for any other purpose, such as pointing. Infants were not to be beaten with canes, and girls were not to be beaten in front of boys. In general, at least half an hour was to elapse before the cane was applied for a particular incident, but on no account was the school to be assembled to witness a caning. These rules and regulations sound curiously like the prison regulations for corporal punishment and capital punishment and convey an archaic atmosphere.

It was generally agreed that teachers whose relationship with the pupils was based on mutual respect and regard and who exuded self-confidence and competence rarely used corporal punishment. Wherever certain pupils and certain teachers came together in a disciplinary situation, however, the matter inevitably ended in physical punishment.

Highfield and Pinset listed three types of problem children to whom we can refer as disturbing, difficult and disturbed. The disturbing children were usually delinquent, acting-out, maladjusted and psychopathic; they were constantly disrupting the class group through their cruelty, bullying, destructiveness, obscenity, indecency, defiance, dishonesty and impulsiveness. The disturbed children, on the other hand, were the ones that needed psychiatric care. They were described as pathologically shy, seclusive, indifferent, listless, apathetic, inattentive, silent and easily discouraged. The difficult group were the "old familiars" who beset any school teacher any day in any country. They were overactive, careless, irresponsible, distractible, talkative, inaccurate and, alas, incorrigible. The incidence of problem children was most frequent at about the ages of nine and ten, and they invariably came from homes with poor living conditions and equally poor discipline.

The problem teacher could also be classified in a similar way. The disturbing teacher was authoritarian, sarcastic, deflating, sadistic and a bully. The disturbed teacher was shy, ineffectual, impotent, easily disorganized and, often, indifferent and abstracted.

In discussing the beating situation I shall speak specifically of the parent-child relationship, but my observations can be extended very easily to the classroom situation. In this section, I have focused my clinical attention on the oft-repeated, hypocritically sounding remark, "It hurts me more than it hurts you," often prefaced by some such sentence as "I just hate to do this because—" which sounds equally questionable. However, I intend to use it to analyze in greater depth the question raised by Highfield: why did the teacher punish, and why did the child misbehave?

To do this, I shall explore the thought, feeling and fantasy going on in the minds of the participants at the time of the beating and after.

First of all, let us deal with the beating parent. In discussing the different aspects of his motivation, conscious, pre-conscious and unconscious, I am going to have him think aloud for us.

The reality aspect. "You deserve this punishment because you deliberately contravened the order I gave. It is necessary that I punish you to preserve consistent law and order in this home and impress on you the necessity of obeying your elders and betters. In this sense the beating will help you later in life when you have to deal with bosses. I like you very much, and, therefore, it really does hurt me to hurt you, but I know that it is for your own good. I see it as a deterrent for you, and as an example to your brothers and sisters. At the same time, I am trying to be just by fitting the beating to the degree of your misbehavior. There are some authorities who believe that the punishment was immanent in your crime and that no further action is necessary; your football broke your own bedroom window and you will suffer from cold drafts until your pocket money repairs the windowpane. In my opinion, however, I think it is wiser to go further than immanent justice and allowing the punishment to fit the crime. I want to impress it more effectively on your cortex, and I will do this best by an actual painful stimulus. Since I have read the latest books on psychology, I know that I am acting contrary to much enlightened thought. This worries me because there is a possibility I might be doing wrong." At this point, the Hegelian rationalization comes into full force. "But, you have every right to be punished. It signifies that I am treating you as a reasonable, rational and responsible human being, and I would be the last to deprive you of this privilege. Incidentally, you are getting so big that it certainly does hurt my hand to have to spank you in this way. It seems to be getting more and more painful each succeeding year. The noise that you make will, of course, inform the neighborhood that something has gone wrong in our house and may even gain me a reputation of a bad parent, especially in this liberal community. I would take it as a favor if you kept your yells down to a minimum. I would not like my reputation to be injured." A. S. Neill has this remark about this situation: "The parental disciplinarians believe that a bad child wants to be bad, that he has a free choice of being good or bad, and that he can be made to be good with the help of a big stick. One can conquer the devil with appropriate flagellation. One can gain submission but lose the child's love. Rather than beat the bad out, you will beat the hate in."[12]

The scapegoat aspect (displacement). Here we have an unhappy family, frequently at the point of crisis and disruption. The parents are at variance with each other on all matters big and small, but especially on matters of discipline. Out of desperation, they find one unhappy, unwanted, unplanned and unloved child, and load all their hate, hostility and criticism onto him. This keeps the family from breaking up, but it puts the burden on the child whose tender shoulders are not at all strong. This is what his father is telling him: "I really hate your mother, and I would like very much to degrade, humiliate and injure her in some way. I am afraid to do this for several reasons; among others, she is likely to retaliate somewhat ferociously, and this is likely to make the family atmosphere unlivable in the weeks to come. It is not worth my hitting her because the whole family has to suffer for so long. It is very much easier to direct all this unpleasantness on you. I know it's wrong to do this, and it hurts me very much to have to do it, knowing it's wrong. It may make your suffering easier if you realize that you are playing an important role in preserving our family against all odds. I apologize for having to hit you rather than your mother."

The narcissistic aspect. There are two elements to this, and we will take them one by one. Here again is a sample of the father's inner speech: "It angers me that you dare to challenge my way of life and disturb my peace and quiet. You are challenging my authority and trying to substitute your ways for mine. However, I am bigger and stronger than you are, and my way must prevail. I don't like bullying you in this fashion, but there can only be one boss in this house, and you have to learn that you can't have your way when it conflicts with mine.

You must understand that your challenge threatens me. I am a decent guy, but if I don't put my foot down, you soon will be lording it all over the house. This means that I have to get the better of you even though I would rather that you simply accepted my particular regime."

Freud once spoke of man's historically lost narcissism. The first or cosmological blow was when Copernicus shifted his planet from the center of the universe. The second or biological blow was when Darwin placed him among the series of animals. The third or narcissistic blow was when Freud demonstrated fairly conclusively that his ego wasn't the master in his own house; man was a slave to his instincts, and there was a large part of his mind that he didn't even know about. Here the father is trying to recapture some of the lost omnipotence of his early childhood, and he is uneasy about it. He is now a small, dull, shoddy, inconsequential person, but on this occasion he is able to say: "I am controlling the world with at least one small individual who is totally dependent on me and of whom I am lord and master. He has to perform and conform according to my dictates. It is the only way I have left to me, and I have to take it, but part of me realizes that it is a futile and degrading way to relive past and vanished glories."

Aspirational aspects (ego ideal). The father has failed as a man and feels emasculated and impotent: "I have failed in accomplishing anything in my life, and now I am going to make sure that I fulfill my ambitions through you. I failed once, but I will not fail a second time. I am going to make certain that you get somewhere I failed to reach. I shall then at least be able to enjoy your success as if it were my own. I don't want to beat you, and it hurts me to do it, because it more than emphasizes my impotence—hitting kids is not a man's job. But I have to hit you, because I cannot risk being a total flop."

Aspects of shame (ego ideal). The father speaks again: "I am beating you for things that I do myself as an adult and as a man. I swear and curse and fornicate and lie and cheat. But I beat the life out of you for doing approximately the same things, simply because you are a child and I am an adult, you are female and I am male. There are four standards of morality operating in life, one for the old, one for the young, one for the male and one for the female. I did not put them there and I feel ashamed to live by them since they are so grossly unfair. However, one must be realistic, and I am merely following the cultural line. I am doing what is expected of me. It still fills me with shame that I have to do it."

Sado-masochistic aspects (superego guilt). Here we again have two subaspects to deal with. There is the masochistic satisfaction or identification with the victim: "As I have you over my knee with your pants down, I can feel every twitch of pain in you, as if it were part of my own body. It provides me with exquisite sensations almost equivalent to pain. I can tell you that it really hurts me more than it hurts you, and this is the way that I want it. In my dreams and fantasies, I am always being tortured and beaten, but it is so difficult to procure this in real life. I can only obtain it secondhand through you."

The sadistic satisfaction is so closely related to this former one that it is at times difficult to separate the two. There is no doubt, however, that the beater is enjoying himself immensely: "I love beating you, especially on your buttocks. I want you to please show me how much it hurts you by screaming and crying as much as possible since this adds to my satisfaction. There is no pleasure so pleasurable as the pleasure in another's pain. But one cannot get away with it completely. Somewhere a great deal of guilt follows on this sadism, and I am frequently burdened with remorse. I feel especially guilty that I sometimes get an erection and even have a climax during the beating. This is vile and hurts me dreadfully."

Transference aspects (projection). Father has a burning moment of insight: "You are really my little brother (or sister) whom I resented so much when he came along and spoiled my beautiful relationship with my mother. I hated him and took every opportunity directly and indirectly to harm him. I had, however, to watch out for my parents. They would frequently attack me if I attacked him, and this added to my resentment. At times I see him in you so much that I can hardly keep my hands off you. I really want to smash you up. You should understand and forgive me. It really hurts me terribly to have to do it because it seems so irrational. My rage is out of proportion to any provocation from you. Tonight I shall have a nightmare that it is really my brother (or sister) that I am attacking. Once again I shall hear my mother's (parents') condemnation and experience that devastating loss of love. I simply cannot bear her (their) implicit anger and punishment, and it really hurts me more than it hurts you."

Seduction aspects (the id). The father (or mother) again has access to a deeper insight: "I really feel bad because I incite you to do all the sinful things that I have kept under control all these years. I stimulate you to do them, enjoying your doing them and then beat you for doing them, so that the satisfaction is a very complicated and full one. In addition, I am especially frightened when you do these things that my own defenses will break down and that there will be a breakthrough of my own impulses. I have to beat you in order to keep down my own impulses and to satisfy my own overly strict conscience that has deprived me for so long of so many pleasures. In this situation, I can both have my cake and eat it. I can act out the essential action vicariously through you and, at the same time, enjoy the moral pleasure of punishing you for it. Nevertheless, I feel guilty about getting my satisfactions in this distorted way and to use you, my own child, for this illicit purpose. I should really be beating myself for my villainy, but in beating you, my conscience really takes it out of me."

Now we turn to consider what is going on in the mind of the child during the beating episode. 1. The child is often aware at some level of consciousness that he is providing satisfaction to his parents and that he is gratifying them, through both his bad actions and their punishing him for them. To quote Lippman: "The entranced parental facial expression apparent to the child describing a stealing episode, a sexual misdemeanor, or a hostile attitude towards a teacher, conveys to the child that the parent is achieving some pleasurable gratification. No amount of subsequent punishment will act as a deterrent against the recurrence of the acting out. A child wishes to do the one thing which he senses gives the parent pleasure, even though he may be punished."[10] Baruch adds: "It is startling to observe to what degree parents seduce children to behavior that is improper enough to create serious conflicts in the child or adolescent. The parents may erroneously believe that repression is bad, and this may lead them to permit children to act out their impulses freely, to the parents' covert satisfaction."[2] 2. The episode may represent a mode of attention-seeking on the part of a much neglected or rejected child who has reached the deep, unconscious conclusion that it is better to have a negative or a painful relationship with his parents than none at all. 3. The child may consciously and psychopathically contrive such beating situations in order to reap the rewards of the parents' subsequent remorse expressed through emotional bribes or concrete gifts. There are also more distorted conscious wishes. A child confessed to me that he once heard that a father fell dead from a heart attack whilst beating his child. He so hated his own father that he hoped that something similar might happen and was prepared to provoke and undergo chastisement for this end.

In his classic paper on the beating fantasy, "A Child Is Being Beaten,"[5] Freud traced its history to the very early years of life, certainly before school age and not later than in the fifth or sixth year. He found that it was a very frequent fantasy in cases of hysteria or of obsessional neurosis, and it usually culminated in masturbation. It occasioned great feelings of shame and a sense of guilt in the child. Later, when the child was at school and saw other children being beaten by the teacher, the fantasies, if dormant, were again called into being. At this time, there was no longer one child being beaten, but an indefinite number. In high school, although the children were no longer beaten, the beating fantasy was influenced by accounts given in books, and these reinforced the fantasy. The influence of the school on the fantasy was so clear that, at first, the patients themselves were tempted to trace back their beating fantasies exclusively to these impressions from school life which dated from later than their sixth year.

The fantasy was invariably charged with a high degree of pleasure, but not the real experience of a beating at school. Seeing another child beaten at school occasioned a peculiarly excited feeling which was probably of a mixed character and in which repugnance had a large share. In a few cases the real experience was felt to be intolerable. The curious thing is that the individuals who had these powerful fantasies were themselves very seldom beaten in their childhood.

Very carefully, Freud disentangled the elements of the fantasy. To the question: "Who was being beaten?" came the answer: "A little child is being beaten on its naked bottom. I am not the child, and I am not the beater, but the child is my brother (or sister)." The beaten child can, therefore, be either male or female. At this stage, the fantasy is neither sadistic nor masochistic, since the child producing the fantasy is neither being beaten nor doing the beating. At the next stage, the beater becomes clearly recognizable as the father, and the fantasy now takes this form: "My father is beating the child"; with the further addition: "My father is beating the child whom I hate." In the next phase of the fantasy, a profound transformation has occurred. The beaten child has invariably become the child producing the fantasy, which is now unmistakably a masochistic fantasy: "I am being beaten by my father." In the final and later phase of the fantasy, it becomes nebulous again. The fantasy-maker is now looking on whilst a number of children (boys in the case of girls' fantasies, and vice versa) are being beaten in complicated, elaborate ways. Often, other punishments and humiliations are substituted for the beatings. The fantasy now has a strong and unambiguous sexual excitement attached to it and is accompanied by masturbation.

In some cases, a boy's beating fantasy is somewhat different in that its first form is: "I am loved by my father, but I am being beaten by my mother." This fantasy is, therefore, passive from the very beginning and is derived from a feminine attitude toward the father. In both cases, however, the beating fantasy has its origin in an incestuous attachment to the father. In the case of the girl, the unconscious masochistic fantasy starts from the normal oedipal attitude, in which the father is taken as the object of love. The boy evades his homosexuality by repressing and remodeling his unconscious fantasy. The remarkable thing about his later conscious fantasy is that it has for its content a feminine attitude without a homosexual object choice. The boy's original fantasy: "I am being beaten by my father," clearly corresponds to a feminine attitude; the girl's original fantasy: "I am being beaten (loved) by my father," also represents a feminine attitude and corresponds to her dominant and manifest sex. The fantasy is very likely to occur in unmanly boys and unwomanly girls. There is no doubt that it is the feminine trait in the boy and the masculine trait in the girl which produces the passive fantasy in the boy and its repression in the girl. In both, the fantasy is altered through the mechanism of the masculine protest, but this does not help our understanding too much. I want, however, to emphasize that this is a very complicated situation for the child. If he is suffering from a neurosis of obsessional or hysterical type, the beating experience is going to reinforce his fantasy, and thus reinforce his neurosis. It is, therefore, important to treat rather than to beat the neurotic child, and it is, therefore, important to learn how to distinguish between naughtiness and neurosis in childhood.

A brutal beating can leave marks that persist for weeks, and, with the child's constant inspection of them, they impress themselves deeply on his mind. They leave, as it were, a permanent scar on his psyche, even though the body wounds heal successfully. After a beating, some stress-sensitive children may develop, for a while, such minor phobias as fears of the dark and of falling asleep and may even have a sequence of traumatic nightmares which repeat the original situation. For the younger child, the traumatic event may be repeated in his play until he has mastered his anxiety connected with it. In this phase, there may be psychosomatic symptoms such as vague abdominal pains, headaches, urinary frequency and even diarrhea and vomiting. The child may show an increased aggressiveness in school (identification with the aggressor) and may even resort to bullying. Just as likely, he may show unusual fearfulness and isolate himself from any situation possibly leading to injury. In therapeutic play, we would observe that his castration anxiety may be enhanced.

In the parent, following such an episode, there is much evidence of guilt reactions with obvious remorse, making up to the child, or even bribing the way back to a good relationship. In sadistic cases, there may be guilt over the orgastic satisfaction and dreams relating to this. Occasionally, a parent may have marked psychosomatic symptoms, such as headaches, vomiting, giddiness. Many are actually exhausted by a beating episode and take to their beds for a while. Other consequences of such an episode that I have met in my practice include anginal attacks, slipped discs, a dislocated shoulder and a parent who died from heart failure. The effect on the children, as might be imagined, are disturbing and complex and require a great deal of working through.

In dealing with the negative effects of the more pathological expressions of discipline, I have been assuming that these are invariably bad, and that a great deal of disturbance in the child can be attributed to this negative training. However, we psychoanalysts must remember that our main preoccupation is with the internal situation, with the internal conflict that unfolds during the course of development. However benign the external situation is, there are certain vicissitudes that prove hazardous to the child. It is difficult to think of ideal situations for the child, but many psychologist parents often imagine that they provide the perfect environment, an Eden, for their child, and are then surprised to find a serpentine complex inside it.

Piaget's daughter, Jacqueline, had been brought up in a democratic regime without any strict punishment. Her parents had never demanded any sort of passive obedience from her without discussion, and they always tried to make her understand orders instead of laying down categorical rules. On one occasion, she was put to bed and given a laxative, the effects of which had been described. In spite of her mother's precaution, especially designed to avoid any reaction of shame or guilt, Jacqueline was greatly upset when the medicine worked. Her face assumed an expression of distress, her eyes filled with tears, her mouth drooped; she was obviously experiencing the same feeling she would, had the soiling occurred because of her own negligence. As Piaget remarks, it was staggering to find in a little girl who never knew what authority was and whose parents made a point of cultivating autonomy of conscience in their children, that the orders received should have led to so stubborn a moral realism and sense of overwhelming responsibility.[14]

In the case of A. S. Neill's daughter, Zoe, the child had been brought up as the epitome of the Neillian child, free to express herself in every way possible way, without threat or punishment. Yet, lo and behold, she developed a real phobia for a cow, in the manner of little Hans, which lasted for a few weeks. (It is Neill's assumption that in the unfree child, it would have lasted very much longer, and he may well be right about this.)[12]

An eighteen-month little girl goes to the seaside for the first time. She has just achieved bowel and bladder control and is proud of her achievement. She runs to the sea with her bucket and spade and squats down to fill her bucket. A wave comes and wets her pants. She runs to her mother in great distress and is inconsolable. She has not been trained punitively, but things have been going on inside her which, if we knew them, make her disproportionate reaction much more understandable. It is well to remember that we cannot ascribe everything to the rejecting or punitive mother, the bad teacher, the awful medicine, the frightening cow, or the terrible sea.

BIBLIOGRAPHY

1. Baldwin, A. L. "The Effect of Home Environment on Nursery School Behavior." *Child Development*, 1949, 20:49.
2. Baruch, D. W. *New Ways in Discipline*. New York: McGraw-Hill, 1949.
3. Frenkel-Brunswik, E. "A Study of Prejudices in Children." *Human Relations*, 1948, 1:295.
4. Freud, A. "Psychoanalysis and Education." *Psychoanalytic Study of the Child*, 1954, 9:9.
5. Freud, S. "A Child Is Being Beaten." *Collected Papers II*, London: Hogarth, 1946.
6. Harris, D. B., H. G. Gough and W. E. Martin. "Children's Ethnic Attitudes: II." *Child Development*, 1950, 21:169.
7. Highfield, M. E., and A. Pinset. *A Survey of Rewards and Punishments in Schools*. London: Newnes Educational Publishing Co., 1952.
8. Kent, N., and D. R. Davis. "Discipline in the Home and Intellectual Development." *British Journal of Psychiatry*, 1957, 30:27.
9. Lewin, K., R. Lippitt and R. K. White. "Patterns of Aggressive Behavior in Experimentally Created 'Social Climates.'" *Journal of Social Psychology*, 1939, 10:271.
10. Lippman, H. S. "The Role of the Probation Officer in the Treatment of Juvenile Delinquency in Children." *The Juvenile Offender*, C. B. Vedder, editor. New York: Doubleday and Co., 1954, 360.
11. Maccoby, E. E., and P. K. Gibbs. "Methods of Child Rearing in Two Social Classes." *Child Behavior and Development*, W. E. Martin and C. B. Stendler, editors. New York: Harcourt, Brace, 1962.
12. Neill, A. S. *Summerhill*. New York: Hart Publishing Co., 1960.
13. Phillips, E. L., D. N. Weiner and N. G. Haring. *Discipline, Achievement, and Mental Health*. Englewood Cliffs, New Jersey: Prentice-Hall, 1960.
14. Piaget, J. *The Moral Judgment of the Child*. London: Kegan Paul, Trench, Trubner and Co., 1932.
15. Sears, R., E. E. Maccoby and H. Levin. *Patterns of Child Rearing*. Evanston, Illinois: Row, Peterson, 1957.
16. Whiting, J. W. M., and I. L. Child. *Child Training and Personality*. New Haven: Yale University Press, 1953.

CHAPTER 12

A Tribute to Anne Sullivan Macy: A Great Teacher of Discipline

RUDOLF EKSTEIN

DISCIPLINE IS THE INNER STATE OF MIND which we set as a goal for our children to achieve as well as one of the means of education through which we hope they can achieve this goal. I will examine the account of a famous teacher and her work which illustrates the need for and the use of discipline in the learning situation. I am using material drawn from William Gibson's *The Miracle Worker*. Gibson's sensitive drama beautifully reveals the dynamic undercurrent of the struggle that took place between the impulsive child and her dedicated teacher.

A teacher of discipline, Anne Macy, née Sullivan, was the woman who accompanied Helen Keller through many years of her life. She helped Helen Keller move out of the emptiness of chaos—the complete lack of inner discipline and ignorance—into a world of life and knowledge, speech and wisdom. She accomplished this in spite of the fact that Helen could not hear; in spite of the fact that Helen was blind.

For a teacher, it is helpful to think about personality organization in terms of learning readiness: a potential for learning which shifts and changes with the growing child. The child who comes to school at five or six years of age is one who should be prepared for learning, but is not always ready for it. The school and the teacher must be prepared to take what comes.

The child of this age has grown through a number of conflicts. These conflicts, stemming from the early relationship with the mother, center around trust and distrust. In general, they express themselves around the issue of control—outer control, inner control and rebellion against control. Conflicts also cluster around the desire for initiative, and about the guilt connected with such initiative: they may focus around the newly achieved capacity for industry, which is sometimes replaced by apathy or laziness or inability to work. Each child brings the results and resolutions of these conflicts to the school and teachers. The child with whom Anne Sullivan worked was a special kind of child. She was about seven years of age at the time when Anne Sullivan became her teacher. She had resolved none of the conflicts described above. She had not resolved the issue of trust even though she had primitive faith in her mother. The blind trust she gave her mother was based on the need for instant gratification. It was mixed with wild anguish, with rebellion against any kind of frustration, and it was worthless because it was not paralleled by self-trust. It was but the response of a wild animal that jumps instantly when it is not gratified.

When Helen came to Anne Sullivan she had neither control from within over her own body nor from the outside world to keep her in line. Her parents felt so guilt-stricken and yet, sometimes, so filled with hate towards her that they could neither control her with discipline nor let her go to somebody else who might control her. Anne Sullivan found a child who was full of initiative, but since it was a destructive and violent initiative, mixed with hate, with anger, and with guilt, it led nowhere. Since Helen had resolved none of the other conflicts, she had no industry but that of grabbing and taking—an impulse-driven way of trying to master life.

What Anne Sullivan had to do when she entered the Keller home was to bring about in a short time what six years of education normally accomplish. And she had to do it with a person who was deprived of the usual capacities that normal children have. Fortunately, Helen Keller was also a person of unusual intellect and perseverance.

When her parents discovered Helen was blind they were desperate. Burdened with the usual ambivalent feelings of parents who face such a discovery, deep unhappiness and guilt, they pledged themselves to make up to her for her afflictions and to do whatever they could to keep her with them. As the child grew older, it became more and more apparent that they might not be able to keep her at home unless, somehow, she could be taught. She was as yet unteachable: she could not be controlled, and she had no inner discipline or self-control. The parents wrote everywhere for help. Although very little about teaching such children was known anywhere, the Kellers found out about a home for the blind in Boston where a great deal of experience had accumulated. There had been a case at the Boston Perkins Institute for the Blind, fifty years earlier, in which the famous Dr. Howe had trained a blind and deaf individual to communicate. This person was still alive. When the parents heard about this, they wrote to Boston and the Institute sent Anne Sullivan to the family.

The life of this teacher is of interest to us because her determination to help Helen had to do, of course, with her own life struggles. We know that many professional occupational choices have to do with one's own background, and the obstinacy and the devotion of this teacher developed out of her own basic experiences. These life experiences were gripping and often crippling.

Anne Sullivan's father had been an irresponsible alcoholic who had beaten her mercilessly; eventually, he had put her and her gravely ill younger brother into an almshouse. Her own eyesight was failing during the time her little brother was dying. The brother had had nothing in his life to hold onto but his sister. He pleaded, "Can't you make me stay alive?" and, frightened of dying, begged her never to leave him. She grew up with two overwhelming feelings: guilt, as if she had made him die; and determination to go to school and learn, as if she might make him come alive again and thus fulfill his dying plea. For her, therefore, learning was not only a goal to fulfill her promise to help him but it also represented atonement for the deep sin of having deserted him. When she heard about little Helen she was determined to accept the position because she knew that such a child faced a mental death unless she could be taught. The dying voice of her brother had become a part of her conscience and committed her irrevocably to this task. She was twenty-one at the time she took over.

When the average teacher gets a group of six- and seven-year-olds, he walks into a classroom with an established discipline and a list of rules from his administrator. The administrator requires and supports the teacher's discipline and gives him the security of a defined job, hours, salary and tenure.

This young woman, without family, with the brother's death on her conscience, went from Boston into the deep South. She took a job of which only the most general limits were defined, a job at which the pay and tenure were to be arbitrarily established and tendered. Her employers were not only her administrators, as it were, but also parents who constantly interfered with the structure that she needed to establish in order to teach this child.

Her first problem was to wrest authority from the parents in order to set up a situation in which she could teach. The parents, of course, were less interested in teaching than they were in a concept of discipline which would make an orderly little girl out of Helen. They were less motivated in seeing that Helen would have a new world open to her than in relieving their own guilt by having done everything they could. When the teacher came in and sought to establish her authority over the child, they were instantly involved in this struggle in which they could not be impartial. They were torn between their guilt toward the child and their strange love for her—and could love for such a child be anything but strange and tortured? They were constantly driven to undermine the teacher whom they could pay but whom they could not give authority because they had none to give.

Anne Sullivan was involved in two struggles at the same time. On the one hand, she had to establish her authority over the child and, on the other hand, she had to wrest permission for this authority from the parents in order to create a situation in which teaching could take place.

The scene in which she gives the child the key to the suitcase is a beautiful symbolic portrayal of what she wants to do. With it she tells Helen: "Here is something new, and you may open it if you can find it. You will find in it a doll that has eyes. You may find love in it. You may find knowledge."

The first answer of little Helen was to take the key, lock up the teacher and throw the key into a deep well. The first gift was thus refused, because at that time the teacher was experienced as an enemy. It became clear to Miss Sullivan, however, that Helen had intelligence and determination. She could perhaps be redeemed, provided there was authority.

Anne Sullivan wrote in a letter to her former teacher that the greatest problem she had was to discipline Helen without breaking her spirit. Without any knowledge of psychoanalysis, she knew intuitively that the notion of discipline was one of establishing an inner self-control in such a way that the spirit is not broken and the child does not become a submissive slave, but rather develops into a person who has the internal discipline necessary for learning.

Miss Sullivan also thought that discipline is the gate to knowledge, and without discipline there would be no knowledge. A struggle ensued, a struggle in which the child countered Miss Sullivan's efforts with hate, with aggression and with a constant attempt to regain the over-indulging, helpless mother. The mother also was trying to restore the previous way of life in which impulse could triumph but in which learning could not proceed. Miss Sullivan was determined to prevent this. Although, sometimes, she herself wanted to escape, to go back to Boston where she had what passed as a home of her own, where other blind children would love her, she could not go back. Whenever she was tempted, she heard the voice of her brother saying, "Do you know how it pains when one is dead forever?" And having been temporarily blind, she knew that to be blind and also without knowledge means to be dead. She identified with the child, as does every good teacher who must live himself, as it were, into the mind of his pupil. At the same time, she could keep enough distance between herself and the child to allow for the change that occurs if outer authority is accepted and identified with.

Miss Sullivan's next move was to come to some kind of terms with the parents. They were on the verge of letting her go because they could not bear the pain of watching their child's struggle with her. She got them to provide a schoolroom, a cabin, outside of the main house. She literally and physically had to establish something we take for granted because we get our children when they are capable of separating from the parent. Miss Sullivan had to fight for such separation and to insist that she be given two weeks within which to establish control over the child. This control she knew could be established only if a condition would prevail so that she could bring the word, communication, language, to the child. For we must always remember that language is based on some form of separation, on some need for give and take. Anne Sullivan had to create such an authority situation, even though it meant cutting the child's supply lines to the free but chaotic, uncontrolled flow of food and love, as well as sporadic despair, from the mother and father.

She said to Captain Keller, "Yes, it's going to be a war," and a war can only be won with control of the supply lines. She determined to control the supply lines to this child, since this was a war of the child's mind but also in the child's interest. It was a war waged by love.

Her campaign was one of endless repetition, of endless conditioning and of endless teaching. Repetition rather than insight was necessary; repetition pushed to the point where the child realized that this person who insisted was not intent on crushing her nor taking her core identity away from her, but, rather, was seeking to give her speech—communication—and individuality. For one can be oneself in this world only if one can accept another self, and one accepts another self only when one can communicate with that other person as a truly separate object. That battle, waged by love, is won at the truly moving moment when, for the first time, Helen can not only spell the word "water" but understands it as an abstract concept. She can then communicate. She has conquered the symbolic function.

After that, the teacher returned the child to her mother, but the first thing Helen asked of her mother was to let her go to Teacher. She had discovered that Miss Sullivan was not her enemy but her teacher; she had learned to spell "teacher" and had become, as it were, identified with the learning process.

It is a truly touching moment when the little girl can give the key back to the teacher and can allow the teacher to use that key in order to unlock the closed mind.

What I have been trying to say is that discipline, as psychoanalytic knowledge confirms, is not coercion, even though coercion and a terrible struggle between human beings may sometimes be necessary to establish the only true discipline, inner discipline. Discipline gives each of us a key to choice, and only in a society in which there is choice can there be true discipline. Societies that have no choice, that are unfree, know not discipline, but merely coercion.

I speak then about discipline that is based on love, that knows choice and permits choice. When discipline is considered a capacity for choice, a free society can replace the egotism of blind impulsive behavior and the stagnation of coercive control with the thoughtfulness of deliberated action and the freedom of knowledgeable creativity.

CHAPTER 13

Management of Discipline Problems in Normal Students

FRITZ REDL

THE MANAGEMENT OF DISCIPLINE PROBLEMS in normal students is not given enough thought. Learning is a task which requires a great deal of control from within—for all students. Accordingly, the learner is confronted with the task of managing those needs which are temporarily excluded from the learning situation. Because the healthy youngster sometimes is so well involved in the learning process, he may pose problems in management of his behavior. I wish to speak about these students: they are not problem learners and do not need treatment. Rather, they have problems about learning because of their involvement in it.

In my early years of teaching, I noticed occasionally that a pretty nice kid would suddenly get furious, ball up his paper and run out of the room. At first this looked to me like downright rebellion. Upon a second look, and it didn't need a long one, I could see the difference. This was a child who was so excited, so involved, so anxious about producing and so afraid he might not really live up to expectations, that he was suddenly hit with an awareness of the possibility of failure that he could not take. Had he not been such a good learner, so involved and so interested, he might never have bothered.

Another example of a student in a panic-producing situation is one who has an upsurge of an early experience brought on by what's going on in the class. This would not have happened right at ten in the morning unless he had been involved in that learning situation.

He may have to do something to keep his self-image halfway uncontaminated by the feeling that he is no good or that everything is taken for granted anyway. This includes his having to compare his self-image with the expectations that his parents and other people have of him.

The problem of success and failure . . . the reaction to it . . . ruminations on where one is going . . . where one comes from . . . what others think of one . . . all of that is in the learning task, and somewhere along the line, these are the things that throw the healthy learners. Their very interest is suddenly punctured by the emergence of any one of these emotional problems. When this happens, the teacher has to deal with it if he is to be supportive to the healthy learner and the learning process.

Sometimes the most wonderful, most normal child, in the process of growing up and being involved in group learning, faces something which may make him temporarily "go off his rocker," though he has no right to do so and no diagnosis to justify it. A student who runs out or says something nasty to the teacher, out of his excitement around the learning situation, is one who is in this state.

Everybody has the need to go off his rocker occasionally. We all have certain neurotic or other anxieties get hold of us temporarily and then we take hold of ourselves again. That is life. However, don't let anyone tell a classroom teacher he does not have to handle that. If he is in the room at the time, it is his problem to help the child get back on the track and to prevent the rest of the students from getting sucked into the contagion chain.

For instance, something bad happens during recess, and two youngsters get mad at each other. By the time the teacher walks in, they are both so hot under the collar that temporarily they do not see him nor hear him nor even know he is there. They are ready to sink their fangs into each other; the teacher must do something to stop them right now. That does not mean they are crazy, but right now what must be done is comparable to what would have to be done in a ward of psychiatrically disturbed children. Except those youngsters, if the situation is handled correctly, in a short time will be back where they are supposed to be.

This is what they don't tell a teacher when he signs his contract, because he is not supposed to know how to handle a child who is in deep panic or anxious or in a depression and suicidal, unless he is going into a class for very disturbed children. Yet normal children sometimes are temporarily in a similar state though they have a reasonable amount of snap-back ability. This ego resilience means that a youngster who has had a blow-up doesn't take very long until he is back in the saddle again. And normal children have good resilience.

In the group life of children, individuals who are otherwise quite "well adjusted" learners sometimes get entangled in group processes. That means they get excited and get into what we frequently call contagion chains, where what one person does seems to produce similar behavior in other members of the group. This may develop some contagion potential way beyond what we otherwise would expect. We may find that youngsters are hit by the general mood of group psychological intoxication; in which case, they act as unreasonably as adults can act when they go to a convention in somebody else's town. Since the teacher is the group leader, even though his main task may be curriculum and the related learning process, he must do something about it.

One of the biggest problems which most teachers run into sooner or later is the task of stopping a contagion chain without making a mess of it. What does one do if the group is just at the point of psychological intoxication? How does one handle it without too much waste of time which is, curriculum-wise, expensive and, learning-wise, important, without leaving a mess that someone else must wipe up?

The general stereotype which is maintained in educational circles is that basically good curriculum planning ought to take care of the healthy learner. And, if the curriculum is well planned, it is true that the teacher has a better time than if it is not. But even so, the teacher still has heavy doses of the task of handling behavior problems. Then the question is, "How do I deal with it reasonably effectively, without creating problems somewhere else, while rescuing the learning process right now?" This is the big task of the person who is learning-oriented. One cannot handle behavior by, say, bouncing five of the students and yelling at the rest of them. This might enable a teacher to have his themes in on time, but who will learn in that kind of a group?

Teachers have to learn to spot behavior which only seems inappropriate to the learning process while it actually is a psychological condition for great concentration. Only as long as certain children can sit that special way or finger this gadget or what not, can they really concentrate. This is quite different from behavior which doesn't fit the learning process and actually is disturbing. I think good research and observation on this differential diagnosis are highly indicated.

I know quite well that we psychoanalysts try to get people away from putting too much emphasis on "surface behavior." We try to help people feel that they shouldn't always worry about "do you do this or that?" but about the real relationship. But I want to confirm the respectability of being interested as an adult in what to do in a given situation. Now, obviously, what a teacher does, if he punishes a child or praises him or criticizes him, isn't the only thing. What is also important is the relationship between him and the child and how he means what he does. We psychoanalysts have emphasized this now for the last forty years and that's good because it's necessary. But in our enthusiasm about the importance of the basic issue of relationship, we sometimes forget that what a person does is not a matter of indifference.

For instance, if one loves a child and means very well, but gives him half-a-pound of arsenic, he will still be dead. In such a case, the behavior matters, not the atmosphere and the relationship.

If a teacher loves a child and is enthusiastic, but does screwy things, he's going to create a mess. He's going to put the youngster in a position where he is confronted with an experience which is too much for him to take and which throws him into pathological production, or throws him, period. Not only the people who don't like children and rejecting mothers mess them up. It is also people who love them and are wonderfully motivated who mess them up with idiotic and inappropriate behavior. So, it is not unimportant what one does, even though I grant that what one does must not be interpreted only through describable behavior, but also through the message that comes with the behavior. Unfortunately, and here the big communication problem comes in, sometimes the behavior and message are perfectly all right, except that by the time they reach the consumer, they either fall flat or the consumer packs them with stuff from his own case history, causing distortion and trouble.

I remember, for instance, how frequently kids from a tougher area considered peculiar the nice lady who wanted to be really friendly and tried to show she liked them by touching or patting them. For those kids, that didn't mean a darned thing. In that case, the distortion set in at the inappropriateness of the form of the message in terms of the receivers' Unconscious or his neighborhood mores. The point I'm trying to make is that it is interesting and necessary to know what we really do.

I'm in favor of developing something like a pharmacopoeia of educational influence techniques. That means, we have to know what techniques we put together in what way with what kind of dosage, so that before anybody is made to swallow them we can predict what will happen when they hit his stomach. Which patient needs what kind of technique or which student needs what type of behavioral handling still depends on how well we can predict what a specific behavior on our side will release in the child to whom it is directed.

Behavior is not superficial, provided one looks at it with open eyes and not merely with a counting machine. It does make a lot of difference how we manage situations, because the specific situation we create for a child by the way we handle him may be the decisive factor in whether or not he can cope with it. From our point of view then, behavioral techniques of handling children's behavior are not just superficial.

Let us assume I am a teacher primarily interested in the basically healthy learner and focusing on the learning situation. From time to time, I may get into a situation where I will be confronted with some form of aggression which seems to be inappropriate on one or another count. This needs to be stopped, but how? I could shoot the offender and accomplish that. But how do I stop it so the learning process isn't disturbed and no other damage or problem is created in the youngster's life beyond what is appropriate and relevant in terms of an increase of his involvement in the learning process?

This is what I call a technique of behavior intervention. The real problem is that anything I do will really be out of my hands the moment I have done it. I can only create a situation with which the child has to cope. The real success or failure of what I do depends upon what the youngster will do with it. Our problem is to create a situation which the child's ego can translate into a constructive experience that increases his learning potential.

One of the difficulties for most teachers occurs when something happens in the back of the classroom, say, where five kids are just starting off on something. The teacher has to figure out with whom to start, whether he should let it go or what. He does not want to waste time on it. On the other hand, he does not want it to reach the point where everybody else will be interested in the side show and not listen to him any more. Thus, he must size up whether to intervene and how.

The child behavior we have in mind, by the way, doesn't have to be wrong or bad or pathological. The most normal behavior in a given learning situation is temporarily inappropriate if it interferes with the current part of the learning process. Part of the trouble is that we frequently demand opposite types of behavior from children just because a bell rings. For example, during composition class, they must be creatively productive with an imagination a pathological liar could envy. That kind of pathological liar's imagination must last from 9:00 till 9:40. At 9:50 they are in mathemathics, where they must exclude all imagination, fantasy or feeling. And the teacher must try to create a specific situation for each kind of learning and all behavior inappropriate to each must be considered as disturbing behavior.

In short, youngsters sometimes produce behavior which, at that moment, is inappropriate for the learning task. In that case, the teacher has to tolerate some of it. Sooner or later, however, a point is reached where he wants to know how to stop that behavior without any child feeling that either he or his behavior is disliked. Also, the teacher wants to give him the strength to control his behavior himself. This is important because only physical restraint stops him from the outside. Otherwise, self-control is up to the child. Unless a child utilizes energies for self-control by getting his own ego to use energy for the control of his behavior, the teacher is stuck.

In fact, most of the behavior-intervention techniques which teachers have available are actually no more than an "invitation to a dance." The youngster still has to mobilize his own resources to control himself from within.

The real question for a teacher is, "How am I supportive to the kid's ego, so that anything I do has a better chance to succeed than to fail?" For instance, a teacher has to criticize. When necessary, he had better criticize or the youngster will think the teacher is a dummy. Or the teacher may have to use something like a threat of failure. The youngster is then exposed to an experience of displeasure, a negative self-image, and he doesn't like it. The reason for doing this is not just to make the child feel mad, not to give him what he has coming, but to rattle him. If rattled, he may become more aware of the real issue at stake and may muster enough energy to change his behavior. Two things result for the child: 1) he experiences displeasure (unless he is a masochist and enjoys it, in which case it's a poor technique: he isn't supposed to like it); and 2) there is a minimum upsurge of anger or, rather, the normal human reaction to displeasure or pain, the rallying of possible counteraggressive forces.

What happens from now on depends on the child. But there are several steps in front of any youngster exposed to anger or displeasure because something unpleasant happened.

He has to perceive the difference between the cause and the source of his trouble. He must be able, in his ego, to make the distinction between the outside source of his predicament and the actual cause which, both basically and to a large degree, lies within him. This gives the teacher a good criterion for what to watch for; if he is happily triumphant at telling the youngster where to get off, then, to the child, it looks very much as if the teacher is not only the source but also the cause of his trouble. The teacher can be sympathetic with the youngster's predicament, but he must make it clear that his interest is in the final outcome, especially as it facilitates the youngster's perception of the situation. Thus, the youngster can see the teacher as one who is admittedly the source of his trouble but, in actuality, not its cause. The teacher gave him the low grade, but was not the cause of his trouble because he ran around on his bike instead of working.

The next thing the teacher must do is decontaminate this experience from other bad ones. It is normal and natural for cornered or threatened people to throw the rest of their case history into the pot and stir it around. The teacher must remember what trouble it must be for some of his students whose people at home are constantly triumphant and just knock them around. When the teacher comes along with his benign criticism, these children are suddenly supposed to perceive that in this case the unpleasant experience is only the source and not the real cause of their trouble. What a difficult distinction to make! But without it, obviously, a given experience gets immediately contaminated with similar ones which make it easy to alibi this particular situation, and, therefore, to ward it off negatively rather than react to it productively.

The third function of the ego confronted with failure, criticism or with an implied threat is, of course, to internalize at least part of his anger. The child is mad right now, but he shouldn't be mad only at the teacher but at himself as well. Being a little mad at the teacher helps him cope with some of his anger by letting it out. A teacher should give his students a five-inch range in which to puff off anger so they don't have to internalize the whole issue. That would be either phoney or really self-destructive in that they feel, "I am no good; I am not worthy of anything anyway; why should I try?", etc. and there will be no change. Thus, a certain subliminal range of aggression ought to be directed at the source which creates the discomfort and which is normal, but the major part of the anger ought to be directed internally.

The teacher has to be able to guide the internalized anger so that it becomes issue directed. The child must get mad at that part of himself which is connected with the learning issue about which he was criticized and not about everything else. Some youngsters will over-internalize, so that the moment they are criticized they think, "I'm no good, I'm too dumb, I'll never amount to anything." That means that they immediately turn all their anger toward their whole personality rather than to that part which produced the problem, namely, the last two weeks when they didn't work and were riding around on a bike.

So, the ego has to be capable of draining off some of the anger on the outside, but directing the rest of it only to that part of the personality involved in the specific problem. This is quite an elaborate function. The situation the teacher picks determines whether he facilitates it.

Obviously, it is not enough if a child is angry at himself. He has to be able to neutralize that anger into energy which can be used for self-control. Any interference, including punishment, makes sense only if it rattles the youngster into the capability of translating the aggression produced in him into workable energies which increase his self-control.

The next important step is to produce an inner experience which, in non-clinical terms, one might call repentance and New Year's resolutions. The hope is that the youngster realizes, "I wish I wasn't in this boat, I wish I had avoided it, I'm sorry for it." It doesn't mean repentance in a big guilty way but a pious thought like many a New Year's resolution. If it does not occur, the rattling has been wasted.

The next item is that the youngster has to be able to store the present experience for use in a future temptation situation. Otherwise, it isn't productive. That is a big problem. Some children have no storage ability;

what happens now is gone or it is stored so pathologically that they can't work at all and become paralyzed.

The child must also be helped to restitution, recovery and re-establishment of a more comfortable frame of mind. Very often I find that teachers are quite skillful in making the youngster quite aware of how idiotically and inappropriately he acted but leave the rest to chance. This is like stuffing something down his throat and assuming the stomach will take care of it without watching to see whether it can. The question is, what does the situation have to be like so he can forget the incident after drawing the needed resolution from it? The restitutive processes mean that the youngster can close the experience but use its results next time without pathological associations or effects. I certainly also hope that the youngster's ego is capable of making restitutional gestures to the surrounding universe: that is, he is able to convince the teacher that he has learned something from the experience. That, by the way, is an additional task for the teacher to help the child with.

This is a rather complex picture of what's going on inside the child any time he is confronted with a situation in which he is criticized heavily, challenged severely or threatened by implication with something unpleasant unless he changes. The assumption that the ego of the child takes it all for granted, no matter how or what the teacher does, is, of course, false.

Obviously, there are ways of criticizing which will be supportive for some of these steps and wrong for others. Furthermore, some children are more ready to take any of these steps if their home life is supporting. Other youngsters, not so supported, have a life situation that spoils the teacher's communicational soup. It isn't that something is wrong with the soup. It was cooked well but the parents threw some cockroaches in it. In short, the type of experience the teacher produces for the child in order to influence him may merge with, or be contaminated by, elements inserted by the child or by his other life influences.

Complex as this is, no teacher has to think it through each time a situation occurs. Each time one breathes, he doesn't think of all that goes into breathing. However, now I am talking about what goes into it. And, what I am saying is that I think it is possible to develop a somewhat more specific model for examining the kinds of experience helpful to a child or a group.

A teacher must go by his perception or apperception of which behavior paralleling a given learning process is actually a danger to the learning process and which of it is relatively safe. To list these techniques, by the way, is also an oversimplification. It's as if one had a pegboard with a lot of nice instruments, but if one does not know how to use a chisel or a hammer, obviously one will mess up the material.

One then shouldn't blame the screwdriver or the plane. It happened because one did not know how to handle the tool. So, the question is not only what technique is indicated, but what is an appropriate way of using it and what other message is unknowingly being packed into it?

Teachers not only want students to stop undesirable behavior, but also to remain motivated, interested and capable of learning while tampering as little as possible with the basic learning process. This last is a challenging issue for many teachers. Frequently, they get so excited around a specific incident, which they handle all right in some way or another, that the rest of the learning atmosphere is destroyed. The real question is how the teacher's behavior can convey the right message to the student. Since the biggest problem between adults and children is that both parties have trouble handling their own feelings around what they are doing, the ability to be comfortable with a wide variety of techniques, rather than the few one happens to be familiar with, is most helpful. It is also helpful to know which emotions block us when we are supposed to handle a situation reasonably well, and which we have to get hold of in order to be supportive. But probably the biggest issue is whether the experience the teacher provides is such that from then on, the child's ego can take over and perform the important tasks well, so that controls from without are slowly replaced by controls from within.

CHAPTER 14

The School's Role in Discipline

SYBIL T. RICHARDSON

AS EDUCATORS COLLABORATE with psychoanalysts, they gain new insights into teaching and discover new dimensions of its understandings and skills. The school's role in discipline is a topic well suited to this team study. Both groups are dedicated to the development of healthy personalities who attain self-controls enabling them to manage their impulses and to use freedom wisely.

The central task of education is the development of human intelligence and its application to human problems and behavior. In the past twenty-five years, interest in discovering the principles of mental health and psychology and in applying them to teaching has been widespread. Critics seem to have gained the impression that modern education is essentially non-intellectual in its efforts and commitment. Teachers know well, however, that their major task is to release human intelligence and to develop human potentials. Their concern about children's social growth and emotional problems is part of this responsibility. Some children are afraid to learn or are too preoccupied with personal problems to respond. The teacher's skill begins with awareness of these barriers and reduction of them so that a child is enabled to learn. First things must come first. The alternative between developing happy, well-adjusted people with little knowledge and developing competent intellectuals who are unhappy neurotics is not a choice for teachers to make. They are, rather, charged with the development of an integrated personality that will function intelligently. Teachers today know more about personality development than did teachers of the past. They have, therefore, greater responsibility to examine ways of helping children to understand their feelings and actions and to grow in self-discipline.

The teacher is the first cultural agent outside the home whom the child perceives as a symbol of authority. As a cultural agent, the teacher is in long and steady contact with children and adolescents. If children perceive the teacher and the school as unfair and unjust, they may

147

quickly generalize that this is the way of life—this is the way of the world. Each teacher, therefore, must evaluate classroom climate and procedures in the light of children's learnings about authority and self-government. Democratic citizenship cannot be learned by years of sitting in class groups which are small autocracies.

In developing self-discipline, teachers have advantages that the parent does not have. For example, teachers may be more objective and rational in approach. Past events influence the parent's dealing with his child, often making him more emotional, more sympathetic and more indulgent. While responsive, the teacher can be more objective in observing the child as he is now and in contrast with others of the same age. In the classroom, the teacher has the advantage of working with a group of similar age and interests and can use the powerful incentives of group approval and prestige. At home the parent faces the confusion of adapting rules and standards to family members of different ages and interests.

In helping the child develop self-discipline and inner controls, teachers are directly in touch with each individual's strong urge to grow, to learn and to achieve. Teachers have almost complete control in setting the learning task by selecting the activities which give the learner opportunities for mastery. This selection determines each child's growing sense of confidence and pride when he succeeds, or of shame and anxiety when he repeatedly fails. Through a carefully planned program of success and difficulty, a child develops the self-respect which enables him to control his behavior and to accept group standards.

A main concern of education must be the growth of each learner's insight into the causes, logical or illogical, of his own and others' behavior and into the consequences of each upon the other. When the elders in a society feel unsuccessful, guilty and insecure, they do not resolve to work harder and to be more self-disciplined. They turn to youth and insist that youth must work harder and accomplish more. At these times, schools face criticism and pressures. People demand quick results and become impatient with the time required for teaching important ideas and for understanding.

As a result of these pressures the use of corporal punishment in schools is increasing. Adults attempt to hide their shame at such punishment by using terms as "swats" or "spank" rather than harsher but more honest words as "beating" or "whipping." Some people rationalize its use by saying, "Well, that's all they've had at home, that's all they understand!" But especially for these children, the capacity for reflection on the causes and consequences of behavior, the acceptance and management of feelings, and the rational approach to human problems are essential. These children may never, unless at school, encounter the use of intelligence rather than physical force in solving conflicts. The use of corporal punishment should not be countenanced in the school. The climate of fear and resentment which accompanies emphasis upon punishment, rather than guidance toward self-understanding, interferes with learning.

Education as an institution is part of society's long, slow progress toward a more humane and civilized man. When the school stoops to coercive efforts, including corporal punishment, it fails in its central task and responsibility. It fails to help young people use their intelligence in the control of behavior. It coarsens the sensitivities of both the punished and the punishing. Within the long and loving relationship of parent and child, corporal punishment can be understood and forgiven. In the impersonal setting of the school, pervaded by judgments of worth and achievement, the impact is quite different. If the school's purpose were to develop youth who would form gangs and carry knives and clubs, what better means could be found than the systematic use of force and physical pain?

The school's role is to extend children's experience with authority beyond the home and to prepare them to take part in the broader community. To guide pupils in developing constructive citizenship and self-control, including group living and learning in the classroom, teachers have found specific techniques.

1. Teachers study the previous experiences of a particular group of children. They do not use a stylized picture of how sixth graders or tenth graders should behave, but study the social behavior actually learned in the home and community. The group begins, therefore, with standards and rules which the children can reach and meet successfully. If not, the classroom atmosphere is immediately pervaded with disapproval and punitive corrections.
2. Teachers try to establish a personal relationship based upon knowing students as individuals, for one of the greatest controls of social behavior is an awareness of being known. The individual thus has a sense of who he is and what he represents. The greatest relaxations of control come when persons are incognito. When on vacation, many teachers do not like to be known as teachers, presumably for this same reason. The sense that the teacher knows him and is concerned about him is in itself a support to a child in his struggle for self-control.
3. Teachers act on the awareness that the adult's ways of behaving toward children are reflected in the children's behaviors and attitudes. Children surrounded by considerate and controlled adults become considerate and controlled. Discourtesy to children is apparently normal in our society where adults respond to children as they never would to one another: "That's enough from you!" "You talk too much." The very fact that such discourtesies

persist in many adults indicates that adult society is often not helpful in encouraging the self-respect basic to self-control.

4. Teachers schedule and time classroom activities and plan for arrangement of equipment and belongings to minimize children's conflicts. The teacher's study and control of these managerial details aid children in developing orderly and thoughtful behavior. To develop self-discipline, teachers must establish an environment appropriate for the needs and interests of the age group. Through their own experience, children discover the need for rules and standards. Adults, however, find it difficult to let mistakes happen. The incident of the spilled paint or the fight on the playground should be welcomed as a "teachable moment" which can help children identify with authority as an abstraction and feel increasing responsibility for their own behavior.

5. Teachers must consider children's feelings, regardless of the conflict; how the child feels about what happened is as important as what actually happened. A child who is already feeling guilty and remorseful is only further disorganized by scolding and punishment. He needs to be shown how to make amends and to do better next time. The child who is angry and resentful needs time to regain control and help in dealing with his feelings.

6. Teachers must analyze and identify incidents in which discipline or order breaks down. Which children were involved? At what time of day? What were their previous activities? What new activities were beginning? The knowledge gained from such analysis is essential in establishing an environment conducive to self-discipline.

In educating for self-discipline, many adults are troubled by the problems of consistency. Consistency is often thought of as a list of rules coupled with a list of penalties; if this rule is broken, this penalty results, regardless of who breaks the rule and under what circumstances. Psychologically this is the height of inconsistency; the punishment should not fit the crime but, so to speak, should fit the criminal. We are consistent if in every incident of behavior we apply a rational approach: What were the causes of our own behavior and others'? What were the consequences in others' feelings and behavior? How might this be avoided next time? The steps of reflective thinking are the keys to consistency in understanding and controlling behavior.

Teachers are also harassed by the pressure of time. They say, "How can I spend time setting up classroom standards, discussing the rules of the student council, or analyzing the incident on the playground? I have a reading period with three groups, and math coming afterward and then singing. In short, I have to cover the content."

Team-study conferences emphasize that there are learnings as important as any taught in reading or arithmetic. Essential for these learners and for society is development of insight into the causes of behavior, sensitivity to and responsibility for its consequences. The role of the school is to insist upon the increased use of intelligent behavior to help children apply moral principles to everyday life. This is the only way to develop citizens who will show initiative, who will be able to use freedom, and who will assume responsibility. Courses in citizenship or senior problems will not accomplish this goal. The way in which each teacher handles the day-by-day incidents of children's conflicts and helps them take the next small step toward more intelligent behavior will, however, profoundly influence the future.

CHAPTER 15

Some Reflections on the Problem of Discipline

GEORGE V. SHEVIAKOV

I ALWAYS TELL MY STUDENTS that I do not pretend and do not believe that what I am saying is the final truth. It is just the truth as I see it this morning. I hope some of my thinking will continue to be revised in the future as it has in the past.

To many people the word "discipline" and the word "punishment" are synonymous. This is most unfortunate because punishment is only one of the many ways of reinforcing certain behavior in youngsters. Punishment in itself is a terribly complex problem which I shall not discuss here except to say that, yes, sometimes adults have to punish children in their care. But there is a great difference in whether a youngster is punished as an act of revenge on the part of the adult, or the punishment is a logical, realistic consequence of the abuse of a privilege. While it may be a lot of fun to throw spaghetti around in a school cafeteria, the adults in charge cannot allow it. We don't have to beat the child to discourage repetition of such behavior, but for a while he should lose the privilege of being with other people and have to eat alone. This is my idea of punishment. As much as possible, it should be a logical consequence of the youngster's abuse of some privilege.

There is a second problem: getting obedience from youngsters while also fostering self-control or controls from within, as Fritz Redl called it. This is a complex problem in which I see much confusion on the part of parents and teachers. I am not against obedience. When the school firebell rings, for example, I think it would be silly to discuss with the youngsters the history of bells, the effects of fire, the desirability of leaving the classroom and then vote on a course of action in order to teach them self-determination. Nonsense. Youngsters simply have to learn that in certain situations we just obey set rules. That doesn't mean, however, that we require automatic obedience in all kinds of other situations where we could really do some reflective thinking with the youngsters—to their benefit and our own.

Parents and teachers have the right to have their own value systems. The meaning of discipline can be shaped by these systems. Suppose a parent, perhaps an influential businessman, believes sincerely that he wants to raise a good organization man. I could write a prescription of methods for raising this future organization man. I could also mention to the parent the dangers of my prescription, since there are dangers, of course. Opposed to such a parent is the father or teacher whose goal is to free the youngster to be able to actualize himself, to make choices. For this educational goal, the prescription must be quite different, and there, too, the dangers of some methods must be thought through.

In educating youngsters, one must consider two internal forces which control primitive impulses. One is commonly called the ego, the second is the superego or conscience, if you wish. The youngster is born with the potentiality to develop these inner standards and values, but they have to be developed. How this is done is very complicated and beyond the scope of these remarks, but some aspects of both must be mentioned.

In considering the ego, it is necessary to stress the functions of the sense of reality, the understanding of causes and consequences which has nothing to do with the moral sense with which the superego deals. As we provide different techniques and different experiences for the youngsters, as we discuss them objectively, each one will be able to make wiser choices and to understand why he makes such choices. He will be able to do this, not from any sense of guilt or fear, but from his sense of reality. It bothers me that many parents and classroom teachers are so afraid to spend time with youngsters in discussing the "whys" of human conduct. In my work with teachers and children all over the country, I have learned that most youngsters when not preached to but when invited to think seriously and allowed really to discuss among themselves the pros, cons and consequences, somehow come to pretty reasonable conclusions. Most important is that these then become their conclusions and have real meaning for them.

As for building the superego, I think we use essentially two quite different methods. One is fear or intimidation, whether psychological or physical, which unfortunately works. Some youngsters acquire a very cruel, inhibiting, strong superego. The parents thoughtlessly have done too much—and the wrong kind—of a good thing; in such a superego one finds guilt and all kinds of personality-damaging byproducts. The other method is not using fear but identification with the adult. This, of course, is a much harder job for the adults. Here we have to present ourselves to the youngster as a sort of desirable model like whom, more or less, the child would like to be. This is often why coaches are greatly admired by boys and have a much greater influence on the value system of youngsters than some personnel in counselling, guidance and, as some youngsters call it, "social slop"—social studies.

Many years ago when my boy was in second or third grade, I was on a very hectic schedule lecturing on "How to Be Good Parents and Teachers." I began to notice that I was not getting the same results with my boy that I used to. I finally decided to take a day off and spend it alone with the boy on the beach. We did. We played with balls and kelp and did all the things one does on the beach. At the end of the day I was completely exhausted and even my boy was kind of tired—but extremely happy. On the way home he said quite suddenly, "Didn't we have a good time?" After I agreed, he said, "You know I am going to do everything you ask me to do from now on."

That was his reaction with no beatings, no lecturing, no reprimanding, just having fun together. Not just fun, but time and interest and help in developing competencies meaningful to him. I think this is something that teachers have to take quite seriously. What kind of image, what sort of prototype of an adult are we presenting to youngsters?

This question concerns every adult responsible for a child. It is of special importance, though, to the school administrator whose responsibilities include not only many children but also the community and his staff. The administrator must learn about his community and its values. He must work at educating it to support a mutually satisfactory school. He must select a staff on the basis of criteria that go beyond the applicants' gradepoint averages. And he must continue to help educating it by presenting himself not so much as a boss whom they may or may not fear but whom they must obey, but rather as a consultant with whom they may consider alternatives.

I think that establishing a climate in which more teachers can make more choices and decisions is the big job of the administrator. While this might involve making mistakes, the administrator as consultant is a safeguard against the serious ones, and we learn from our mistakes. If the teachers are not afraid of the boss and he behaves like a consultant, they are more likely to discuss things with him. This is something I learned from Fritz Redl years ago when he ran a camp for so-called delinquent boys and girls. Every evening he had a staff meeting which he would always start by telling his counsellors what mistakes he had made that day. Thus, they could bring up for discussion their doubts, questions and mistakes. And this made it possible for discipline to be seen in light of the camp's purpose.

I think we school people must consider discipline in terms of the extent to which we assist people to make choices, to examine the alternatives rationally and to feel free to make the mistakes that are part of personal growth.

PART IV: Solution of Learning Tasks or Resolution of Emotional Conflicts — Teaching versus Treatment

The children could only be cured if there was a love relationship between the teacher and the pupils. If there were love, there would be jealousy, and only a good teacher knew how to evoke the love without evoking the jealousy.

J. C. HILL

CHAPTER 16

The Boundary Line between Education and Psychotherapy

RUDOLF EKSTEIN

BEFORE 1938, TEACHERS AND CLINICIANS trained together in the Vienna Psychoanalytic Institute. Though not large, this group was distinguished by the fact that it represented a variety of different practitioners: elementary-school teachers, kindergarten teachers, child analysts and teachers specializing in working with severely emotionally or mentally handicapped children. We were all studying together to see whether psychoanalysis had something to offer the educator. During this training there was no clear boundary between psychoanalytic therapy and psychoanalytically oriented education.

I believe that the lack of clear differentiation had to do with the fact that psychoanalysis was then so new and so occupied with the causes of emotional illness and its prevention. The cause of emotional illness was seen primarily in the educational system, and I am referring now to the parent as educational agent as well as the formal school system. The educational system was considered over-strict, Victorian and traumatizing. The benefit derived from psychoanalysis was seen in an educational movement which stood for less restriction, for sexual enlightenment and for an effort to avoid traumatization of children. In those days we had achieved a sort of fusion (or, occasionally, confusion) between psychotherapy and analytically oriented education. Only slowly did we learn that this concept of education did not completely hold.

I could perhaps best illustrate this through an incident from one of the schools which we had organized at that time in Vienna. It was a progressive school with psychoanalytically trained teachers. One of the teachers told the following story about a little girl of eight who was highly disturbed. She had just been brought to this school in order to benefit from its system after she had gone to one of the typical strict elementary schools. This little girl now found herself in a school where

157

the children were asked: "What would you like to play?" "What would you like to learn?" The little girl answered, "I don't like it at all. As a matter of fact, I am very unhappy here. I like my old school much better." The teacher was puzzled. "Why?" And the little girl burst out, "Because in the old school the teacher helped me to be good."

I think that this anecdote tells us clearly that psychoanalytically oriented education has to do more than undo traumata, has to be more than a reaction to outmoded educational techniques. Since those days in Vienna, representatives of both disciplines have worked toward clearer boundaries between education and psychotherapy.

As I use the word "boundary," I suspect that it suggests the idea of limits beyond which one should not go. Such connotations are not very useful if they are colored by notions of hierarchy and status. My use of "boundary" is inspired, rather, by the concept of different functions, of different applications of the insights derived from psychoanalytic knowledge. I believe it is our task to note clearly that between teaching and healing, between education and psychotherapy, there is a boundary line not in terms of understanding the child, but rather in terms of differentiation of function, of purpose and purpose-geared technique. In the case of a child, who has acquired certain symptoms, the expressions of conscious and/or unconscious conflict, there is the need for psychotherapy. It is the task of the therapist, through psychotherapeutic intervention, to restore the lost function. It is the task of the teacher and the educator not to restore function, but to develop functions by helping the child to acquire skills, knowledge and correct attitudes.

From that point of view, one might say that the teacher's job, the educator's job, is a much broader and more important one. What the psychotherapists do is remove the inner obstacles which have been created in the child and which prevent him from making use of what life has to offer. The teacher comes to the child with a different purpose. The purpose of the teacher—and the parent—is to help the child to acquire various kinds of learning. One might say that the educator brings controls from outside, from without, to help the child to learn techniques to live. The psychotherapist helps the child—to use Fritz Redl's phrasing—to restore inner controls which have broken down.

Despite the attempt to differentiate between the function of the psychotherapist and the function of the teacher, frequent overlapping does occur. As a matter of fact, the younger the child or the more complex the illness, the more these functions do overlap. But I would like to emphasize that there are two different functions, as defined here, and both can or may make use of the generic knowledge which psychoanalysis offers.

Ordinarily, when we speak about psychoanalytic knowledge, we have only therapy in mind because psychoanalysis has become most widely known through its application as a therapeutic technique. When the first group of educators was training with the analysts in Vienna, they wanted to see whether psychoanalysis could be applied not only as a therapeutic technique but could also be used by the teacher as he helped the child acquire skills and knowledge and useful attitudes toward life. When this group left Europe after the first experiment in modern democratic government in central Europe had failed, a good many of us went to England. The first meetings that we had in England are relevant to the possibility of wider application of psychoanalysis. At them, Anna Freud addressed a large group of the recently arrived Viennese and many English friends who had joined us. The three addresses made by Anna Freud in London, in the fall of 1938, were for teachers. Many hundreds had come, and I think it is not incidental that she chose to address teachers first. I think she did so because psy-choanalysts have always felt, even when they were primarily interested in therapy, that the therapeutic function makes social sense only when psychoanalysis can be applied to the educational process and is not utilized for therapeutic purposes alone.

In this social use of psychoanalysis, inquiry is needed. A task for psychoanalysts then is to help teachers distinguish between problems which are educational and those whose solutions are beyond the educa-tor's sphere. Educational techniques might fail in certain situations be-cause the appropriate technique may be a therapeutic one. Related to this task, therefore, is knowing how to refer parents and children to appropriate resources.

There is an area which teachers and analysts should investigate together. This is the area of collaboration in dealing with children who need treatment. Some of these children, even though sick, neurotic or psychotic, can and should continue their formal education with modified techniques. Most important, teachers and analysts must discover how to apply psychoanalytic knowledge in teaching itself. Concerns common to both disciplines include: the nature of learning; the differences be-tween the kind of learning based on repetition and that which is based on insight; and the role of teacher-student relationships.

As some contributors to the field maintain, psychoanalysis has never offered a learning theory of its own. I will not challenge this contention seriously but—with tongue in cheek—I must insist if it does not offer a learning theory, psychoanalysis could well be considered an unlearning theory, since it brings about a kind of education in reverse. Freud spoke of it as *Nacherziehung*, a second education. He referred to its propositions concerning therapeutic change of symptoms, the pathological formations which had been "learned" and then, under the influence of therapeutic action, unlearned. If these propositions concerning unlearning could be turned inside out like a glove, they would pertain to the acquisition of functions through education, rather than the restoration of functions through therapy. They would then describe a learning theory.

I believe that pessimism concerning the applicability of psychoanalysis to formal education has much to do with the development of psychoanalytic theory. This pessimism derives from the history of both its application as therapy as well as the place that it held until recently in our school systems.

When I speak of its development as a theory I refer to earlier phases when instinct theory was dominant. At that time the topographic model of the psychic apparatus stood in the way of developing a theory which included the serious study of cognitive functions. Earlier therapeutic use stressed the emotional aspects of treatment: affect discharge, regaining mastery over instincts, making the unconscious conscious, reliving the infantile neurosis in the transference neurosis, etc. Consequently, school systems primarily saw the use of psychoanalysis in mental hygiene attempts, preventing emotional disorders and helping children who suffered from them. Desirable as these uses are, they have defined and limited the use of psychoanalysis by the educator, despite the changes in modern psychoanalysis.

Since Freud's inception of the structural model of the psychic apparatus, we have developed ego psychology, including a psychology of adaptation, as part of the total theoretical framework. This has influenced treatment techniques to the point that "to make the unconscious conscious" is no longer an adequate description of its goals. Freud's "Where Id was there shall Ego be" is a better summation; that is, higher psychic functions should be restored and brought to dominance. These higher functions include the concepts of insight, capacity for delay, capacity for problem-solving. The resolved unconscious conflict frees energy for ego function. Thus, instead of the compulsion to repeat an old conflict or an old and vain attempt to solve a problem, the capacity to solve new tasks is now available. These tasks include those of learning. The freeing process of therapy has given us an opportunity to observe the restoration and the use of cognitive functions. We now pay attention to problems in these functions as well as to emotional and interpersonal problems. It is no mere coincidence that psychoanalysts are now slowly catching up with the work of Piaget.

In previous considerations the emphasis was on conflict; equally stressed now is the task implied in a conflict. Conflict and task are but two sides of the same coin. The therapist is more concerned with conflict as he attempts to help the patient. The educator is more concerned with task, as he helps the student. The difference is one of focus, and each focus requires different skills since it implies different goals. Psychoanalysis practiced as a therapeutic technique is unlearning theory. Utilized in education, it is a learning theory, albeit presently available only in fragments, many of which are not very well tested or tried.

Erikson's "phases of growth" apply to this interrelationship between conflict and task, particularly the one that characterizes the latency period—the time when formal schooling starts. Erikson—who tried to describe in psychosocial terms what Freud had described earlier in terms of instinctual psychic development—has described the latency period as a time of conflict between inferiority and industry. Although "conflict" is a word that appears quite frequently in psychoanalytical literature, in my opinion it is not completely appropriate for facilitating the fullest understanding of the psychological issues involved. The word "conflict" is usually associated with ideas of psychopathology. It reminds one also of war, of something painful, of something that had better not take place. Thus, if we speak of the young child's conflicts, we may see him torn between the forces of industry and inferiority. In such a conflict, the parents or teachers certainly want industry to win over inferiority in order to permit the work required for the learning task. But such an outlook refers to the result of a process rather than to the process itself. I suggest now that this process can be better understood in an educational perspective if we refer to what takes place not only as a conflict but as a psychic task as well.

The child will meet this task well if he has resolved previous psychic tasks. He must have acquired basic trust, autonomy, the capacity to accept controls from outside—inner and outer discipline—and socialized initiative. Such a child was not crushed in the oedipal struggle; has learned to renounce early instinctual wishes; identifies with the role of the parent of the same sex. He is thus ready for the school task and for learning, so that he can someday fulfill the same functions as his providers of today who take care of him, on whom he is dependent and from whom he must finally grow away.

Latency rather than being a quiet period, is actually a very active one in which ego growth takes place. Defenses and adaptive psychic organizations develop. Then character formation takes place, and a readiness to learn becomes available.

But this learning readiness, which is discussed in chapter 6, is unsteady. Its acquisition, a slow process, is experienced at times as a serious struggle. The child who learns looks up to the parents and teachers, compares himself with competing peers, looks at the volume of work, and finds that he is wanting. Regardless of how well he will come out in the end, he must go through phases where he feels that he cannot do it, that he will never reach the educational goal. This anxiety-ridden feeling of inferiority can now become either the driving force towards learning, towards industry or the goal-inhibiting force. As the latter, it may force the child to become a dropout, a passive and inhibited learner, a school failure, an under-achiever, or whatever name we may choose to give him. But if he had no feeling of inferiority, if he thought of himself as somebody who already knows everything, he could not learn. He would then live in a megalomanic fantasy world, as our clinical work reveals many youngsters unfortunately do, and would achieve only in fantasy what he is unable to bring about in reality.

The complete lack of self-appraisal; the inability to know what one can do; the belief that one can do everything—in other words, the absence of any kind of sense of inferiority—would lead to an autistic world. This might be a universe of great success—within the skin; a kind of LSD Utopia; a new religion which would fall apart as soon as it had to be matched against realistic achievement. A certain sense, then, of "I do not know it as yet nor do I know if I can master it" is a necessary accompaniment to learning. The outcome of the oedipal struggle will dictate whether this new conflict can lead to the acquisition of the capacity to work and study, to learn and to master school problems. The conflict then is essential to the task, and, in many ways, is the task.

Educational methods have made use of this psychological fact. The system of grading, the competitive arrangement in the school situation, the use of that conflict, that particular attitude towards the task of learning within the socialization process, each is well known. Sometimes we see education only as external manipulation and forget about the intrapsychic meaning of the conflict. We then see education only in terms of a conditioning process, something that is being done to the child. In doing so, we miss the active tasks involved, the active conflict in which the child is engaged, and the intrapsychic events which take place in order to solve the problem.

In stressing the intrapsychic work necessary, the psychoanalytic contribution is to see the teacher not simply as a taskmaster. Rather the teacher is seen as someone who initiates in the child those processes by means of which learning and mastery can take place. The child then gravitates between the "I cannot" and the "I can do it very well." He has his ups and downs since he is constantly confronted with new tasks. As long as these tasks are only external tasks, he will meet them in the manner that one bears burdens. If these tasks become internal tasks, however, he will not only meet the tasks but also develop the capacities needed to solve them. The system of external rewards will be replaced by internal gratification. The work for love will turn into the love of work. It is at this point that repetition learning can begin to be replaced by insight learning and the pleasure that is gained from the development of cognitive processes.

Education, then, cannot avoid conflict, nor should it avoid conflict situations. The task grows out of conflict. The task is the child of conflict. One might well say that the capacity for the solution of tasks grows out of the resolution of conflicts. An inner world without conflict could not lead to growth and mastery.

A systematically defined psychoanalytic learning theory would need to encompass propositions concerning individuation and separation, concerning the resolution of conflict, concerning internalization processes, concerning the parallelism between insight-learning in therapy, and problem-solving in education. This is to name but a few of the processes of development and maturation which are the professional concern of analysts and educators in their common quest.

While Freud said teaching, healing and governing are three impossible professions; he also said, "The voice of the intellect is soft, but it is persistent."

I think that the psychoanalysts and the teachers who are working together at present are united, both in the sense that they have chosen an "impossible" profession, as well as in the sense that they believe in the power of the searching intellect. In this union we are, then, soft but persistent in the pursuit of our "impossible" dedication: serving children through the fields of education and psychotherapy.

CHAPTER 17

The Referral of the Emotionally Disturbed Child

RUDOLF EKSTEIN and ROCCO L. MOTTO

TO THOSE OF US PARTICIPATING in research concerned with emotionally disturbed children, the issue of referral may almost be seen as a prerequisite for our activities. The presence of such children in a classroom and the various effects they can produce make referrals a subject of equal concern to teachers. What we will touch on, consequently, is the referral process in the school setting.

A short digression is called for here. The authors' present joint efforts have to do with collaboration between psychoanalysis and education. A major necessity in such a collaboration is mutual respect for different functions. Such an explicit statement is necessary in considering the present subject since it must be overtly said that a referral is usually experienced as a defeat. This is true whether the referral is made by an educator, a general practitioner, a psychoanalyst, a psychiatrist, a social worker. Everybody has problems about referrals.

With this understood, the first question is what would the problem be for the referring person in the school system. That is, the personal problem, the problem that one has when one deals with a parent or the child and admits that one cannot do it. This is the motivational issue that is involved in a referral.

The first points the person in a clinic reacts to are those of the referring person and his or her particular feelings about having failed with a particular system. This means the clinic person is thinking, "In the school system, there has been a failure on the part of the child in terms of either academic performance or social performance. The system can no longer cope with this or tolerate it." Depending upon other factors within the system, the receiving end becomes aware of various attitudes. One may be likened to army medicine. The whole attitude of army medicine is that the individual does not really count; only the

164

system does. One organizes all therapeutic efforts in the system of army medicine with that in mind. While the school system is, thankfully, not identical with the army system, it does have its own organizing principles. The referring person must know his system as well as possible, then, working within its framework, see what can be done in terms of the individual who is right there before him.

Those on the receiving end of a school referral of an emotionally disturbed child recognize that quite often the referral has a cry for help as its base: "Help us, help us out of this dilemma. The problem that we have cannot be tolerated within our system. Please rescue us." Now everyone knows what happens with rescue fantasies. Regardless of the years of analysis and the degree of the success of the analysis, when someone approaches the clinician with the cry of help, wings begin to sprout. His halo forms and he begins to think that maybe the thought "I'm not really like God" isn't quite true. He wonders if perhaps he can go in and really bail somebody out. But to respond on that level means that he is off on a bad footing, an unsound footing, in terms of the individual.

Yet this cry for help does serve some purpose. It is completely impossible for the clinician to go into an area of emotional disturbance unannounced or uninvited. The cry for help, even if its source is a feeling of failure, is an invitation of sorts. Referrals from the school are in the academic sphere, in the behavioral and in the social. Something about the child's development is awry and makes it impossible for him to become a part of a classroom group. The school says, "This child never participates, is withdrawn, silent, off in a corner. Is there something we can do about it?" On the opposite side of the scale is the child whose behavior is so destructive that the group suffers from the constriction imposed on its functioning.

Let us take a look at an imaginary—but not unreal—referral situation to get an idea of what is involved for the referring source, the person who takes the referral and the parent. The situation involves a child in junior high. From time to time he is overwhelmed with rages so great that not even the teacher who tries to separate him from the child he attacks can do so without some other help. The rages are such that one has the feeling the boy does not know what he is doing, that he is in an almost psychotic-like state. The rages endanger other children, and the boy must be constantly supervised. He goes to an ordinary public school in which there are the usual numbers of children and supervisors. He is a bright child, accepts the fact that he should not get violent, but he says, "I cannot help it."

From time to time he puts the school into an untenable situation. The school finally calls in the father. He is a man with considerable experience in the social sciences and is an intellectual and gifted person. This father is suddenly confronted with this enormous problem. Of course he knows about the child's outbursts but he doesn't quite know how bad they are because at home the child can be controlled. He gets the description from the school administrator, who finally says to him, "We can only keep this child in school if you get psychiatric treatment for him." He then locates a psychiatrist, sets up an appointment with him. Let us follow him as he keeps it.

Mr. Brown: My name is Mr. Brown, Dr. Smith, and I am coming to you for consultation about my child, about Johnny. I guess you saw from the school report that he gets these wild temper outbursts. He has them sometimes at home, but they are mild in comparison to what the school describes. As a matter of fact, I have my doubts about the school. You know how it is; they have too many youngsters in each schoolroom. There was one teacher particularly the other day who was terrible. She reminded me of my mother —absolutely impossible! Nevertheless, my boy tried to cope with her, I tell you, he really tried. He did the best he could, you know. You see, the fact is if you say he needs psychotherapy, Dr. Smith, of course his mother and I will try to see he gets it. But it means a tremendous sacrifice for us. I've got a small salary, we're in debt, but of course I'll do it if you advise it. Quite honestly, what I really feel is this: psychoanalysis is something you do when you're desperate. It's about the last thing you ought to try. You go into the depths and get the child more upset than ever because you do this. From my experience, I know psychoanalysis will be experienced by the boy as proof of absolute failure, so he'll do even worse in school. You see, I'm deeply convinced it's not the past that's important in the life of a person; I've come to this from my anthropological studies. I think what is important is a change in the environment. I think that in his school environment they're constantly down on him and are so critical of him, it's devastating. I feel that if you would write a letter to the school that, perhaps, someone should supervise him between classes, why then I think, we could solve this whole problem. But as I said, if you think he needs psychotherapy, I'll follow your advice, Dr. Smith.

Dr. Smith: Mr. Brown, I'm quite impressed with the amount of feeling that this has stirred up within you. I wonder though when you say that your son would accept therapy or react to it as evidence that he has failed. Would you?

Mr. Brown: Would you see a failure in this, Dr. Smith?

Dr. Smith: Now you see you've brought it closer to the question that I was about to ask you. Aren't you really saying that you feel you have failed as a parent? As a father? Weren't you trying to bring this up to—

Mr. Brown: Now you sound exactly like Mrs. Miller in the school! She said it's up to us parents.

Dr. Smith: When you tell me that I sound like her, then she and I probably have one thing in common: the ability to stir up in you the feeling that you have failed as a parent. Therefore, you are finding it quite difficult to proceed with your aim of finding out what is best for your child. I don't know right now whether psychotherapy is the answer or if psychoanalysis is needed. I had hoped to be able to sit down with you and investigate and explore the total situation, but I see that we—

Mr. Brown: But if he stays out of school, things are going to get worse! This kid is at home. He is very depressed. The school is driving him into an illness!

Dr. Smith: Yes, and I can see that you have a need to drive us into considerations that are outside of the child. Take this matter of writing a letter to the school asking that they have an extra supervisor to watch over him. I will accept that this might, for a time, handle the situation, but it seems to me that you're really skirting the issue here and trying to keep us from getting the best understanding of what's going on with your boy.

Mr. Brown: Well, you see I believe that it's the field forces outside which are responsible for what a person does. And I think that with this child one can see how the outer forces, the school authorities, the teachers, the other children, bring these provocations. As a matter of fact, you prove it because you're saying maybe I failed as a parent. If so, it was again an outer force that was involved. How would the investigation of his past help any but to stir him up and get him sicker? I have seen people in psychoanalysis who get sicker from this so-called treatment. Why, in the newspaper the other day, there was an editorial. . . .

It is apparent that it would be almost impossible to get out of the impasse of this situation. It is even more apparent that there must be a weakness or defect in such a referral procedure. This transaction between parent and psychotherapist has been precipitated. It has been forced upon a parent before he has really been helped to accept the idea of an involvement in it or even the idea for the need for it. What can people in a school system do to facilitate matters? This would have to be done in the time between first bringing the need to a family's attention and the time when they are in the therapist's office. The weakness, therefore, would be in the area of the school people's skills or experiences in that they might have to help the parent accept the idea that there is a need within his child for this next step. This means some additional energy on their part, and additional work. It means, further, the process of referral has in it more than just confronting the parent with, "We want you to get psychotherapeutic help because we think there's a problem with your child."

Quite often the mother or father is very compliant and says nothing in response to such a statement from the school. The explosion comes in the therapist's office. When the therapist discusses this with the school people, they are amazed. The family, they say "weren't like this at all." But the family's behavior reflects an attitude that the parents have with authority which, in such a situation, is represented by the whole school system. The parents' whole effort is to try to keep their child within the system, therefore, they're not going to start "bucking" right in the school. There, they will be docile, accepting, compliant. They will say, "Oh yes, do I have his name spelled correctly? Do you think you could phone so that I could see him tomorrow, could you help facilitate matters, perhaps, if you called first?" Mr. Brown's dialogue reveals more accurately what they really feel.

What Mr. Brown calls to our attention is that everybody involved is exasperated; it is an emergency situation. The school felt exasperated because it did not know how to keep the child; the parent was exasperated; certainly the child was exasperated; the doctor who had to listen to that father after making emergency time for him was exasperated, too. So often the referral by the school is characterized by emergency and pressure, frequently by panic. The family's attitude is: "I would never have come to you but the school sent me. What can I do? If I want to keep him in the school system, I've got to obey. But I know it's the school's fault, not ours." The exasperated emergency aura envelopes all the participants. It is not only that Mr. Brown gets exasperated with Mrs. Miller and Dr. Smith. After a while, Dr. Smith and Mrs. Miller, reporting to each other, are also exasperated. She, because he could not sell psychotherapy. He, because she does not realize the problems he had to cope with. To recommend psychotherapy to that kind of father would be impossible. Nor would the psychiatrist tell Mrs. Miller—and we certainly think he should not—to take the child back in the school.

That leaves a lot of frustrated people without any answers. One of the most important problems of research in the area of referrals is to discover how to time them so that they do not become emergency situations, particularly since today's therapy resources, both private and public, are not in any position to take on emergencies. There are just not enough clinics around, so unless the referrals are done in a meaningful process in which something can unfold, nothing can truly be accomplished.

What seems to have been the most important mistake in the particular referral cited above is something which could be corrected in speaking to school administrators. This was to tie up permission for the child to continue in school with therapy. That is, when psychotherapy becomes a required, enforced condition one puts the parent in the position of a criminal to whom one says, "We will put you on probation providing you go to a psychiatrist." Connecting the decision to seek psychotherapy with something outside, rather than inside, has very little chance for success. Of course, someone like Mr. Brown could get so desperate about the fact that each school refuses to take his boy that he might eventually attempt psychotherapy for the child anyway, but he would not do it out of insight. Only as a last resort should such conditions be set, because most referrals of this sort would go wrong. But actually, can we blame the school? The dilemma for the teacher or the administrator in this situation is that it has already come to a point where one should say that the child cannot be maintained in a public school. Nevertheless, out of sympathy for the child, one feels that one should do something. What happens then is that one ties up, as it were, the required with the permissive and it cannot work out.

While this was an extreme case, extreme situations are useful as learning devices. What is needed most is to study both the nature of referrals and the numbers that are really successful. Usually the referral is made: then we are rid of the problem because it is off the desk. What is needed is a follow-up to see if the people really kept their appointment and whether the treatment was started and was successful. What went right and what went wrong with these referrals would need to be studied. Mr. Brown's experience illustrates the quality that is born from emergency and necessity rather than a spirit of growing insight.

The nature of this emergency situation cannot be stressed enough. In medical and surgical training, the accident or emergency ward is a fascinating place where one is constantly asked to repair things—and quickly. After a while, one begins to see the same individuals returning and is doing the same kind of surgical repair (of course, this is what led to an understanding of the accident-prone individual). There are times when one must act quickly. Too often, however, there is the urge to rush in to "do" which ignores the possible reality that there may be many factors in the history of a particular child and family that indicate that emergency action is really not going to be the final answer.

In analyzing the referrals made to us, we have begun to ask "What happens to a specific kind of child—the autistic, the borderline, the schizophrenic—that has been coming to us in relatively large numbers in recent years (as so often happens when the community begins to get the idea that there is some interest in this)?" We are able to absorb relatively few of these cases and there are surprisingly large numbers of them. We are beginning to ask ourselves, "What happens with these families to whom we give three or four names of other agencies, and perhaps four or five names of individuals who might be interested in this particular diagnostic category?" We don't really know and we don't think we should be satisfied with the answer that there is so little available in this community that they probably don't get any further help. That may be part of the answer, but there is also the matter of, "How much can families with these extremely sick children make use of this referral process when one has had perhaps just an hour or two to deal with them?" Another recent question of ours is, "Is it possible, that if we had staff energies to work with them over a long period of time, even though we do not have the therapist available to work with the child, that we might be able to do something with these families?"

We find, as portrayed by the imaginary Mr. Brown, that even with the frank evidence of an extremely sick, psychotic child, families would still have this negative reaction. In other words, if the treatment resources are on the scene and available, one cannot have the feeling that the family is necessarily going to step right into them and make use of them. And we think, with so few of us in the field of child psychotherapy, we must refine the measures to help these families become prepared for and able to make use of what there is on the scene.

Earlier we noted that the unrealistic expectations of some people with a child in such difficulties have to do with the fact that when people are helpless, they frequently turn to someone and expect a miracle. Everyone understands that and we don't want to sound as if we entirely blame the help-seeking person—the teacher who quickly calls us, or the parents, or the child. Rather, we have to share the blame with them. In recent years in order to convey what they can do, psychiatry and psychoanalysis very frequently have overpromised. One effect of this is that unanswered questions loom enormously in the subject of referrals. To find the answers is an issue of mutual concern to psychoanalysis and education so that we have a more reliable basis for successfully working together in aiding emotionally disturbed children.

In this social use of psychoanalysis, inquiry is needed. A task for psychoanalysts, then, is to help teachers distinguish between problems which are educational and those whose solutions are beyond the educator's sphere. Educational techniques might fail in certain situations because the appropriate technique may be a therapeutic one. Related to this task, therefore, is knowing how to refer parents and children to appropriate resources. There is an area which teachers and analysts should investigate together. This is the area of collaboration in dealing with children who need treatment. Some of these children, even though sick, neurotic or psychotic, can and should continue their formal education with modified techniques. Most important, teachers and analysts must discover how to apply psychoanalytic knowledge in teaching itself. Concerns common to both disciplines include: the nature of learning; the differences between the kind of learning based on repetition and that which is based on insight; and the role of teacher-student relationships.

CHAPTER 18

The Acquisition of Learning Readiness: Task or Conflict?

RUDOLF EKSTEIN

THE PRESSURES OF OUR SOCIETY are exerted on the learning child, his family and the school system. When this occurs during a time experienced as crisis, they produce reverberations among clinicians and educators as well, and give rise to questions on every level of inquiry. In recent years we have been concerned with the Sputnik complex: the demand that we push serious study of scientific subjects into the earlier grades in order to compete in an international contest full of danger for our civilization. We are concerned with dropouts, teenagers, segregation problems, disadvantaged children, Head Start programs. We face immense problems with rebelling adolescents, their often aimless search for purpose and identity, and their peculiar communities which express in bizarre forms their alienation from adult society. We frequently feel that we are powerless to bring them back into the educational process, regardless of whether we think in clinical, educational or social terms. So great are the numbers of those afflicted that in our own ranks we have developed a new tendency towards interest in mass problems, large social problems, which has even given rise to new clinical movements such as social psychiatry. It is against and in spite of this background that I am dealing with the development of the learning capacity of the child, and the educational and clinical help which must be offered him.

In considering learning problems in terms of the individual, my outlook is the one which has given psychoanalysis its vital strength. It is the outlook that has led to the development of techniques and of educational and therapeutic resources, which, in turn, has given impetus to the solution of the other, much broader questions. Schopenhauer suggested once, "Wo das Zaehlen anfaengt, hoert das Verstehen auf": "where counting starts, understanding stops." He was very pessimistic as to whether the kind of mass answers that are possible in other areas

172

of science are truly applicable to considerations in the social field. While I would not agree any longer that the qualitative methods of psycho-analytic research cannot or should not be supplemented by quantitative notions, I do believe that we should turn matters around and start to understand before we start to count. If we are to understand the enormous problems of modern education, we may well start with an individual situation. We may then see whether the understanding Schopenhauer talks about cannot best be enhanced if we look once more at the single case in order to learn something about the learning difficulties which many children encounter today in school.

A recent clinical experience had to do with Ricky, almost ten years old. He came to our attention when he had completely failed in school, and when the public-school system did not want to promote him from the fourth to the fifth grade. I will use this boy's situation as an illustration of separating, if possible, two kinds of learning difficul-ties. That is, there are those learning difficulties which are normal growth processes and which can be considered as the average task every child experiences in developing his capacities for learning and bringing about learning readiness. There are also truly pathological difficulties which are regressions or fixations to or at a level where there is no learning readiness, and where the solution of a task is made im-possible because of the lack of capacity for resolution of conflict. I have suggested elsewhere (chapter 6) that the solution of learning tasks is mainly the domain of the teacher, who must match the child's learning readiness with his own teaching readiness. The resolution of inner con-flict, however, is the domain of the child's therapist who deals with the restoration of those capacities defined as learning readiness.

Ricky's parents were advised by the school counselor to ask for psy-chiatric help. He is the oldest of four youngsters and has been described by the parents as very antagonistic towards his teachers, even in kinder-garten, and refusing to do his work. All reports describe him as a young-ster with a superior intellectual potential, but they state that his per-formance is erratic, and that he gives the impression of dealing with his own hostility in a passive-aggressive way. He struggles against parents and teachers while, at the same time, using that struggle in order to reach them. He came to the current therapist at a point of total impasse.

He had been seen earlier by a psychiatrist who had responded instantly to the charm of this boy, who has a way of easily winning one over. The psychiatrist had evidently felt that he would be most useful to the child if he were to accept him fully in the treatment situation. He seemed to decide that the basic therapeutic intervention should consist of giving advice to both the parents and the teachers in order to bring about an entirely different social situation which would then permit the child to function. He seemingly made the decision to use the therapeutic material of the consulting room in order to get cues by means of which to change the child's environment. Many of his activities then consisted in replacing the child's passive aggressiveness, his unwillingness to function, his not listening, not hearing, not performing, through the active intervention of the adult, who thus became a kind of auxiliary professional ego for the child. Regardless of how much tact might be used, the outcome of that kind of battle is clear. I am reminded of "The Faults of Parents," an early work of a pioneer psychoanalytic educator, Pfister. He saw children's difficulties in terms of mistakes that parents and educators make, and his attempt, of course, consisted in influencing the adults; that is, in treating the problem as an external rather than an internal one.

This attitude is still prevalent. I leave as an open question whether it stems from a countertransference towards the child; an over-identification with his plight; an unconscious need to identify with him and to fight against parents and teachers, or whether it is professionally mature insight into some of the external difficulties which may have to be changed. There is, of course, an external side to any kind of learning difficulty, and I am not suggesting that the psychotherapist who perceives a child's problem in that way is necessarily wrong. The child will see such a therapist as a kind of magic helper stronger than the school and the parents. This magician is on his side and will help eradicate his difficulties. Obviously this is not enough; external manipulation is hardly ever enough.

In Ricky's case we dealt with a father who had high ambitions for himself and for the child. He believed in excellence and was very demanding but, at the same time, aloof, except for the times when he would be experienced by the child as angry and threatening. We dealt with a mother who needed to be protected by her husband. She looked up to him like a child to a father and had not been able to develop some sort of maternal autonomy on her own. She had literally to be given permission to allow herself to be spontaneous and tender towards Ricky. Her past dealings with him had been such that the emotional climate between them needed the constant protection of procedures of emotional antisepsis. Every word of love, every touch, every spontaneous act or expression of tenderness was filtered through objectivity, through diffuse anxiety, in search of permission or prohibition from professionals. It was as if she wanted to be guided in every step even while she reacted to the guidance—just like her son—with passive aggression, with an inability to use the advice. The first psychotherapist then experienced these parents as constantly opposing him. After a while, the situation between the therapist, on the one hand, and the teachers of the public school and the parents on the other, was a replica of the basic relationship between Ricky and adults. They all had arrived at a dead-end street.

This impasse led to a reassessment and a new effort by the present therapist. The impasse described raises many questions concerning the kind of collaboration indicated between therapist and school. (Some of these have been touched upon in chapter 19.)

Ricky's first session with the therapist did not reveal much except that it gave the therapist an opportunity to allow for some tentative identification with the helplessness of the parents and the teachers. All they had told him and that he had found in the different reports seemed to be confirmed. The child was charming, aloof, jocular, pleasant, without any particular insight as to why he had come or what he was supposed to want from the therapist. He maintained a level of humor, of little tricks here and there, with an air of being completely unconcerned. While one could not help but "take" to him, there seemed to be no way to focus on anything. There was no overt anxiety, but rather a pleasant, manipulative air about him. He meant to convey that he had the therapist wrapped around his little finger.

As he explored the room and the toys, he tried everything and nothing. He touched the things, inquired about them, but like a butterfly that roves from flower to flower, he went from toy to toy and from question to question, barely beginning or touching something before leaving it. He interrupted and disrupted the play or game before it even started. His attention span seemed to be very short, and he almost made the therapist feel that the impression of the parents and the teachers was absolutely correct. The professional helplessness that such patients arouse expresses itself frequently in the question as to whether one really wants to treat the child, or refer him elsewhere, since surface impressions leave one feeling so shut out. But there was also an eager indication on this child's part that he wanted to come back, that he wanted to explore some more and find out about all the other things that he had not yet seen. The therapist was able to use this as a bridge which permitted him to indicate that he, too, wanted to explore some more and find out about all the other things that he had not yet seen. He could even suggest some concern about how little fun Ricky could have when he started so many things but could not enjoy the outcome.

The first session made one temporarily identify with the "diagnosis" of the demanding environment, namely that Ricky did not want to solve a task. At the same time, indications showed that the truer problem was one of understanding this behavior as symptomatic and as an indication of inner conflict. The therapist must confess surprise as to the sudden, and actually unexpected, turn of events that took place as soon as the second hour started.

Before describing what happened, I want to comment on the therapist's bewilderment about the change of events. Upon reflection, one might perhaps say that he underestimated his influence on the child. He underestimated the fact that he did not impose a task on the child but gave him permission to say whatever he wished to, such as expressing through erratic beginnings without endings what the problem really was. In really being given permission to say what he wanted, Ricky tried out the therapist first by a way of talking in sentences that began but didn't end. I am, of course, referring not to his spoken word but to the language of his play. The therapist thus had established the basic rule of the hour, rather than identifying himself with the parents who wanted to establish the basic rule of the learning situation where one completes a task. In therapeutic action he identified with the therapeutic situation, even though in assessing the child's behavior he felt a fleeting identification with the helplessness of the parent. If that identification had been the dominant and overwhelming one, he might have done exactly what the first therapist did; that is, become active, if not vis-à-vis the child who gave him a feeling of helplessness, then vis-à-vis the parents and the school whom he might have thought he should dominate and manipulate because of his professional authority and authoritativeness.

During the second session, the boy inquired about a basket filled with crayons. When Ricky was given all these crayons, and paper as well, he wanted to develop a story like funnies in a newspaper and tell the therapist something funny. The therapist thought, of course, that this attempt to draw a story would end up exactly the way all other attempts had ended, and was quite prepared for a beginning without any form of ending. He thought that anxiety would prevent Ricky from completing the task that he had set himself. But from then on Ricky was a changed child.

Actually, the beginning of the hour itself gave the therapist a cue. The therapist had opened the door to the waiting-room, since the glowing red light indicated that someone had walked in. As he opened the door, he saw no one; but Ricky who had been hiding at one side, quickly sneaked into the room, rushed to the button which controlled the red light and turned it off. The therapist found the boy under the desk and shared his pleasure of having tricked the therapist.

Crayons in hand, Ricky decided that he wanted to develop a story about a young boy and wondered about a name for the hero of the story. The therapist suggested "Tricky the Trickster." Ricky was delighted with the name and from then on for a number of weeks he developed his

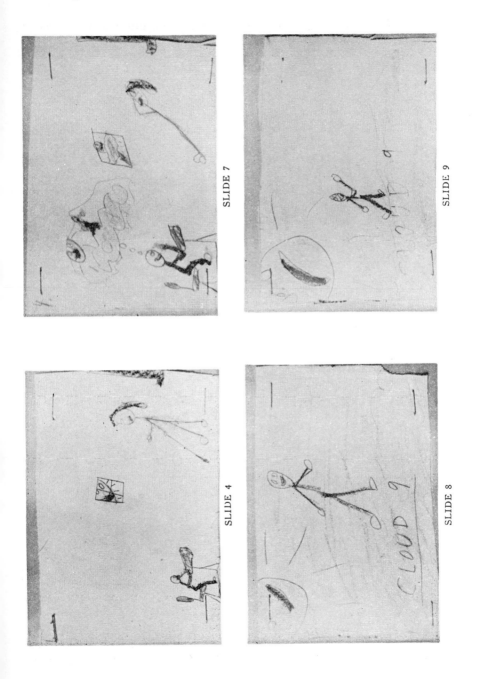

little book of many pages. Sometimes he compulsively redrew and re-worked his story in order to come out with his idea of perfection, but he never let up. Frequent slips of the tongue indicated clearly that the story of Tricky the Trickster was an autobiographical account of Ricky the boy with a severe learning difficulty. What follows now concerns the work of a number of weeks, during a situation which had not yet led to a full commitment concerning a treatment program. This is an important fact because the material that follows must be understood as Ricky's insight into his difficulty, his acceptance and understanding of the therapeutic situation, and his way of committing himself to treat-ment, his way of "promising" to make use of the treatment situation.

Tricky starts to draw a classroom scene. A little boy sits at his desk, head in his hands, and faces a tall teacher, more than twice his size, in front of a huge blackboard, a long pointed stick in her hands; between them is a small window through which the sun is shining. (Slide 4) The boy does not work, the teacher gets excited and yells, and the draw-ing of the child on the second picture gives one the impression that he is sort of falling apart, exploding. He wants to play a trick on the teacher. Ricky accompanies the different drawings with comments, and some-times writes comments into the drawings. His hero, Tricky the Trickster, thinks of the wonderful sun outside. He knows magic tricks and decides that he will trick the teacher by disappearing so that he can be with the sun. (Slide 7)

He flies right toward the sun, and the sun is smiling. (Slide 8) But just when he seems to have achieved his end, escaping from the demand-ing teacher and fulfilling his longing for the smiling sun, he discovers concern on the face of the sun: (Slide 9) a terrible thunderstorm is starting. It rains and there is lightning, and he has to escape from the thunder, and the sun is covered by black clouds. He is back in the dreary classroom facing the teacher again. She does not know what is happening and seems to be helpless vis-à-vis the magic of Tricky the Trickster and angry, at the same time, that he isn't paying attention to her. While the helpless teacher wonders what to do with Tricky next, the boy sits at his bench and has a fantasy.

In this fantasy he is concerned with how to get around the problem of having the terrible thunder and rain between him and the shining sun. Tricky the Trickster is a clever boy and he knows about science. He thinks that if he could stand on top of the clouds, (Slide 10) they would not be between him and the sun, and the rain would not drive him back into the classroom. He could be reunited with that shiny sun. He again uses all his intelligence in order to outwit the teacher, and uses his magic to escape once more from the dreary schoolroom, and sees himself on top of the clouds with the shiny, smiling sun. But as he starts

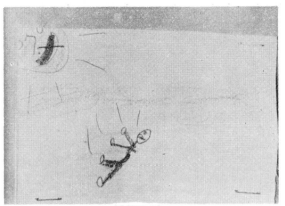

SLIDE 10

SLIDE 11

SLIDE 12

to enjoy his triumph, he again sees distress and concern on the face of the sun. The smile turns to worry and anxiety, since the sun has discovered that the cloud was starting to rain and was thus melting away. The boy had no base to stand on, and again could not remain with the sun. As the rain cloud melted away, he started to fall down through the sky. But Tricky the Trickster, even in terrible moments of distress, is not without resources. A parachute is opened and his life is saved. (Slide 11) He slowly comes down to earth, and although he gets stuck in a tree and has lost the sun, he finally saves himself. (Slide 12) But there he is, back in the classroom, again facing the dreary teacher. What a beautiful illustration of phobic and counterphobic mechanisms!

Frequently when Ricky could not cope with the learning situation and did not obey orders, the teachers had sent him to the principal, who often sent him home. There, he had to face the anger of the parents while he wanted to be reunited with a loving mother. The child thus gravitated back and forth between the demanding image of the teacher whose demands he cannot meet, and the longing for the smiling image of the mother. He sees her primarily in oral terms, without demands, without rules that guide the life of the school child. His need for love does not include the need for the child's work, the development of learning capacity, performance of age-appropriate task. His conditions for love are to receive unconditionally, and he is constantly driven back into situations with conditions which he cannot or does not want to meet. It depends on one's diagnostic estimate as to whether one assumes he cannot meet conditions for approval, or whether he has an option and chooses stubbornly to refuse to meet them. The educators and the parents experience his refusal, his escape into the fantasy world, as stubbornness, while he tries to convey the lack of need-satisfaction which causes him to feel isolated and to be alienated from the parents and teachers. Moreover, this is a situation that had been observed as early as kindergarten and was most likely true even in earlier years.

Tricky the Trickster faces the teacher again. The teacher tries once more to force him to do his work. The next picture reveals a change. The window and the sun are gone. Instead of the cloud that keeps him from the sun, there is now a similar huge area drawn in red, and in it once can read the words: Do your work. (Slide 14) Tricky is described now as someone who must look for a new way out. He does not try to escape again to be united with the sun. He decides to do magic work. As he submits this magic work to the teacher, she looks at it and becomes very angry. Ricky writes on the next page: Magic work fails, and draws a dejected little boy who has gotten a failing notice. (Slide 17) He must leave the schoolhouse and take the marks home. As he comes home to show the report card to his parents, he crosses his fingers for magic protection, full of anxiety as to what they will do with him. Ricky describes Tricky the Trickster as a boy who has his own fantasies as to what would happen to him. Ricky stresses that this is not what really will happen, but that these fantasies of Tricky the Trickster are just on his fantasy hero's mind.

One notices here a subtle reference to the boy's capacity to differentiate between fantasy and reality. But fantasy is so strong that it is almost like reality. As Ricky discusses his pictures and story, his creation of the thoughts of Tricky the Trickster, he makes sure that the therapist realizes that Tricky the Trickster does not always know where the fantasy begins and ends, and where reality begins. It would be too far-reaching for the purpose of this discussion if I discussed in detail certain of the finer points of psychic organization which are described through the accounts that Ricky gives of his hero. Suffice it to say that Tricky the Trickster expects that his father may hang him or shoot him or, worst of all, may kill him by a guillotine or by chopping off his head with an axe.

I believe that the development of the story shows clearly how insight grows. It becomes clearer and clearer that the maternal principle, split by his conception of the demanding teacher and the smiling sun, is understood in terms of helplessness. The teacher cannot get him to do the work, and the smiling sun cannot stop the rains and the thunder, nor convince him that he is loved and that he can do the work, and thus magic must fail. The paternal principle, described through the thunder and clouds and the threat of falling, becomes humanized towards the part of the story when Tricky cannot escape any more to or above Cloud 9, but sees himself facing angry parents for having failed the work. Ricky sees himself as being threatened with annihilation, with castration, and finds it impossible to cope with his anxieties, except for his hope that all the threats he faces will not really come true and are only in his mind. They also mean, perhaps, that the parents never quite mean what they say and do and are, therefore, in many ways as helpless as parents as the teachers are as teachers, and as he is as the learning child.

In one of the next scenes he describes what really happens to Tricky the Trickster. What an interesting account that is of the differentiation between reality and fantasy within a production of fantasy! The mother looks critically at the report card, and the boy is "mildly spanked" by the father. (Slide 22) Tricky the Trickster goes back to school and hands in to the teacher the report card which was signed by the mother.

During all of this time the therapist has only admired the many wonderful tricks that Tricky the Trickster has devised and voiced sympathy for the fact that these tricks did not work in getting Tricky what he

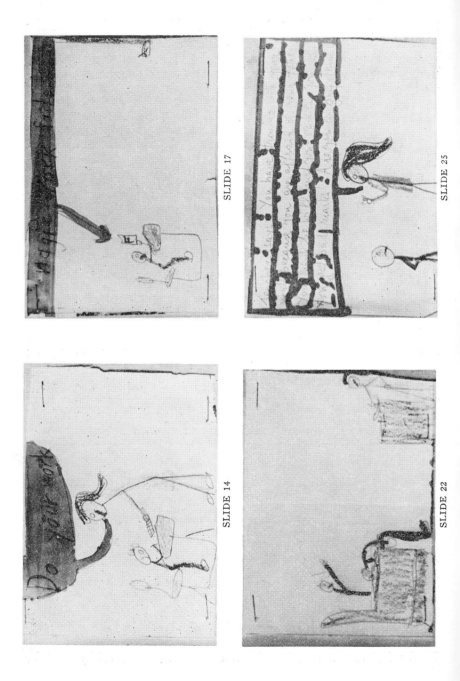

wanted. He did not moralize but identified with the position of Tricky and always wondered what he could do to be and to feel accepted by teachers and parents, and really to enjoy the smiling sun. Therapist and child, thus, enjoyed together the wonderful tricks of the hero. They responded to the thrills, the dangers, the adventures as if they were a fairy tale, while the therapist left it entirely up to the child to develop that part of the story which would be considered the cautionary aspect in a fairy tale. Over a period of weeks, Ricky showed the hero being punished, being tamed, finally accepting reality. He showed himself, when given the initiative, as actually identified with the demands of reality; he wishes to please the therapist and to indicate what the purpose of the therapeutic work should be.

As Tricky the Trickster is made to come back to the teacher, a discussion ensues between Ricky and the therapist about the words the teacher may use in order to be of help to the child. It was only at this point, after a number of weeks of developing the story theme, that the therapist helped Ricky in developing the teacher's part of the story. Their little book contained these words: "Teacher says: You have trouble with your work because you are afraid of your father. You think he will hurt you or kill you if you get bad marks. Are you angry at him?" (Slide 25)

On a later page the red area which offers space for the teacher's words now carries her new message to Tricky: "Tricky is the best worker in the class."

One year later—an interesting "prediction" on the part of Ricky concerning the effectiveness of therapy for him—Tricky has a test and the teacher tells him that the work is good and she gives him an A. (Slide 27) School is out. (Slide 28) The child runs home with his report card while the beautiful sun shines and smiles at him. His mother, who has on a yellow dress like that sun, says: "Oh, darling!" (Slide 30) and his father gives him rewards, green dollar bills, while Tricky, seeing all that money, says with delight: "Oh, boy!" (Slide 31) There is another page indicating that this is the end of the story, except that he writes a postscriptum on a final additional page. This picture shows how Tricky takes all the money and takes it to the store in order to buy candy.

This story sounds almost too contrived to be true, too much like a textbook story, a cautionary tale with moralizing built into it, but nevertheless it is the free invention of this child, completed by him. The new division of labor is one in which the therapist turns into the one who admires Tricky the Trickster, while Ricky turns into the person who sort of creates in his fantasy figure, thereby joining the adult world; a new conscience, a vital superego, and an effective capacity to work.

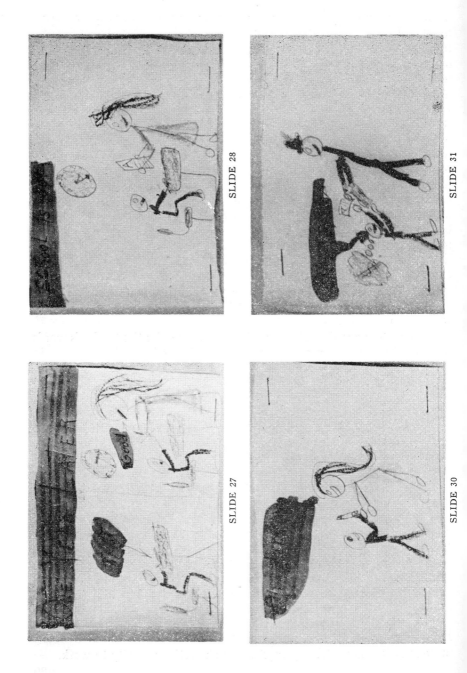

SLIDE 28

SLIDE 31

SLIDE 27

SLIDE 30

As the story of Tricky developed, it became much easier to ask Ricky to what degree he was really functioning like Tricky. It became possible to ask to what degree he worried as Tricky did about terrible punishments and even if he thought that his wishes to be close to the sun, to be tender with the sun, might have much to do with the hope that mothers should never demand, should only feed and satisfy and what happened to such hopes when countered by the stern anger of all those who expect something of him. We started to work slowly on all the issues that prevented Tricky the Trickster, that is, Ricky, from doing his work and forced him to believe in magic and flying to Cloud 9. Can he really keep that promise, or was that promise just a way to restore love, to make the world, the sun, and the mother shine on him again? But there was some reality in that promise, inasmuch as the work itself that he accomplished during these next few weeks showed that there could be concentrated effort and that, at least in psychotherapy, this capacity for prolonged attention was undermined only rarely.

But it was undermined on one day. The father had brought the child to the waiting-room. As the therapist opened the door, the father stopped him in front of the child and said that he wanted him to see a note that he had received. He handed the therapist a failure notice from school. The therapist tried not to pay too much attention to it, beyond acknowledging it, but during that therapy hour the boy was diffuse. He was full of anxiety again, and interpreting did not help. The hour was under the sway of the disruption that had occurred when the father tried to make the therapist into his own extension, and to expose the child's weakness. This time there was no story about Tricky the Trickster, but only aimless attempts at random activities.

I believe that the summarization of this case provides rich material for conjectures and inferences concerning the contributing factors in this example of a learning problem. The demanding teacher and the smiling sun are but different aspects of the mother figure. That smiling sun could never be reached, and that demanding teacher never succeeded in establishing inner discipline. One may well wonder why it is that for such a long time Ricky must maintain this split in his way of looking at the maternal figure. One might also wonder what is revealed about his relationship to the father, and what is revealed about the paternal object representation, when the father in the story of Tricky the Trickster is shown as an impersonal threat—thunder, lightning, rain and clouds, dangerous parachute jumps, etc.—and only much later appears, as does the mother, as a real person.

Much of the material has the coloring of the oedipal situation—the longing for the possession of the mother, and the castration threat. Yet, many of these elements are really of a non-phallic nature and have to do with much earlier problems in the development of the ego organization. Some of these problems perhaps go back to a time where there are only unsteady object representations, and when occasionally there is a kind of autistic isolation from the paternal figure.

I should like to document this through a few additional illustrations from the therapeutic material. At the point when Ricky got Tricky off the hook and had the parents reward him, we learned that the reward was expected in tangible services. Tricky got money, a kind of impersonal expression of the father's esteem, and went to buy himself some candy. It was at that moment that Ricky discovered a little Tootsie roll play candy machine among the many toys, and got the therapist to stock that Tootsie roll machine. He developed a candy store. During the next few weeks he dealt with the candy store as he had dealt with the story at first. He worked painstakingly, using whatever doll furniture he could use, boxes, etc., in order to build this candy store. Some of the things to be sold were actually candy while others were make-believe candy. Ricky and the therapist stocked the store, and he now had a subtle way of getting the parents to join the play. He would sell them some candy for a penny, or would buy himself some candy, or the therapist would buy candy, and the next few weeks were a kind of stagnant situation, looking more like playing out a kind of candy feast. He suddenly and spontaneously wanted to feed the therapist candy and take some candy for himself. There were harmony and happiness but there was, for a while, no movement in the story. It seemed that he had regained attachment to food, and occasionally, when opening the door to the waiting-room, the therapist saw the child sitting very close to the parents. They were telling each other stories, and the mother had found a newly gained spontaneous capacity to react to the child with tenderness and acceptance, and the same was true for the father.

At some given moment, Ricky added the doll house and the dollhouse furniture to the candy store and brought in a disturbing element. It seemed that the period of working through and the establishment of a new basis had ended, and as if he were now ready to face new material. In that doll house were all kinds of family dolls, and among them tiny doll babies. He took the doll babies and had them go into the candy store during the night. They were supposed to sleep on the candy, without parental supervision. Tricky the Trickster, or should we now say Ricky the Trickster, introduced new humor, anal humor. The babies would do all kinds of "doo-doo" in the candy store, and Ricky would sell the therapist or his parents candy which actually was left there, he suggested by the babies, mixed perhaps with the "dirty things" that babies do at night. Hilarious laughter characterized the giving of these new gifts, and his having tricked everybody in play into accepting as candy what was really fecal matter from the babies. These were the tricks of babies, of phantom twins. Then he began to build the doll house. At first he worked on the babies' room. These babies, a strange dual expression of himself, took furniture from every other room. In their room, there was some living-room furniture, bedroom furniture, and kitchen furniture. They had a refrigerator there and all kinds of food, liquid and solid. They decided to barricade the room. The babies were isolated and fenced in, and the parents and other children were not allowed entrance. Whenever the therapist made some comment about the babies' isolation and how they might be longing for the parents, Ricky insisted that they had everything. Theirs was an autistic paradise; they were completely independent, and the parents would never be allowed to go in there. Paul Bunyan never enjoyed such advantage in his quest for omnipotence.

The therapist commented that these courageous and independent babies, rebelling successfully against any outside force that might take away their freedom, must be lonesome and helpless sometimes. Would they not want their parents at night, to reassure them, to tell them fairy tales, to talk to them, and the like? Ricky countered this with his certainty that they did not need the parents and did not want them. He denied any dependency need on their part. As a matter of fact, the rest of the home was described as chaotic. He would simply turn all the other rooms of the house into messy storage-rooms. When the therapist wondered what had happened to the rest of the family, and whether the babies had destroyed them and had made themselves really completely independent, Ricky developed another theme. The house and the other rooms slowly emerged. There were all the siblings, and there was a dining-room where the family would gather together happily to have a beautiful meal, except that the babies maintained their vigilant barricade against the other members of the household. Their isolation was described as one caused not by the parents, or other children, or the outside world, but arranged and desired by them alone. The therapist's interest in the babies' potential lonesomeness led, in future hours, to the child's comment that some day they might give up the barricade.

A situation developed, according to Ricky, which indicated that the babies were sick. Finally, something had to be done for them. The rest of the family was not allowed to enter, but it seemed that the babies or somebody had called a doctor. Though described as a friendly doctor, he really had to work his way into that multiple-purpose room of the babies. He could not come in through the door nor through the ordinary windows. He somehow got to the babies only after quite a struggle and sort of guaranteeing that nobody else could enter the room. He was a friendly doctor, and he wanted to help the babies with drugs and with foods. All his help was oral in nature. The time had now come for Ricky's therapist to introduce the doctor as somebody who was not just interested in drugs and food. He wanted to understand the babies and see what really was on their minds. Slowly, he was allowed to be more than a friendly doctor. The babies and he talked together. By the time this happened, Ricky himself seemed to have more access to the parents, the rest of the family, to other children, and seemed to have made a better beginning in the new school year. The friendly doctor was on his side as well as on the babies' side, and it was frequently possible to tie up the story with Ricky himself. The barricades are not down yet, but there is a bridge between that autistic world described and the parents outside. The friendly doctor is that bridge.

I am not able presently to carry the case further, and I feel like Ricky at the time he developed the first storybook about Tricky the Trickster. I have given just a part of the story and cannot tell exactly what might be coming, but there seems to be a trend toward higher integration.

No single case example can encompass all the questions concerning learning problems, but I hope this one can illustrate a more systematic way than usual of asking questions about pathological learning problems: the treatment issues, as well as the educational issues. Learning problems are indeed the most frequent complaint and/or symptom brought to the attention of clinicians. There are so many different types of learning disturbances that one will do well to keep in mind that as soon as the psychoanalyst goes beyond the symptom or the presenting facade, such a diffuse classification is not very useful. One might say that learning difficulty can be compared to work difficulty in the adult personality. It is simply an external sign of an emotional or mental disorder which has to be understood in dynamic, economic and structural terms; in terms of object relationship difficulties, ego disturbances, etc. Ricky's case is no exception. I could well see that one could discuss this case as a mere clinical entity, in terms of transference and resistance, and in terms of the usual vicissitudes of treatment.

Freud's definition of mental health in terms of the capacity for love and work can be paraphrased in the case of the child to: The child's mental health can be defined in terms of his capacity to love and to learn. Learning is his way of working. Thus the notions of love and learning have to be examined in process terms. These notions are not static, absolute concepts, but change as the child's mind develops.

Throughout this book, I have referred to the Freudian and Eriksonian concepts of emotional development in order to define the ingredients necessary to bring about learning readiness. This, too, is a notion that I want to be understood in process terms. Every phase of the child's development develops a new ingredient for learning readiness which the child will bring into the school system in an integrated way. The first ingredients are very much tied up with his capacity for love. One might say that the small child who develops trust out of the separation-weaning conflict lives through at that time a phase where learning and loving, love and work, are merely two sides of the same coin and are not as yet truly separated. This phase of orality—the loving of, the working on, the separation from, the search for, the finding of the breast—somehow combines love and work. There for the first time, as the child learns, loving and working, uniting and separating, he moves toward the capacity for basic trust in others and trust in himself.

The clinical material concerning Ricky indicates that this establishment of trust, this learning via trust and self-trust, is indeed on shaky grounds. His long story of Tricky is one of vacillating between facing the strict taskmaster and escaping to the smiling sun, between magic and true effort, between the hope for unconditional love and the fear of terrifying separation and sadistic punishment. The isolated and barricaded babies mix food and feces, do not want parents and claim that they do not need them. All of these give us beautiful clinical demonstrations that Ricky, at the age of ten, had not brought about, or worked through, the issue of trust, the important ingredient the teacher needs to inherit from the parents when formal schooling starts. He starts to live in an isolated world, and prefers to live on Cloud 9, in the hope of reaching the warm, smiling sun. The thunderstorm, the rain, the melting of the cloud, drive him back to the impossible task, a little version of Don Quixote between the windmills and Dulcinea.

I need not emphasize that the issue of trust, its specific outcome in this case, can also be used as an indicator of the particular child's capacity for object relations. The fantasy material is full of examples in which the object is depersonalized, is barricaded against, is seen as strict and sadistic; whenever the child does reach the object in a positive way, it is seen primarily in oral terms. The rewards consist of money and candy; and the long phase of play activity around the candy store, around the babies' use of food during the night, refers to oral and anal need gratification, most of the time without objects. Only toward the end of the phase described in our material do we see objects emerge. They move from food to personal friendliness, from drugs to verbal interaction, and to some feeble attempts to reach out, to let the babies reach the external object world of parents and siblings.

An examination of Ricky's problems with autonomy and control would indicate that the trust deficit described earlier has created immense difficulties in facing that second phase of development. What he will bring to school will be almost autistic autonomy. Free in his internal fantasy life, he has no autonomy for learning, for the use of teachers and of the school. He sometimes makes sporadic attempts, and since he is a bright child, he occasionally makes rapid advances, but he cannot sustain them.

Just as he cannot maintain more than autistic autonomy, he cannot accept control. His inner control is poor, and his capacity to accept control from others always leads to a deadlocked struggle. He becomes inaccessible. No punishment helps, and he escapes over and over to Cloud 9 and the fantasied mother, the sun that smiles and feeds. Sometimes he tries to get himself to work by inventing powerful, sadistic control interventions on the part of the adult world. It is as if he wishes to have castrating, punishing parents, as if the threat of being shot, of being hanged, or being guillotined might get him to work. He almost prescribes control activities to the teachers, and provokes sadistic, angry behavior on the part of the parents. This part of the fantasy material is not only an attempt at reconstruction, but also describes his attempt at solution. But the solution of conflict fails. Therefore, he cannot solve the learning task. He is still deeply engaged in the resolution of inner and external conflicts.

This conflict situation leads him towards an attempt to bring back the anaclitic object, to restore unconditional feeding love by means of promises which he cannot keep. The learning by magic, the work by magic, are promises made in order to restore love but they must fail and cannot be kept. The struggle between autonomy and control finds him developing intensive stubbornness, and whatever capacity there is for relating to objects is involved in tricking the object, and then coping with the ensuing anxiety. All his learning initiative, his curiosity, is in the service of tricks, of attempts to escape, of developing fantasy solutions; and whenever this initiative is turned into an attempt to cope with the real task, it breaks down and leads to a sense of inferiority, a feeling of incompetence.

Any attempt to identify with the aloof but demanding father fails, and every attempt to regain the mother's unconditional love fails as well. He becomes isolated like the phantom babies who live in the barricaded room.

Anna Freud[2] and her co-workers at Hampstead have developed a psychoanalytic profile by means of which the development of the child is followed through these different phases in such a way that inferences can be made concerning the therapeutic task. This profile goes beyond the ordinary workup of a child. It is oriented around psychoanalytic thinking and tries to assess the child's strength and weaknesses.

I suggest that a similar undertaking could be tried with regard to the learning failure of a child. In following Ricky, it is possible to develop a psychoanalytic profile around all the aspects of the living situation, and design it so as to serve the work of the therapist. But it is also possible to write the profile primarily in terms of focusing on the learning difficulty itself to try to see how every deficit, as well as asset, contributes to the learning difficulty, and eventually, to its solution. Such a profile concerning the learning difficulties could be developed not only for the therapist but also for the educators and teachers who work with such a child as Ricky.

As Ricky enters the school system, that phase of developing capacity for industry which, as Erikson suggests, turns into a feeling of inferiority if the establishment of that ego capacity fails, is one that Ricky has not passed through with a sufficient degree of stabilization. From his beginning in therapy, it can be seen that he is not without capacity for industry, not without capacity for compulsive and orderly working, but this capacity is severely impaired. It is a capacity which is available to him only temporarily and in the service of resolution of conflict. If it is primarily to be in the service of the task imposed by the outside world, he escapes to search for the warm and smiling sun, and he becomes unavailable to the teachers and for the learning task. In turn, of course, he arouses in the teachers strong feelings of their own failure and inferiority and of wishes to control him as if he were already capable of accepting and using their control.

It is interesting that the first therapist thought in terms of controlling the teachers. The second therapist also had some contact with the school system, and used it to bring about some mutuality of purpose without dictating or suggesting what the school should do. He made few comments about the child and encouraged the school staff to live with its own limits. The school people countered this with their own suggestion that they would recommend a social promotion, rather than set him back, and that they wanted to give him a full year in order to see whether he could catch up. They added they would be very happy to get together with the therapist and exchange information. Interestingly, they then started to describe some of Ricky's assets. They found that frequently he really knew quite a bit about this and that but could not put it to work; that is—he could not deliver in terms of the demands of the adult world, but obviously achieved quite a bit when he was permitted to be more or less in his own world. That is, of course, exactly what happened in psychotherapy when the condition of producing something was in terms of his own needs, in terms of the equivalent in child analytical work for the basic rule in adult analysis. It would be interesting to discuss what teachers could do were they to know the learning profile of such a child, described and developed along analytic lines such as the one the therapist attempted to use.

As I have indicated in many places, I wish to separate the functions of psychotherapy and of educating or teaching. I suggest that teaching techniques can be developed for such a child, to go side by side with the therapeutic process. Cues for teaching techniques could be derived from the learning profile of this disturbed youngster so that the teaching task would not have to be given up. In this particular case, the mere indication on the part of the therapist that he did not wish to interfere with the autonomy of the school instantly brought about a supportive change in attitude. But occasional case conferences, in which psycho-therapeutic secrecy is maintained while allowing for sufficient contact, would help in the development of a learning profile which teachers could use and apply to their own functions. The psychotherapist, in turn, might gain immensely from observations which would go beyond the usual factual reporting of success or failure. The advantages of such co-operation are obvious in our complex world where many professional people carry different functions, work in different places and agencies or in private practice, and generally seem unable to maintain the kinds of co-operation needed to bring about an optimum program for such a child.

The work with this child suggests a model of professional co-opera-tion, as well as the kind of co-operation to be worked out with the parents.

What seems to be particularly important in the case of learning dif-ficulties is to bring about a new kind of collaboration between the teach-ing and clinical professions. I can envision activities which will bring teachers and clinicians together, in which learning difficulties will be discussed around a child's learning profile. His ways of learning and of resisting learning will be described in terms of the therapeutic problem as well as in terms of the teaching problem.

The developmental knowledge that we have today about ego develop-ment; about the growth of psychic structure; about the development of object relationships; about the development of capacity for imitation and identification; about developing learning readiness and the developing capacity to use teachers, should be utilized in such a co-operative process. Isolation must be broken down and a meeting-ground established for the educator and the psychoanalyst wherein both can benefit from the same basic model—the learning and non-learning profile of the child—without interfering in their respective functions, and while maintaining their respective professional identities.

One could get to Ricky's problems in more than one way: the order-ing of data is always related to the techniques available. Much that can be applied to the learning and teaching process, the developing capacity of the learner, stems, strangely enough, not from experiences with children but from experiences with adults. I refer now to the education and training of professional people. Teaching devices that have been elaborated as supervision of professional skills, such as psychotherapy, psychoanalysis, social casework, and the like, provide examples. The concepts involved, I believe, can be applied to Ricky and children like him and older.

Wallerstein and I[1] referred to certain typical aspects of supervision which exert a regressive pull on the professional student as typical constellations repeating themselves over again, and we called them "problems about learning" and "learning problems." The former ones were described to me by Peyton-Jacobs as learning resistance, while the latter ones were described as the student's typical learning style. They may be useful or may actually turn out to be an obstacle if this style is not appropriate for the subject to be learned. Peyton-Jacobs has also referred to these problems as "blind spots" and "dumb spots." Blind spots would refer to inabilities in the development of a capacity to learn, having much to do, for example, with certain inhibitions, as if the material were taboo and should not be known. There are, for example, children with reading difficulties who have difficulty reading anything in order to avoid learning about things which would create anxiety in them. Some of Ricky's difficulties are of that nature. Dumb spots refer to lack of knowledge and lack of skill, and frequently also to learning styles which are inapplicable to the subject matter.

These characterizations made me think about the monkeys who could see no evil, speak no evil, and hear no evil. The blindness would refer to incapacity to see or to understand certain things because of inhibitions and taboos; the dumb spots would refer to lack of knowledge, lack of learning skills, etc. The addition of deaf spots would refer to difficulties with teachers, with authority, with parents. These generic characterizations, somehow a part of every learner, can also be used in order to develop a learning and non-learning profile of the child. Ricky, for example, could not allow himself to see certain things as long as he felt that the adult would oppose this knowledge, would be critical of him, etc. We see, for example, that during treatment certain desires, such as the babies mixing feces with candy and the like, could only be discussed when he felt that he could trust the therapist; at first, they were taboo subjects, a difficulty that indeed would show up in his developing learning inhibition. His learning style was best characterized perhaps through the name of the hero of his fantasy life. Tricky the Trickster had a way of learning, of trying to achieve autonomy, knowledge and skills, even though it got under the skin of adults. His learning style was actually in the service of learning resistance. It was a means of opposing parents and teacher, and thus, of course, was a cramped learning style inasmuch as he could not really use the school and the teacher and thus developed deaf spots. Much of his learning style is typified through his depiction of the autonomous babies who barricaded themselves against the adult world and tried to develop their own self-sufficient, Paul Bunyan-like world of learning, without the need for teachers or any adult. Such babies, of course, have no one to identify with or to imitate, and much of their learning remains hidden from the adult world.

The teachers never saw these private learning worlds of Ricky. They could not give him credit for them, nor could they exploit his learning style and match it with a teaching style appropriate for him. A major requisite for teachers is the development of a teaching style which takes into account whatever the child has available at a given time in order to learn. In other words, the teacher should be in a position to utilize the child's own learning style rather than to expect a learning style for which he is not yet ready. In Ricky's, the teacher would also have to use the child's resistance to learning, and it becomes clear, of course, that a learning profile for Ricky would have to be matched by a kind of teaching profile to fit him. Such individualized teaching and learning would try to adapt the teaching style to the learning style. This would prevent a child's learning difficulty from provoking teaching resistance.

Much of the learning style of the child, any child, has to be understood as an investigation of his capacity for insight, his ways of acquiring insight, his creative methods of problem solving, his cognitive style, etc. These functions, studied so well by Piaget, and also important for psychotherapy based on insight, have not been given quite as much attention in our work as they deserve. We have to catch up with that part of psychology which has so far remained a stepchild in psychoanalytic work, in spite of our frequent reference to the work of Piaget. Most tests of youngsters in the realm of intelligence, achievement and cognitive functions, unfortunately, are usually deficit-oriented rather than positively based.

It seems to me that a continued collaboration between teachers and clinicians around a case like Ricky's would not only benefit the child but would help us to create models of collaboration, magnifying models of studies around the issue of learning. While many children can be helped without such co-operation, the more serious disturbances certainly will need it. Ricky's case was comparatively easy, and the case material I selected certainly was straightforward. But whenever there are more difficult situations, particularly where there are cognitive deficits or cases in the phase of puberty and adolescence, the issues cannot be solved well without that collaboration. Many a failure is due to professional isolation or to many unco-ordinated individual efforts.

Learning during puberty and adolescence contains a new ingredient which will decide the way in which the youngster learns and the way in which he resists learning. As the adolescent is increasingly confronted with purpose, with goals, with identity struggles, with conflicts over separation from the home, these will either enhance or cramp his learning style; that is, they will add a new variable to the total learning profile. These struggles are a part of learning rather than its obstacles.

Ricky's purpose in learning, beyond the joy that he experiences playing tricks, presently seems to be entirely one of trying to restore the shiny sun, trying to restore love, and trying to restore the supply of candy, of oral gratification. There are still no dominant functions which indicate that his ego has turned passivity into mastery, imitation into identification, or that he is beginning to develop the pleasure function of learning—the joy of discovery and of mastery.

Siegfried Bernfeld once described the teacher—and he may as well have included the psychotherapist—in terms of certain narcissistic preoccupations, of certain tendencies toward professional megalomania, that made him think about his task in over-idealized rather than technical terms. Bernfeld suggested that the teacher could be compared to the gardener who thinks that he makes flowers grow, when all that he does is remove stones, fertilize the ground, provide water, and create conditions for growth. It is nature that causes the seed to develop into a certain flower; the gardener merely provides appropriate conditions. I think it is useful to add to his simile that a gardener will do best if he knows a great deal about the seed and if he can develop something like a growth profile of the different plants he wishes to grow. If he had such a growth profile he could then develop a profile which could describe his own activities on behalf of the plant.

In presenting the struggle of a little boy against and towards learning, against and towards the teachers and the parents, I have tried to indicate how the elaboration of a learning profile, both in terms of mastery of a task and the resolution of inner conflict, should prove helpful to teacher and therapist in developing teaching and therapeutic styles adequate for the task. Learning disturbances, as well as normal learning conflicts, have to be understood along developmental lines. To follow these developmental lines in relation to the learning task and the unresolved learning conflict, Ricky's case was used in two ways. Reality, that is, the task of the teacher and the parents; and the child's inner psychic development, that is, the task of clinical intervention, were both considered. These tasks should not be completely separated nor should they be entirely merged. Both must be carried on without destroying their functional difference. This will require an intensive effort in collaboration between educators and therapists, both in actual practice as well as in research.

BIBLIOGRAPHY

1. Ekstein, Rudolf, and Robert Wallerstein. *The Teaching and Learning of Psychotherapy.* New York: Basic Books, Inc., 1958.
2. Freud, Anna. *Normality and Pathology in Childhood; Assessments of Development.* New York: International Universities Press, 1965.
3. Pfister, Oskar. "The Faults of Parents." *Zeitschrift für Psychoanalytische Pädagogik,* 1929, 3:172.
4. Schlesinger, H. J. (1964) "A Contribution to a Theory of Promising: I. Primary and Secondary Promising." Unpublished.

CHAPTER 19

The Borderline Child in the School Situation

RUDOLF EKSTEIN and ROCCO L. MOTTO

PSYCHOANALYSTS HAVE FREQUENTLY been invited to set forth their views on matters which are important to the professional educator, to those responsible for the development of our school facilities, for public education. Very early in the history of psychoanalysis we find it exerting an influence on educational philosophy and educational technique. But it is a rather new development for psychoanalysts to contribute opinions, knowledge and skill to the *education* of children who are regarded as emotionally or mentally ill.

The earlier concept of the "problem child" seems to be a vague notion; it has never been made clear whether we refer to illness in children or whether we speak about the educational problems that such a child creates for parents and teachers. A more recent notion of the "problem parent" puts the emphasis on new factors, and one may suppose that future notions will deal with the "problem teacher" and perhaps some day, when the public no longer needs to think omnipotence into the psychiatrist or psychoanalyst, we may seriously talk about the "problem psychoanalyst."

The stress on individual differences is a recent emphasis of our society. In the twenties things looked rather different to Bernfeld when he discussed education in terms of two decisive limits. The educator, the teacher, and the parent were helped to see that certain fantasies about educational function, the notion of the molding of the ideal character, needed new adaptation to reality considerations which were societal and psychological in nature. In his definition of education as the "reaction of society to the facts of development," "development" referred primarily to these aspects of human growth which are understood today through the term "maturation." Society reacts, then, in terms of its own patterns, its own needs, which are defined by its values,

197

its social structures, its economic opportunities. Developmental and maturational aspects of children have been studied by analysts, but the developmental and maturational aspects of society have been hiding, in the early years of psychoanalysis, behind the concept of reality. This early work of Bernfeld acknowledges the fact that the reality within which the child grows up is not a static one but is ever-changing and follows its own laws.

More recent expression to this thought has been given by Erik H. Erikson in his *Childhood and Society*.[3] He demonstrated through the study of educational devices in different primitive and modern societies that these educational means serve the maintenance of characteristic personality patterns which reflect the goals and aspirations of the group. Bernfeld and Erikson refer to two sets of circumstances which limit the educator and teacher in their educational task. The first set refers to the limits society imposes on the school system, the second to the inner limitations in growth potential, in learning capacity which the child brings to us.

The school system some twenty-five or fifty years ago was not geared to pay much attention to individual differences. It addressed itself, as it were, to the average child. All other youngsters, whether they were considered to be particularly gifted children or slow learners, whether they were emotionally or mentally ill children, had really no place in such a school system unless they were capable, more or less, of adjusting themselves to the average expectation which the school imposed upon them. Erikson's volume poses questions as to the type of innovation which would be necessary were the school system to develop special techniques and special programs for special groups of children. Such considerations are the outgrowth of a society whose basic philosophy expresses faith in the individual, a responsibility toward each individual, strong or weak, and readiness to carry this philosophy into practice. Indeed, more and more American communities have developed within their school systems special programs in order to meet the needs of children who cannot keep up with the program which is designed for the fictitious normal or average child.

Psychoanalysts who are to contribute to these special programs must keep in mind Bernfeld's two limits. They are usually aware of the first: the psychological limits of the child. Actually, as has been pointed out, for example, by a number of contributors to the volume *Ortho-psychiatry and the School*,[4] the main strength of the psychiatrist or the psychoanalyst in relation to the schools concerns his function as consultant, his diagnostic ability which leads to decisions for therapy. The other limit of education, namely, the readiness of the public and of the school authorities to assume responsibility for nonaverage children in the school system is a problem with which it is much more difficult for analysts to deal. The greatest difficulty stems from the fact that few psychoanalysts have ever intensively studied the methods of education, the problems of learning, and the problem involved in the training of teachers. Therefore, they tend to stress family problems, interpersonal issues, therapeutic issues, and certain dynamic aspects of group action. They tend to look at the classroom as a potential therapeutic agent, and they usually do not differentiate between *treating* a sick child and *teaching* a sick child.

The tendency of teachers, whether they meet the borderline child in the nursery, in kindergarten, or in elementary and high school, is to expect help in the management of the child which can be given properly only if the consultants separate teaching and therapeutic functions rather than try to make a therapist out of the teacher. This separation of function represents a serious problem which is only slowly being tackled in professional circles.

What is a borderline child? This new diagnostic category refers to children who at times give the impression of normality, or of classical neurotic adaptation, and at times develop a state of mind which reminds us of the psychotic organization. The seat of the disturbance thus would be the ego organization of the child: unstable, fluctuating back and forth between comparatively normal states and very abnormal states. These abnormal states might include occasional fugues, seizures, loss of orientation in time and space, disturbances of reality testing, occasional delusional or hallucinatory phenomena. Many of these symptoms may not be detected in the classroom, but usually the teacher will become aware of those children with wide fluctuation in their capacity for adjustment, for learning, and for getting along with their peer group as well as with other teachers. Some of these children may at times show signs of extreme anxiety or rage, and may suddenly withdraw from the school situation. As a matter of fact, any of the neurotic disturbances may become visible and grow to extreme proportions, which indicates tremendous strain and a breakdown of the capacity for adjustment and adaptation. We wish to stress, though, that these children at times give excellent impressions and may return to modes of functioning which are more related to the normal or neurotic child. The most difficult children for teachers are those with borderline conditions in which there is no fluctuation, children who are shy, silent, passive and withdrawn without being completely isolated from the group situation. These children are not the troublemakers per se, but they are extremely troubled and need to be detected if one wants to save them from more serious difficulties during puberty and adolescence.

The teacher who is confronted with a borderline child looks to us for management devices which are supposed to help the child toward adjustment. Or the teacher who is confronted with a borderline child whose bizarre behavior may upset the rest of the classroom and whose emotional crisis must provoke fear and anxiety in children, parents, and teachers alike frequently wishes just to remove the source of anxiety and disturbance. It may well be that some teachers might not be able to work with such children, regardless of how co-operative the school administration may be. Teachers who respond with considerable upset, with personal anxiety to such children, will most likely be less suitable for such work than teachers who are patient and accepting of such conditions.

We have found through individual experience with a number of teachers that it is possible to maintain a number of severely disturbed youngsters, even hospitalized youngsters, in ordinary school programs, and that in many instances personal collaborative experiences between teacher and therapist, mutual respect for each other's function, have led to excellent results. One of the authors treated a borderline child of nine, whose rage reactions, learning problems, and disciplinary problems created difficulties in the school situation. The teacher tried to pay more attention to this child, to the detriment of the other children. She was torn between satisfying the needs of this one child and satisfying the demands of the other children. The psychotherapist's contact with her helped her to leave to him the therapeutic task, which freed her to devote her time more fully to the total group situation without feeling that she neglected the child. This restored her to the role for which she had been trained, while her own information about the child gave the therapist important psychological clues and helped him in turn to carry out his function more effectively.

Frequently, the very fact that the teacher knows a specific borderline child to be in treatment; the fact that an opportunity exists to report unusual events to the psychotherapist; the awareness that the parents are contributing to the treatment situation, encourages a teacher to help a child in school in spite of disruptive difficulties which may otherwise not have been tolerated. The psychoanalyst, on the other hand, has frequently found that the help of the teacher, who sets limits and educational goals for the sick child, has been of tremendous value. A child cannot develop and mature if he is exposed only to the therapeutic environment. Such "hothouse atmosphere" is useful for certain initial phases in treatment, but sooner or later the child must leave the protective isolation of the treatment situation and must start to utilize the treatment within a living environment for the child.

In 1958,[2] one of the present authors, in conjunction with Drs. Keith Bryant and Seymour Friedman, reviewed more than ten years of studies on childhood schizophrenia and allied conditions. Many of these conditions are actually borderline conditions and go through different phases of treatment. Some of the sicker children may start in residential homes or in hospitals and attend the hospital school. They may later move to a boarding school and a boarding home before being returned to their own home and the ordinary public- or private-school facilities. The paper reviews and lists the total literature on training and learning issues with severely disturbed children in residential schools, in certain private schools, as well as in public schools. However, it is well to note that nearly all the studies listed have been contributed by therapeutic workers; comparatively few have been influenced by the professional teacher. We now need contributions which stress the teaching problems. It is true that frequently the issues of teaching and therapy cannot be separated, but it is our conviction that we need additional emphasis on the modification of teaching techniques with such children.

In our own experience, from which we wish to cite a few case examples, it is interesting to note that comparatively little contact has been necessary between the clinic and the educational facility because of the acceptance of each other's function. One may expect the necessity for a great many contacts if the child is very ill and in an acute emergency situation or if either the psychotherapist or the teacher is very insecure and therefore needs the help of the other. Disturbed parents also sometimes may necessitate more active collaboration on the part of teacher and therapist. Ordinarily, very few conferences and occasional telephone contacts or correspondence suffice to maintain relationships in rather complex clinical situations. Occasionally the mother of the child is mature enough to serve as a sort of go-between between clinic and educational facility. While having conferences with both, she can convey the clinical point of view to the teacher and the teaching problems to the therapist or social worker. Such short and infrequent contacts, however, operate only if they are carried by mutual respect and by a mutual acceptance of the other's function.

A few case illustrations may serve to indicate that the school is capable of helping children who otherwise must be considered to be very sick and who in the past could not be assimilated by the school program. These cases represent experiences at the Reiss-Davis Center in Los Angeles.

Jimmy was brought to us at the age of four years, three months. He had been studied at different centers, having been considered first to be a retarded child. At the age of 22 months he was given the diagnostic label of "mild to moderate mental retardation due to primary cerebral hypoplasia." His development was considered to be at the 15-month level. When he was two, another center diagnosed him as presenting an "atypical development of childhood" and psychotherapy was recommended. Family agencies and mental hygiene agencies were approached by the parents, but since the child was still at a preverbal level, no program could be arranged.

We learned that this unplanned baby, after unsuccessful nursing, was put on a formula when he was four days old, and it was discovered that he became exhausted when trying to get nourishment. The mother then noticed that the holes in the nipples were too small. He was also wrapped too tightly, and only later did the mother learn how to loosen the clothing. Such early memories of the mother frequently constitute a clue toward an understanding of the mother's level of functioning, as well as her basic attitude toward the child. She recalled that the pediatrician was "shocked at the looseness of the stool." which previously she had not recognized as diarrhea. The formula was changed many times. The mother described how she kept putting food back into the child's mouth even though he spit it up and that she did so until he screamed so much that she had to stop. She said she was determined to "do everything right if it killed me." She described the child as one who would get "hysterical" if there was any change in his room or in his routine. In the course of attempting to get help for the child, one neuro-surgeon suggested brain surgery, which was performed when he was three years, five months old. Holes were bored into his skull and the surgeon claimed that fluid drained from the brain for several days. In spite of the surgery, the parents saw no improvement. The surgeon wanted to attempt a craniotomy, but the parents opposed this and applied to another clinic.

Jimmy began to speak at the age of two and a half although his speech was repetitive and he mixed up the pronouns. He had withdrawn more and more during the last year, and occasionally when other people came to the house, he would go into a separate room and shut the door to be by himself. While toilet training succeeded, feeding continued to be a problem. He was described as compulsive and ritualistic, experiencing any disturbance of routine as something very painful. He wandered about aimlessly and seemed to be at a loss as to what to do. He had no contact with other children.

The first definite impression he gave when seen at our clinic was one of a "neatly dressed youngster in a corduroy suit, quite chubby, rosy complexion, bright-eyed, small baby teeth, a very definite impression of a baby." As he accompanied the psychiatrist to the latter's office, he made a feeble attempt at offering his hand. The psychiatrist's description follows: "After standing up to greet me, he spun around from left to right, came down the hall with me and then spun around again from left to right as we entered my office. He was verbalizing all the time, but these verbalizations could not be understood." His play activity was highly disturbed and was described: "As he approached the toys he spun around again. He then busied himself with the cars and played somewhat with them, also with the crayons when I offered them, the baby carriage and the baby doll, knocking them off the play table. Then because he heard some noise out in the parking lot that was being repaired by a bulldozer, he went to the window to investigate. As he approached it, he spun once before he could get up on the couch to look out the window. As he approached the window, standing on the couch, he spun once more. As he and I observed the bulldozer, he chattered away in a way I could not understand. Then as he returned from the window he unspun himself over to the edge of the couch, unspun as he got down on the floor, and then returned to the toys. He had spilled a bunch of little colored cubes, and as he felt them underneath his shoes, he began bouncing on them in a 'whoopsy-daisy' baby kind of play. In this his body would be very stiff and tense, but he seemed to be enjoying it, laughing all the time. This continued for some minutes, during which there were one or two distinct words that I could understand."

The psychologist who attempted to test this child stated, among other details, the following in her report: "Jimmy is a nice-looking four-and-a-half-year-old youngster, with a somewhat babyish expression and manner. Although capable of speaking in sentences, he rarely did so. Most of his verbalizations were confined to words and short phrases. He seemed minimally aware of people; only occasionally was there real eye contact with me. He seemed preoccupied with his own thoughts and would answer questions inappropriately. Often, the question had to be repeated several times in order to get him to respond. Sometimes he would respond if I put my arm gently about him. At times, he was surprisingly co-operative and responsive. At other times, he seemed to blot out whatever was said to him, behaving as if he had heard nothing. Then there were occasions when he would aggressively throw test materials on the floor instead of complying with instructions. It was at these moments that he appeared most enthusiastic and pleased. He was able to respond to the more difficult items, such as the leaf, but could not identify a picture of a hand. Interestingly enough, he read the number 8 printed in the corner of the card instead of answering 'hand,' an achievement for a normal four-and-a-half-year-old. Frequently, it took some time for outer stimuli to penetrate, so absorbed was he by his own inner thoughts. At times, he behaved as though no one else was present. This examiner could well have been another piece of furniture, yet physical contact could sometimes bring forth an appropriate response."

The next four years this child was in treatment with a psycho-therapist. During the first year of treatment no attempt to place the child in any kind of group situation succeeded. After one year of treatment he was added to a small experimental group of children with similar developmental disturbances. These children, in addition to their regular psychotherapeutic program, met in a group setting each afternoon for a two-hour period of play. While the psychotherapy dealt with the individual problems of the patient, the group experience constituted the first attempt to expose these children to some formal training and some reality demands. Three years later a remedial teacher was added to the group of adults who worked with these children. We tried to expose the children to formal academic learning, and a formal assessment of Jimmy led us to believe that he was ready for a trial in a more formal school setting. Our own clinical retests and the tests of the psychology personnel at the school revealed remarkably similar findings. His chronologic age at eight years, seven months was matched by a mental age of eight years, four months, thus giving him an I.Q. of 97, based on form M of the Stanford-Binet. The school psychologist reported as follows: "Jimmy is capable of functioning in a regular classroom, starting first with an hour a day and increasing it gradually, and I would recommend him for admission to the B3 at the public school."

Plans were then made to have the clinic group activity come to an end. During the summer this child was placed in a summer day-camp program which was his first group experience with "average" children. We learned that Jimmy functioned fairly well in spite of several trying incidents. At the opening of school in the fall, he was enrolled, and within a short time he was attending this program full time from 9 a.m. to 3 p.m. and remained on a B3 level. At the time of this report he was holding his own, and he created no problems within the setting of the school and the classroom. His individual psychotherapy, twice a week, was continued. There was great evidence that the psychotic process was still present, but under control to the extent that the child could make use of the public-school system. His teachers were aware of his difficulties, and of the treatment program, and the parents worked with both the clinic and the school guidance personnel in order to help him most effectively. There was an exchange of opinion between school and clinic, but this exchange was primarily for information and no attempt was made on either part to recommend techniques. We may well expect that the treatment of this child will continue for a number of years, and it is difficult to predict how much further improvement is possible. The fact that he can deal with an ordinary school program in spite of his illness is proof indeed that the public school has a constructive place in the life of this child.

Data from the treatment of another child, a 13-year-old girl, illustrates a different type of difficulty with which the school setting is confronted in attempting to carry on with the educational task. Helen, an only child, has been hospitalized at a local children's hospital after a psychiatrist saw the child twice in her own home. She displayed acutely disturbed behavior, was overwhelmed by anxiety and by frightening fantasies. She screamed and cried out her fears that she was changing, that she was being changed by her parents, by creatures from space. She insisted that her parents were not really her parents, that things were getting inside of her, etc. These difficulties, which came into the open at the onset of puberty, had been set off several months prior to her hospitalization when she had been molested by a middle-aged man. In reality, the extent of this sexual assault was relatively mild, but for Helen this experience was more than she could handle and precipitated a breakdown. After the incident, Helen became increasingly anxious, withdrawn and depressed, and occasionally would display severe temper outbursts. She would spend many hours watching TV. During menstrual periods her screaming would occur more spontaneously and she would complain about strange feelings inside of her. She began to complain that she was losing her sense of sight, of sound, of smell, and that she felt numbness on different parts of the surface of her body.

Before the onset of the illness she had been, according to the parents, a "good, happy and well-adjusted child." They were confused and frightened by their daughter's behavior, which increased some disagreement which existed between them. This led to a great deal of arguing and threats of divorce. The father suffered from violent temper tantrums, and the mother suffered from agoraphobia. She felt inadequate as a mother, and described her own problems as an adolescent. Since she felt so many difficulties, she had left much of Helen's rearing in the father's hands. She thought of him as wiser and more knowledgeable about ways of handling the child's emotional and social needs. The father was experienced as overprotective and was used by Helen as her confidant and a source of competent emotional support. The mother was seen by Helen as the one who punished, criticized and nagged.

Treatment was begun instantly, after a workable therapeutic relationship had been established with Helen. She started to recognize, with the help of the therapist, what was reality in her life and what was fantasy. She developed psychological strength to a sufficient degree in order to withstand the enormous anxiety she felt. She began to understand the emotional turmoil in her and the new processes going on within her body during puberty. At first, she expressed her problems in a most diffuse, abstruse and disturbed manner. She transformed her relationships to her parents and other human beings, the thoughts and feelings about herself, to fantasies about an unreal world, a world of space, inhabited by fearsome creatures who were certain to harm her. Whenever she had severe attacks of anxiety, she displaced these anxieties through outbursts of screaming and crying at home, at school, on the street and, once or twice, during treatment. These anxiety attacks frightened the parents and left them helpless. They would telephone the therapist for help. Occasionally, it was necessary to visit the child at home. One of her feelings, that she "was changed into something else, a creature from space, through her parents, through space people, through the therapist," were often brought into therapy. She had doubts who her parents were, and she felt that she was "shrinking." She occasionally had the fear that the therapist was shrinking. When her anxiety grew too much, she lunged at the therapist in an attempt to control her wish to scream. She complained also about hearing sounds and voices. She did not want to let her mother out of her sight and insisted that the mother sleep with her. She was also afraid to look into her father's eyes. Her school work suffered immensely. She had always been an excellent student, but now her grades were C and below. It was necessary to help the father and mother in order to make it possible for them to change their attitude toward the child.

After approximately 200 hours of therapy, Helen had again become an integrated person. Anxiety attacks were absent and a normal sleeping pattern had been restored. Her school work had improved to a B average and her relationships with her mother and father had also improved. She had more friends and was able to express her thoughts and feelings more directly rather than through psychotic fantasies. Occasionally, these old fantasies were brought up, but they had lost their intense anxiety of previous days.

It is strange to think that a child may have the degree of disturbance found in this patient and nevertheless be able to function in a public-school program. While she did her school work adequately, she would sometimes during school hours suddenly scream out loud. She would occasionally say that she could not see the blackboard and get herself moved from seat to seat. She even had the same reaction to peers as she had occasionally to her parents, when she felt that they were shrinking in size. During these moments anxiety mounted greatly, and she suffered from short delusional episodes. Frequently the teacher would be unaware of the meaning of these episodes or would not notice them. Sometimes the child would speak about one of these experiences to one of the other children in the class and would be exposed to the child's laughing at her. These episodes fortunately were of rather short duration and were not too frequent.

Helen's therapy began in a summer vacation period and she continued her schooling in the fall and had no interruptions of school during the entire therapy. We have found this to be true not only in this case but in many others as well. Frequently, teachers are practically unaware of the difficulties encountered by the patient. They assume the poor school work of the child to be a problem of "too lazy to concentrate" or of "disinterest" and may never notice that the child is struggling with deep-seated conflicts which may reach psychotic proportions. In other cases, delusional material may spill right into the group situation, but, nevertheless, a tactful, accepting teacher may be able to maintain such a child within the school program. This is provided, of course, that the child is receiving therapy. One can hardly assume that a teacher should or could be willing to tolerate such a child in the school program unless it were known that the child was receiving the necessary care. The child who is helped with a treatment program on the side and is accepted in spite of his difficulties but is, at the same time, given to understand that he must meet certain expectations of the school program will do best. This is, of course, not always possible, and frequently it may be indicated to take the child out of school for shorter or longer periods of time.

The return to school is frequently accompanied by transitional problems, with crisis situations during which some form of co-operation between teaching and psychotherapeutic function is absolutely essential. The formerly hospitalized child, who returns to school after an interruption, is concerned with many questions. He wonders whether the teachers and the peer group will accept him; whether they will or should know about the hospitalization and the illness; whether to let on that he is now having treatment. He will frequently be deeply suspicious, which will not make it easy for the group to accept him. The teacher's task will be to permit the child sufficient time to accept the new situation and also to help him to understand that acceptance by others will be a gradual process. Sometimes the academic task may have to be subordinated to the necessary social task of genuinely joining the group.

A third case, presenting a different difficulty, may round out the picture. The boy, ten years old, when coming to the clinic was described by his mother as suffering from "many fears and he has no self-confidence. He is becoming much too effeminate. He is interested only in feminine things. He has no friends, but wants them so much. He seems to have an extreme mother complex. He is also very immature." Bill had been diagnosed, when seen previously in consultation with a neuropsychiatrist, as a "congenital homosexual." The family stated that the advice had been given to "raise Bill as a girl," that is, to give him dolls, female clothes, girls' names, etc. This doctor allegedly prescribed "male hormones," which Bill took for a few weeks, but one day Bill threatened his mother with a hammer that he suddenly picked up. He was placed in a sanatorium and sedated for a few days and then released.

Further investigation seemed to indicate that his illness was more indicative of a psychological disorder than an endocrinologic one. Bill was the younger of two boys and was a sick and colicky baby with many formula changes. He suffered a period of severe dehydration during the first year of life, but later on had fairly normal development up to the age of three, when "more accidents befell him from the ages of three to six than any child his age should have encountered." The mother described a variety of accidents such as falls, wrist sprains and fractures, laceration of the chin from a fall in the swimming pool, laceration of the eye from a stone thrown by his brother, a fall from a tree, being run over by an automobile, bitten by a dog, and hanging himself with a laundry rope. She described further how she lost all her control after the hanging incident and "just shook the daylights out of Bill." He then stopped having accidents and was always a "mama's boy," that is, he never left her side. The mother felt overwhelmed by his demands for her attention and was plagued by his questions and comments. Some of these questions indicated that he "searched for reality." He played with the younger children in the neighborhood as long as they could stand his "incessant, querulous demands."

From the psychologist's report we obtained the following: "Primitive fears of destruction, with oral sadistic symbolism, were prominent in his fantasies. He confused sexual with aggressive aims and could allow himself only a passive situation which afforded him some safety. He felt that separation from the mother would result in destruction, and he constantly attempted to cope with deep problems of anxiety." His thought processes were described as quasi-psychotic, and it was conjectured whether he should not be considered a preschizophrenic child. In fantasies during therapy he saw himself as a songstress, an actress, a female dancer. He brought female dress-up articles of clothing to his psychotherapy sessions and garbed himself in the feminine attire as well as using cosmetics. He displayed many feminine mannerisms and movements. However, he could limit this dressing in feminine clothing to the psychotherapeutic sessions and was able to stop this activity at home. Occasionally, however, this broke down and he plagued his mother by wearing her evening gowns, her bathing suits, her sun suits, and also by using her lipstick and nail polish. Once when he saw a TV movie in which a heroine cut herself with a razor blade "in order to get attention," Bill made a small one-eighth to one-quarter inch cut in his wrist, also in order to "get attention."

When therapy began, he was doing very poorly in school, both academically and socially; academically his reading was at the third-grade level, and he was doing second- and third-grade arithmetic. His social behavior in school was immature, at times infantile. The teachers described him as teasing other children, as being unable to remain quiet during classes, fighting and quarreling with his peers and preferring to play with much younger children from kindergarten and first grade. He was completely rejected by the children in his class. When treatment started, he was not enrolled in school because his parents doubted at the time that he could make it. But after four or five weeks in therapy, he was started in school and remained there throughout the therapy. There was a gradual improvement in his academic performance, and though his arithmetic performance remained weak, he made great gains in reading. He made a few friends and retained them, and he even went to a residential camp for one summer.

Initially, the parents, who were very difficult persons because of their own problems, sabotaged the treatment, but finally they were able to accept a treatment program for themselves. When this entire treatment situation had to be transferred to another therapist in the northern part of the state because of the father's achieving a better position, the boy's progress was interrupted and he returned to his former symptomatology. He joined a residential treatment center and made considerable progress there, preparing himself to be a rancher since he felt he would "get along better with animals than with people." This boy needed a school program which was combined with a residential setting. Because of the degree of disturbance that he suffered and the degree of difficulties that he created for his parents, whose own precarious adjustment actually stood in the way of his treatment, it was necessary to work toward placement.

A word might be said about the reaction of other children to the borderline child. Of course, one must expect all kinds of group reactions, sometimes such strong ones that the child cannot be maintained in the class. In most cases, though, where the teacher has a fair understanding of the difficulties and can tolerate it, the peer group will identify with the teacher's attitude toward the child. The overconcern of the teacher who tries to solicit through "enlightenment" the help of the group may sometimes lead to unwanted results. The school psychologist will do best if he leaves the initiative to the teacher unless help is solicited. Questions concerning group reactions may sometimes be answered best by someone who is especially equipped to deal with group problems. The reactions of parents who feel that their own children are neglected on account of a special interest on the part of the teacher for a special child are very important. These parents may need help, but generally we do not expect parents to create difficulties in an enlightened school setting provided the teachers do not assume therapeutic responsibilities, the carrying out of which would undermine the teaching task.

We have given three case illustrations in which the public-school system was utilized in spite of a degree of disturbance in the child which a few years ago would have been thought to prohibit the use of public schools. It may well be true that even today the majority of public schools, and perhaps also private schools, could not undertake the responsibility for such children. As schools learn to make use of professional people in the clinical field, however, and start some training of teachers for this type of work, we find more and more situations where this is possible. Frequently, we find that children with severe borderline conditions or psychotic conditions make excellent recoveries, and may then even make outstanding contributions when they have not been deprived of their chance in school. Rather than thinking of such children as nuisances, as disturbers of normal educational processes, we may wish to think of them as hidden assets. But regardless of whether they are hidden assets or not, their acceptance into the school program and the development of techniques which allow us to maintain them constructively seem to us a step toward a richer, freer community. Freedom implies that even sick individuals will be given a chance. The choice available must be of such a kind that they may benefit from treatment, as well as from participation in social activities as much as is possible for them. When the children's true capacity is restored, they will not have lost opportunities for choices because of lack of education. Education and psychotherapy for such children are two aspects, neither of which can replace the other. Either one can be successful only if the other is not disregarded.

Teachers and psychotherapists will help each other best if each will accept the difference of the other's function as a prerequisite to successful collaboration. The maturity of a free society is reflected in the degree to which the notion of the "average" person, the insistence on adjustment to the mass personality, is replaced by the acceptance of individual differences. There is no better place to test the maturity of our concepts of freedom than in our educational system.

BIBLIOGRAPHY

1. Bernfeld, S. Sisyphus or the Limits of Education. Vienna: International Psychoanalytic Press, 1925.

2. Ekstein, R., K. Bryant, and S. W. Friedman: "Childhood Schizophrenia and Allied Disorders." In *Schizophrenia*, L. Bellak, editor. New York: Logos Press, 1958.
3. Erikson, E. H. *Childhood and Society*. New York: W. W. Norton & Co., 1950.
4. Krugman, M. *Orthopsychiatry and the School*. New York: American Orthopsychiatric Association, 1958.

PART V: Tasks in a Changing Society

The information gathered by psychoanalysis can claim with justice that it deserves to be regarded by educators as an invaluable guide in their conduct towards children.

—SIGMUND FREUD

CHAPTER 20

Of Tasks Ahead

G. H. J. PEARSON

THE ATTEMPTS TO APPLY the knowledge gained through psychoanalytic research to the field of the education of children and some errors that characterized some of these attempts have been described elsewhere (see Foreword and Chapter 1). Here, I would like to suggest some of the directions which the combined disciplines of education and psychoanalysis could take in future research. As I refer to education, I do not mean the strong influences that training and rearing have on the development of the child—these have been and are being documented extensively. I refer to the formal education of the child in the acquisition of academic skills.

Psychoanalysis has two important functions—the treatment of the psychoneuroses and the application of the knowledge about the structure and functions of the human mind to the better understanding of many fields of human behavior. The latter is particularly relevant to the field of school education.

Therapeutic psychoanalysis naturally was used for children suffering from difficulties in learning general academic skills. From the study of many such cases, it has been found that the causative factors may range from inadequate teaching or teachers and unsatisfactory relationships between the child and the teacher through the inability of the child to concentrate his attention on his school work because of conscious worries about himself, his impulses, and his relationships with others and the involvement of his ability to learn in unconscious intrapsychic conflicts, the last mentioned being akin to adult neurotic work disturbances. Although there still is much to learn about the influence of interpersonal relationships, of emotions and of the unconscious on the child's ability to learn, educators have not been informed adequately of what already is known. Nor have they been helped sufficiently to apply this knowledge in their work with children, not as therapists but as teachers. When they have been informed, they always have tried to apply their new knowledge.

Progressive education has made the attempt to help the child to learn by utilizing his interests and by trying to make the way he learned as pleasurable as possible. Important as this is, the child must also learn that reality frequently demands that he perform temporarily unpleasurable and sometimes painful tasks in order to obtain a greater and more permanent pleasure in the future. The school has an important function in helping the child to understand reality and to live according to the reality principle. Through this, he experiences the pleasure of success in mastering his academic work and it helps him to channel his interests in a way that will give him the added pleasure of real success in the discharge of his energies. (The chapters in Part III are useful and helpful in directing our understanding of the role that discipline plays in the learning task.) Further research by both educators and psychoanalysts into the methods of utilizing interests as well as accepting reality is also needed in academic education.

The child in the early years of grammar school utilizes many mechanisms as defenses against his unconscious desires. If these mechanisms were seen in an adult to the same degree that they occur in the child, they would cause the adult to be diagnosed as an obsessional neurotic. But these mechanisms are seen in the ordinary behavior and the play of the child in the latency period. If they were carefully described and delineated, could not the educator find places where they could be used to help the child in his academic learning? To achieve these goals, considerable collaboration of the educator, the educational psychologist and the psychoanalyst will be required.

There is the central problem of how learning takes place. Investigations by educational psychologists have produced much information as to the learning methods used by the conscious mind. These are an important part of the theory of learning—a part much better known to the educator than to the psychoanalyst who, until recently, has been more interested in the workings of the unconscious. Experimental psychologists, working with the concepts that the mind thinks in ways resembling a computing machine and that a great deal of learning takes place as a form of conditioning, have gathered another large body of data about how a child learns. The increasing interest in studies of cognition indicates the importance of these concepts. In his daily work, the psychoanalyst has the opportunity to study how the unconscious part of the ego and its synthetic functions operate in solving problems and in other kinds of learning. He constantly observes how unconscious intrapsychic conflicts interfere with the ability to learn. It is well known that the ability to be successful in a desired activity—for example, at work or at school—becomes hampered if it is associated in the unconscious with an unresolved childhood conflict.

Each individual child approaches the task of learning academic skills in his own way, specific to his personality and character, just as each teacher approaches his task of teaching the child in his own individual way. I have wondered if the personality and character traits of each kindergarten child were studied, if it would be possible to predict which children would have difficulty in learning specific subjects? If more extensive studies along these lines proved this idea to be valid, it might be possible to correlate certain character traits and personality reactions with difficulties in learning certain subjects. From this, perhaps, better ways of teaching these subjects to individuals with given character traits could be developed.

The educator has a great deal of knowledge to contribute to our understanding of groups for he deals throughout his work with a group, his class, while the child psychiatrist and psychoanalyst are more familiar with a one-to-one relationship. It is interesting that children in a group of ten quite readily perceive the presence of a maladjusted child in a class and try to exclude him from the group. The teacher, watching the group, soon learns which child has an emotional illness. However, greater collaboration between the teacher and the child psychoanalyst would help the teacher better to recognize the early indications of emotional illness in children. Over the years the pediatrician has helped the teacher recognize better the early signs of infectious disease so that now incipient cases of physical illness are either referred to the school nurse or sent home promptly. A similar training in the early signs of emotional illness would make the teacher more comfortably certain that he is doing the correct thing in advising the referral of a child for study and therapy. He would feel more willing to consult a child psychiatrist or psychoanalyst about the individual child who may have early signs of psychoneurosis or psychosis. From the standpoints of pediatrics and psychiatry, this would be an important preventive procedure.

I believe that it would be highly desirable for small groups of educators, educational psychologists, pediatricians, neurologists and child psychoanalysts to pool their specialized knowledge of children in workshops, similar to the institutes at the Reiss-Davis Center. Such workshops could be formed in various centers throughout the country, meeting weekly or biweekly, possibly over a period of years. Besides the mutual benefit obtained from this pooling of knowledge, the continued working together would reduce the tendency to see themselves as professionals or laymen. Through such workshops, real research into the problems of learning, thinking and development in children could take place.

CHAPTER 21

The Second Education of Teachers: An Experiment in Postgraduate Training of Teachers

RUDOLF EKSTEIN and ROCCO L. MOTTO

SINCE 1961, THE REISS-DAVIS CHILD STUDY CENTER and the Los Angeles Psychoanalytic Society-Institute have collaborated in postgraduate training for teachers in the Los Angeles area.[7] This collaboration was an attempt to add a new dimension to the relationship of psychoanalysis and education: consideration of the problem of learning and teaching readiness. In a recent publication, the authors stated that they think of psychoanalysis as a bulwark of individualism. They believe that the use of psychoanalytic principles and insights in the educational system, including the formal school system, indirectly strengthens the belief in the individual, defines his place in a free and open society and in return fortifies this very society.[3]

Ekstein states (chapter 6) that a society which is only concerned with its adult worries, and which feels pressed to use the child in order to rescue this society's system, is not truly ready to teach. Teaching readiness exists only in full knowledge of the implications of the teaching task, including necessary rectification of past errors and deficiencies. The short-sighted saving of money in the field of education, the ever-increasing size of the classroom, the diminishment of services to students, present tremendous challenges far beyond the strength of the individual teacher. Against this social background, the authors believe that we cannot do more, perhaps, than maintain islands of reason, islands of experimentation, pilot programs, to serve as challenges and potential solutions for the future. In this account, we hope to indicate some of the work going on both to help teachers utilize the insights of psychoanalysis for teaching and learning, and in order to build a bridge between teachers and psychoanalysts and other clinicians.[2]

218

Certain ideas on learning readiness have provided insight into the phase of education which precedes formal learning, the preparatory learning phase by means of which the child prepares himself for the beginning of formal teaching procedures. During this phase of early education, a variety of attitudes develop which, with Erikson[5] we may call ego virtues, and which refer to capacities that will grow out of an intensive struggle between the child and the educator, and within the child. These refer of course to the results of the inner struggle, the developmental phases, which are characterized by the achievement of basic trust, of the acceptance of beginning inner and outer controls, of the beginning of autonomy, and finally of initiative. These inner developmental phases, proceeding hand in hand with the maturational facts of psychosexual and psycho-aggressive development, determine the nature of the available learning readiness at the time that the child enters school.

Thus, the child is seen as bringing a set of qualities which determine to what degree he is able to make use of teachers and schools, to what degree—to use Solnit's phrase—he owns the school (chapter 26). If in each instance the outcome of these phases were solely negative, if neither the capacity for trust or control or initiative were available, we indeed would be faced with a child unable to take advantage of the resources of the school. He would be an isolated fortress, building walls in order to defend himself against all intrusion, thus to live in an inner world. He would be powerless to mobilize the energies that could permit him to make use of both his inner capacities as well as the outer resources that society provides in the formal educational system.

The child's learning readiness cannot merely be measured in quantitative terms, but must be seen primarily in qualitative terms as a steady process of progression and sometimes regression. His ability to solve the task of learning will depend upon the extent that he has been able to develop resources that permit him to resolve his inner conflicts, to achieve learning readiness. Teachers want to use this ever-changing learning readiness rather than approach education as a blind reaction to the children. To help achieve this, we want to use analytic understanding of the nature of learning readiness in order to develop a rational educational philosophy. Such a philosophy will enable us to respond to the children in ways that permit the inner conflicts to be turned into growth conflicts instead of utilizing approaches that crush their capacity to learn. It is in this area, then, that the authors believe that psychoanalysis and education can work together in order to help build a bridge to change blind societal reactions into a rational response, fed by the nutriment of science. Instead of molding the child, as older educational philosophies expressed it, or "conditioning" the child, as some current theories suggest, the authors understand the child as possessing his own internal structure, his own inherent possibilities, and his own reaction to the influences of external forces. He is not merely a block of marble to be turned by the sculptor into an ideal piece of art.

As he enters the formal educational system, the child develops another feature of learning readiness, a phase which has been described by Erikson as the phase of industry. In this he utilizes available trust, the capacity to control himself and to accept control by others, as well as initiative and curiosity, in order to develop skills through repetition, through mastery, and through pleasure derived from successful functioning. This period is one of powerful ego growth. The child brings to the teacher the desire to master, to function, which is stimulated by the pressures of society, the competition with siblings and peers in school, the systems of reward and punishment. He compares himself not only with siblings and peers but also with the adult world. He brings whatever resolution of the oedipal conflict he was capable of, and he is now more or less successfully engaged in trying to identify with the adult world. With his wish to be like the parent, his desire to be as good as the sibling, and his competition with his peers, he finds himself up against inner doubt and against the outside world's question as to whether he can or will succeed. He has not only the wish to master but also the great doubt that he can. He is caught in a conflict between the feeling of inferiority and the desire for mastery (see chapter 16).

The teacher cannot really free him from that conflict; rather, the teacher can utilize this conflict by adopting an educational philosophy that permits him to exploit the conflict for the benefit of the child. Only he can master, and is willing to master, who has doubts about his mastery. Mastery is never conflict-free, even though there may be aspects during the rapid growth of ego facilities which are conflict-free, and which will make the struggle much easier. Initiative and industry must be goal-directed. The striving for the goal, the fear of defeat, the wish to succeed are complemented by feelings that it cannot be done, that somebody else ought to do it for him, that he needs help desperately, etc. Thus, the teacher in the classroom is constantly confronted with children who vacillate between the wish to succeed and the occasional despair that success is out of reach. Ambition and fear of failure are in constant flux, and the teacher will find that the particular constellation between these two forces defines the available learning readiness as well as the available learning resistance of the growing child.

The capacity to master a task, as well as the obstacles to learning, are part and parcel of the constellation that the teacher must learn to utilize in order to develop teaching readiness. The teacher's philosophy must be based on the willingness to give, to offer help, knowledge and skills, while taking into account the facts of development and maturation. This teaching readiness accepts the age specificity of the group, but also considers individual specificity of each boy and girl in the classroom. The teacher must then make use of knowledge of group specificity and individual specificity in order to bring about optimum learning readiness. We referred earlier to the pre-school stages of learning readiness. These are the six internal achievements which are brought about by educational pressure as well as by resolution of age-appropriate inner conflicts and they define the beginning learning readiness of the child as he enters school. These ingredients are capacity for trust in others, as well as self-trust; the capacity for autonomy, as well as the capacity to accept controls by teachers; and the capacity to develop initiative, curiosity, and to be guided by a conscience which contains injunctions as well as aspirations.

In their work with the teachers, the authors have discussed another ingredient, which also consists of a dichotomy with both aspects important for learning. This is the wish to work, to be industrious, accompanied by a sense of not knowing as yet, a sense of inferiority. This sense of inferiority, the pathological extremes of which were well described by Alfred Adler and his associates, need not be pathological but could be considered age-appropriate. Thus, they would be a natural part of the learning process, one of the internal conditions for the wish and the capacity to master. This is the time for school stimulus, readiness for the rapid development of cognitive function, the joy in problem-solving, the need to discover and explore, the opportunity for experimentation and for the slow identification with the teacher. Thus, the need to be approved, to be accepted and rewarded, is slowly turned into the love of knowledge and work, and allows for internalization processes via the teacher's influence.

The development of the teacher would depend on in-service training, and a new orientation of teachers' colleges, in order to lead to teaching readiness, the constant self-development of the teacher. How many educators could say of themselves that they can match the different aspects of learning readiness by functions of teaching readiness? Yet educators need trust in the pupil and trust in one's professional capacity; self-control and the capacity to control the classroom; teaching initiative without hampering learning initiative; a kind of creative industry matched by a constant sense of still not knowing enough, a kind of professional inferiority in the service of professional maturation.

In the midst of junior- and senior-high school the child moves into a new developmental phase, adolescence, a living bridge between childhood and adulthood. All the internal acquisitions already mentioned seem inadequate for the child in the throes of another powerful struggle, a kind of repetition of the individuation-separation phase of earlier childhood. The child now faces the struggle for identity. He must begin to find life goals; a future occupation or profession; a place in the world with social and religious values and convictions; and to separate from the early family unit in order to be prepared some day to create a family of his own.

Erikson has described the identity moratorium, the time of experimentation in which the young person does not know quite who he is, what he is, what he wants to be and what he can be. The struggle for identity vacillates between the wish for premature commitment and premature independence, role diffusion, and lack of commitment. His learning readiness must include the erection of goals, the preparation for commitment, but must also contain the willingness to postpone, to experiment, to keep from permanent commitment. Pumpian-Mindlin describes omnipotentiality, the period of life where the young adolescent thinks he can do everything that he wants, and must slowly discover that this merely means he has not yet made a commitment and wants to try out many roles before committing himself to one.[8] The adolescent suffers at times from megalomania when he thinks he can do just about anything, and at times he suffers from complete helpless inferiority when he thinks that he must fail in everything he tries.

This inner task, the internal struggle, he must bring into the classroom of the secondary school. He has many teachers and really doesn't know which teacher interests him most or which subject is most inspiring and most useful. If he tries everybody and everything, he becomes a promising young man who makes promises and breaks them, nourishes our hopes and disappoints us, encourages himself and is faced by despair. The teacher who works with this age group is merely a transitional ego ideal for the young person, an identity model to which he may or may not remain committed. Thus it is that each of us remembers only very few teachers in his life who were truly important. These were usually the teachers who were finally chosen, half-consciously and half-unconsciously, as the identity models who became decisive for future choices and future commitments. The teacher of this age group must develop a completely different kind of teaching readiness, a kind of preparedness to be accepted by youngsters in this way and then disposed of, and to help them with choices without indoctrinating them or imposing choices. What kind of professional narcissism can be developed in order to bring such tasks about? Teachers in need of followers do not do well with such youngsters. But the teacher who can help them to make choices, and yet does not need to be chosen, will become the teacher of choice. He will develop a kind of teaching readiness that may match the age-specific learning readiness of the adolescent child (see chapter 10).

This phase is followed by young adulthood in which choices of intimacy must be made, but most frequently these choices of intimacy go hand-in-hand, and sometimes prematurely, with the learning and teaching problems around adolescence. A fascinating subject for investigation is the degree to which some people cannot make identity commitments unless there is guarantee for an intimacy commitment outside the family circle. This problem is aggravated by the fact that economic maturity, because of longer and longer periods of learning and study in our industrialized society is often endlessly postponed.

This is but a bare outline of the material that we attempt to master in our work with the teachers. We have found that the developmental and maturational scheme, if constantly focused on the learning and teaching task, permits us to develop teaching techniques which utilize psychoanalytic insight. Such utilization is not merely for prevention of emotional ill health nor for the treatment of children with pathological learning difficulties. It is the means of mobilizing instruments and understandings to further strengths for growth, education and creative development. Anna Freud has shown us how to use developmental profiles for the therapeutic assessment of the child.[6] This same approach can be utilized to construct profiles of learning capacities and learning readiness in a child (see chapter 18).

In continuing this work with teachers, our future ambitions are very much in the nature of a Utopia: they create enthusiasm and inspire us but often strike us as unrealizable. As a matter of fact, while it has been suggested that Utopias express the wish to return to an older state of affairs or an earlier period in one's life, they are also future-oriented and may lead to innovations and improvement.[1] It therefore seems permissible to design a Utopia and speak about our ideal master plan for the training of teachers, particularly postgraduate training of teachers.

At least one aspect of the early teacher training program in Central Europe still seems indispensable although it is hardly ever mentioned in discussions concerning the psychoanalytic training of teachers. This is personal analysis for the teacher. It is only through such an analysis that he can truly understand children, that he can learn to see the dynamics behind the different aspects of learning readiness or learning unreadiness. Out of his own personal experience, he can thus use psychoanalytic knowledge in order to develop the spontaneity, creativity and curiosity required to redefine and redevelop teaching readiness, to invent and to discover teaching techniques.

At present, this is an almost complete impossibility for large numbers of teachers. But we live in a basically generous country with enormous means—technical and financial; a country with a great love for children and an enormous reservoir of latent readiness to support experiments for the improvement of our society.

We seem to live in a time of successive crisis, a time where representative democracy seems to have become blocked, tired, non-spontaneous and static. Could it not, perhaps, be revived through an unbloody revolution within the educational field? Against the ever-increasing occurrence of violence—so often at the base of emotional and mental illness—we must put notions of healing, of education, of reinforcing our school systems with the best that psychological science and educational experimentation have to offer.

If there were the use of government and private funds for this purpose, we would be able to make available not only the technical gadgetry, the teaching machines and educational labor-saving devices, but also the most important ingredient: the personal element that affects the teaching process—the teacher, the professional educator. A profession trained and influenced as we have described could really create a brave new world. Such a profession would envision building the professional identity of the teacher through optimal training by means of psychoanalytic understanding, self-understanding. The teacher who himself had grown through the resolution of his own inner conflicts would now be ready for the solution of tasks.

Such an experiment should start with a postgraduate training program. The participants in such a program would be graduates of teachers' colleges who have had their basic training and their basic work experience in public-school systems. They would be selected as being highly motivated to continue their training in a program that might take between three or four additional years. This program perhaps could be compared to the training program psychoanalysts take after they have had their basic training in psychiatry. We think such training should be connected with an employment situation in a kind of fellowship arrangement with grants available for meeting the financial burden.

The participating teachers would undergo a personal analysis which might be carried out by members or advanced candidates of the local society and institute. Psychoanalytic clinics could finance that as they are willing and able to take low-cost cases, or perhaps scholarships could be made available through grants for talented teachers. This personal analysis would be an intellectual and emotional investment, not a rigid, official requirement for training. Here and there, there may be teachers who might usefully go through such postgraduate training without a personal analysis.

There would be academic courses, seminars and, above all, individual supervision, all of it tied to the practical work situation. A model for this aspect of the program could be found in the training of social workers who do their field work in agencies.

The course would deal with psychoanalytic knowledge and theory relating to children. But the emphasis, over and over again, would be on the application of psychoanalysis to general education, to teaching and to learning.

Related information would be offered from sociology, anthropology and psychology. The prevalent American learning theories would be discussed against a background of psychoanalytic understanding in order to bring about an integration of effort. Particularly valuable in this regard would be the work of such psychologists as Piaget and Bruner. The economic, the dynamic, the genetic and the structural approach would also be integrated with knowledge concerning the family and the interplay between child and parent, child and adult, child and community.

In this ideal training setting for teachers, we have combined service and training. But it seems to us that the concept of such a training center would be incomplete unless service and training were directly related to research. We would want to carry out educational research with our students, and one of the requirements would be a serious paper concerned with research issues in this field.

Most efforts today are fragmentary. Most of our small institutions do not have the professional and scientific strength, and certainly not the financial power, to support a program like this. But even if the unexpected happened and funding were guaranteed, we realize that our utopian demands may go beyond the ordinary sacrifice teachers today are willing to make for postgraduate training. Moreover, our demands may actually be far beyond the actual manpower that we have today as we try to develop *teachers of teachers*—psychoanalytically oriented, open to the other social and psychological sciences, objective and research-minded, but not aloof from the practical tasks. Despite such difficulties, our faith in such a venture has previously been expressed by one of us:

But then we know there is always the yearning in many men and women for real change, for a genuine revolution; there is the search for a true professional identity that gives meaning to one's professional and scientific life. And there are, I know, administrators and professionals who are not satisfied with just "running an institution," but who want to make their mark. . . . .

Since I am speaking to friends and teachers . . . I may ask of you that you believe in the impossible, that you believe in that impossible dream, that Utopia of professional education for teachers; and I want to remind you of a saying, ascribed to Ben Gurion of Israel: "He who does not believe in miracles is not a realist."

BIBLIOGRAPHY

1. Ekstein, Rudolf and Elaine Caruth. "From Eden to Utopia." *American Imago*, 1965, 22:128.
2. ―――― and R. L. Motto. "Psychoanalysis and Education: a Bridge, Not a Chasm." *The Reiss-Davis Clinic Bulletin*, 1966, 1:2.
3. ―――― and ――――. "Education and Psychoanalysis: New Tasks in a Changing Society. *The Reiss-Davis Clinic Bulletin*, 1967, 1:2.
4. ――――. "The Educator's Task in a Residential Treatment Center: Coping with Conflicts of Growth, or Growth of Conflicts." Unpublished.
5. Erikson, Erik H. *Childhood and Society*. New York: W. W. Norton & Co., Inc., 1950.
6. Freud, A. *Normality and Pathology in Childhood*. New York: International Universities Press, Inc., 1965.
7. Motto, R. L., Bernard Bail, R. Ekstein, and Arthur Malin. "Psychoanalysis and Education—the Emergence of a New Collaboration." *The Reiss-Davis Clinic Bulletin*, 1964, 1:33.
8. Pumpian-Mindlin, E. "Omnipotentiality, Youth, and Commitment." *Journal of the American Academy of Child Psychiatry*, 1965, 1:1.

CHAPTER 22

The School Psychologist's Quest for Identity

RUDOLF EKSTEIN

WHILE AN OUTSIDER CANNOT OFFER the school psychologist a concept of professional identity specific to his task, a psychoanalyst is not really an outsider. Psychoanalysts, as their science and their techniques developed, have taken an early interest in education, and have a long-standing and stimulating relationship with the field of education. Their first relationship was a kind of revolutionary attitude in which European psychoanalysts tried to remodel the educational system. This was very similar to what happened in the United States during the original impetus of progressive education under John Dewey. When psychoanalysis found a new home in the democracies at the time of Hitler, its practitioners found that John Dewey and his collaborators had prepared the way. The educator here was less afraid of frustration, less afraid of trauma, less afraid of punishment than his European counterpart. As a matter of fact, it was discovered or rediscovered that the kind of education which knows no limits actually creates dangers for the growing child similar to those created by the traditional type of education.

Since 1938, the development in the United States has been such that the educator looked to the analyst, the psychiatrist, the clinical psychologist and the social worker as the experts who would help with those children who showed any deviation from the norm. In other words, psychoanalysis was used primarily within a clinical context. Thus, psychoanalytic knowledge, during this phase, was not used to revitalize all of education, but was used like a little corner into which one would put all these children who did not fit. Thus, if and when educators got interested in psychoanalysis, it was in the aspect of clinical thinking in order to become quasi-psychotherapists. And too often the school psychologist has been relegated into a corner where he is not connected any longer with the core system, but where he makes decisions about those children who are deviates. From that corner, he must try to find for himself a niche which is more connected with the clinical field than with the educational field.

This brief historical review summarizes the social forces which define both the work opportunities and the identity opportunities of the school psychologist as of the present.

As Motto and I have suggested (chapter 1), we are now ready for a new development. If in the beginning psychoanalysis spoke about itself as re-education; if during the next phase many educators who became interested in psychoanalysis thought of themselves as therapeutic educators, or educational therapists; now would seem to be the time when, in full and open communication, psychoanalysts and educators truly become professional collaborators and peers.

Whenever people communicate with each other they try to identify and learn from each other. Sometimes, unfortunately, the quest for identification only goes one way. A great many analysts of the past, I believe (many may be alive today but are still living in the past), have set themselves up as identity-models. They have turned all school psychologists' problems into therapeutic problems, clinical problems. I think they did so because they—like everybody else—are inclined to fall back on their basic skills instead of understanding that the questions with which they were dealing were not necessarily clinical. I think that psychoanalysts in America forgot that psychoanalysis never was meant to be exclusively a method of therapy. Freud considered psychoanalysis as a basic psychological science which tried to explain personality and could be applied to many endeavors, not only to therapy (which, I think, is just a fringe benefit of psychoanalysis as a science, even though a most useful and worthwhile benefit).

If psychoanalysis becomes what it was originally designed to be, a basic psychological science, its communication with teachers and the educational system cannot merely concern the clinical. Rather, psychoanalytic insights must be translated into practical terms for application to problems of teaching and learning. That this sometimes occurs in the United States today is evident from a number of experiments in which analysts and educators work together. They work not as teachers and students but as collaborators, each both teacher and student, in the effort to bring together the knowledge from education and the knowledge from psychoanalysis into a new unified science, which will help us to meet our tasks better.

It is against this background that I must elaborate on the school psychologist's tremendous problem. He is one who tries to achieve a professional identity through his knowledge of what he stands for and what he needs to know. At the same time, he is identified by the community and the other professions as someone who has a special function to fulfill.

Identity problems have always been with us. They have come more fully to our attention now perhaps, in part, through the harsh dilemmas that confront us in an open, democratic society. In all closed tribal societies there is primarily a tribal identity. As soon as a society becomes differentiated and structured, identity problems arise. This is as true for a medieval society as it is for the days of reformation about which Erikson wrote in his study of Luther.[1]

Wagner's "Die Meistersinger" offers a useful simile. In that opera a young man who is a knight, thus enjoying a well-defined and accepted identity of which he is very proud, falls in love with Eva. Walther finds out that the only way to win her is to switch or enlarge on his identity. Only if he becomes a Meistersinger and is able to join the appropriate medieval guild, a kind of "super union," can he be united with Eva. In applying to the guild organization of the Meistersingers, he brings unusual talents with him. He is very much like the school psychologist who finally tries to acquire his doctorate and finds himself rejected by a great many people who do very much now as the Meistersingers did. Walther has his orals, his preliminaries, and flunks because he is up against a one-man admissions committee. The marker, Master Beckmesser, constantly marks Walther down because he did not want to meet any of the formal requirements of the Meistersingers, although he was identified with creative and productive work.

Walther had about the kind of feeling all of us have before the Ph.D. examination when we are sure that we know our subject better than our professors, but unfortunately have to live up to their bureaucratic requirements. When Walther flunks out, he has a depression and wants to give up his ambitions; he even plays with the idea of eloping with Eva and opposing the will of her father. Fortunately there is among the Meistersingers one Hans Sachs, the shoemaker, who has a great deal of wisdom. Even though he can identify with the Meistersingers, since he is one of their most devoted members, he can also identify with the young hero (by the way, I believe it to be the prerequisite of a good teacher that he can identify not only with the system that imposes rules, but also with those who must submit to these rules and must at times rebel against them). In any case, Hans Sachs, like an expert supervisor, told the young knight that he should not despise these Meistersingers and that he should remember that their rules make sense. No society could function unless it was based on rules. If only Walther could try to adapt his creative gifts in such a way that they could be figured—I almost felt like saying, "into the school system"—into the *Kunstregeln* of the Meistersingers, maybe he could succeed.

The hero does make a successful identification with the demands of Hans Sachs and does not give up his creative talents. He becomes a Meistersinger and gets the girl. With us, unfortunately, it is not that romantic. The university merely offers us diplomas and certification. And acquiring a professional identity requires even more than that.

In order to become a school psychologist or a psychometrist, a student—like Walther von Stolzing—finds himself up against the fact that requirements are many, that guilds are not only made up of shoe-makers, but that there are also tailors in it, and bakers. He must get a teacher's certificate, must be a psychometrist, perhaps ought to be a clinical psychologist, and must meet the academic requirements for the Ph.D. In meeting these and a variety of other requirements, the student gets the feeling that his identity consists of becoming a submissive victim of a variety of unco-ordinated and at times senseless require-ments. He knows that a professional identity is not made of submission, which is solely the identity of a willing slave. What he searches for, therefore, are those ingredients of identity which will give him a true and well defined professional role, which permits others also to identify him and which usually will permit him to identify with a model.

In terms of his functions, who can serve as an identity model for school psychologists as a group? With all the different theories, different ideologies, different job functions, different associations and affiliations among school psychologists, it would prove immensely difficult for a would-be entrant to the field to identify himself with anyone who could serve as a generic model. The great danger seems to be that one cannot achieve professional identification unless he had such a model in his life. School psychologists find that those who ought to be their model stand at least partially for something other than school psy-chologists.

Disagreeable as this is, it is not unique to the school psychologist. It seems to have been the case when the searcher for identity was young Luther, who tried to look up to the Pope but did not succeed in making a full identification; or when it was Walther von Stolzing who tried to look up to Beckmesser and could not succeed; or whether it was the man who described his effort to resolve his identity conflict this way:

> I can throw a little light, for anyone who may be interested, on my own motives. After forty-one years of medical activity, my self-knowledge tells me that I have never really been a doctor in the proper sense. I became a doctor through being compelled to deviate from my original purpose; and the triumph of my life lies in my having, after a long and roundabout journey, found my way back to

my earliest path. . . . In my youth I felt an overpowering need to understand something of the riddles of the world in which we live, and perhaps even to contribute something to their solution. The most hopeful means of achieving this end seemed to be to enroll myself in the medical faculty; but even after that I experimented —unsuccessfully—with zoology and chemistry, till at last . . . I settled down to physiology. . . . I scarcely think, however, that my lack of a genuine medical temperament has done much damage to my patients. For it is not greatly to the advantage of patients if their doctor's therapeutic interest has too marked an emotional emphasis. They are best helped if he carries out his task coolly and keeping as closely as possible to the rules.[3]

The man who could not find a single identity model that really would give him the identity that he finally found for himself was Sigmund Freud. He, however, did have many different identity models. He had Breuer and Charcot and Bernheim and the great physiologist of Vienna, Brücke. He had many such excellent teachers who influenced his future identity as a psychoanalyst, as the originator of psychoanalysis. School psychologists, therefore, can hardly depend on the emergence that perhaps happens once in a hundred years of a man who will be a second Freud or a second John Dewey.

What happens to us when we are being trained?[1,4] Training of clinical psychologists today, for example, is fragmented training. We work toward the Ph.D. We perhaps find identity models during our academic training, but they have little to do with the profession that we choose later. We are exposed to many people, some of whom impress us immensely. We find that the identity models that they offer are, at best, small fragments which we must gather together and with which, as described in the words of Freud, we painfully continue the search for a new professional identity. Nor is the search for identity completed at the end of one's professional training. Rather, I believe, this identity struggle continues to be important for us.

So it was for the young knight who wanted the new identity of a Meistersinger, who had to meet requirements and at the same time did not want to be submissive. The young man who wants to find identity models and has a hard time discovering them frequently will have to use identity models who serve merely as a negative model. This provides an identity to which one does not look up, which one does not want to imitate, but which one wants to outgrow, outlast and be the opposite of.

It is in this everlasting struggle that man finally finds himself if he does. In other words, we shall find that this constant struggle between individualization and institutionalization is a part of the pattern of conflict that may reflect a growth crisis or a crisis of stagnation. This struggle is even more difficult in the life of the school psychologist, since one of the better defined aspects of his identity consists of the dedication and devotion to a system—the system of education, the system of training. I am referring to "school system" in terms of the conviction we must all share, namely, that unless we develop good systems of education we cannot well exist and must become victims of stagnation. Since the school psychologist is dedicated to these institutions which provide a part of his identity, he knows that what he can or cannot do depends in part on what these school systems allow him to do. This covers a great many tasks, a diversity of interests.

What is a school psychologist? What are the conditions that he must meet in order to become someone who knows that he has met the requirements without having become submissive, without giving up the goal of being a person who carries within himself the potential of self-realization? The school psychologist must be a psychometrist; do more involved clinical diagnostic testing; function as a guide for teachers and parents; do some psychotherapeutic work; set up programs for mental health and for the prevention of mental illness; be involved with curriculum problems and with theories of education, learning, teaching. Many of these fragments, I believe, can assume a more complete meaning if the school psychologist thinks of himself as a professional person who is a part of the total educational system.

My general impression is that the school psychologist has been accepted by the educational system merely as a part of the S.O.S. Department. He is called upon when something goes wrong, when the teacher does not know what to do with one particular little Johnny who does not seem to fit in the ordinary school situation. At that moment the school psychologist finds himself besieged with questions of what ought to be done next. Should he talk to the parents? Should he test this child? Should he prove that that child ought to be removed from the school? If this impression reflects what actually goes on, I wonder whether this role which pushed the school psychologist into a corner of the school system was one he chose or one he was given.

It seems to me that a school psychologist should take on a real task. Instead of being in a separate corner of a school system, he should insist on being a part of the total system, whatever his special interests and skills might be. The school psychologist should see himself as someone who is to work within and on the total school system. School psychologists should not only be working on psychopathology, or merely developing programs of mental health. These functions are repair jobs, fringe issues. The real issue today is education as a challenging task in America. So the school psychologist should be a part of the school rather than apart from it, even if he must battle for his position. Whenever the school psychologist does have to battle for his function, he faces a strange and difficult problem because it makes a part of his professional identity taking nothing for granted even after achieving success and victory. His function will be a revolutionary one in the best of American tradition.

If school psychology is so deeply involved with the total school system in such a way that the school psychologist will be forever restless, he will constantly try to help the teachers and administrators improve the total system of teaching and learning. This does not mean giving up diagnostic testing, mental health programs, guidance of parents, guidance of youngsters who have emotional difficulties, collaboration with the child-guidance centers, work with psychiatrists and analysts. But I would like to see this collaboration enriched so not only a small number of children benefit from psychotherapy, clinical thinking, and dynamic understanding, but rather the whole system affected by psychological knowledge.

Learning theory will no longer be considered something that has to do only with animal experimentation.

This view of the school psychologist is not a suggestion for him to go into politics, although there is no school system which is not constantly being confronted by social pressures, by the ups and downs of the political process. But social realities, political dynamics, affect any function, as an analyst well knows. He does not only work with internal pressures and conflicts, but is confronted with social pressures as well. It would be a happy paradise for the school psychologist and the teacher, for all those who work in systems of education, if they could be developed regardless of what happens outside their walls.

We know that our children will constantly bring the outside world into the classroom. The parents will do likewise, and the administrators will do the same, as will those who run for school boards and those who run for political office in the educational field. All these problems enter the problem area of the school psychologist. They mean no more or less than any other challenging task in devising better techniques of learning and teaching, of helping students, teachers and administrators, and of working in such a way that progress is made in spite of the outside pressures that sometimes seem overwhelming.

Social life always affected education, whether we dealt with the training system of a medieval guild, a school in a cloister, or whether we deal with modern schools on the elementary, secondary or university level.

I would suggest that the school psychologist who works on his professional identity will most likely do best with his teachers as his professional identity models. They should be models only in the sense that great men and women are models, not final models which offer themselves for imitation, but transitory ones, fragments of a total identity to be built. Identity models are not to be imitated but identified with. As one identifies with such a person, he will be inspired by his model's search for truth, for knowledge, for new tasks, and this will help one with his own task.

To the school psychologist looking for true identity, I would like to suggest that no genuine identity is merely a copy of a great man or woman. Every professional identity the school psychologist is to acquire must add something to those from whom he learned. If the school psychologist will take from identity models and accomplish with it no more than that which he has taken, he will have actually done nothing with it. But if he will grow he will add to all these identities some "newness," something truly personal that will somehow be more and better than that which preceded it.

I believe that such a concept of professional identity spells out the difference between identities in a closed society, a tribal society, and an open society.[7] All that is required in a closed society is to be exactly like him who has taught one. In an open society, we create a social order which is always open for constructive change. We hope and work, so that our United States will forever be such a society and will never encourage people with fixed identities but will always foster a spirit which produces people who, rather than making premature commitments, commit themselves to core identities which at the same time are flexible and ever-developing.

BIBLIOGRAPHY

1. Ekstein, Rudolf and Martin Mayman. "On the Professional Identity of the Clinical Psychologist." *Bulletin of the Menninger Clinic*, 1957, 2:59.
2. Erikson, Erik H. *Young Man Luther. A Study in Psychoanalysis and History.* New York: Norton & Co., 1958.
3. Freud, Sigmund. (1927) "Postscript." *Standard Edition*, 20:251.
4. Klein, George S. "Credo for a 'Clinical Psychologist.'" *Bulletin of the Menninger Clinic*, 1963, 2:61.
5. Kris, Ernst. "On Psychoanalysis and Education." *American Journal of Orthopsychiatry*, 1948, 18:622.
6. Levitt, Morton. *Freud and Dewey. On the Nature of Man.* New York: Philosophical Library, Inc., 1960.
7. Popper, Karl R. *The Open Society and Its Enemies.* Princeton, New Jersey: Princeton University Press, 1950.

CHAPTER 23

The Education of Emotionally and Culturally Deprived Children

BRUNO BETTELHEIM

EDUCATION IS MAN'S OLDEST and most effective tool for shaping future generations and for perpetuating his particular society. Psychoanalysis is the newest and, up to now, the best body of theory for understanding and modifying human behavior. How strange, then, that education is still not informed by psychoanalysis, and that we still have no psychoanalytic theory of learning.

Psychoanalysis has a great deal to offer and to learn from education. By all rights the two should be intimate partners in a common venture, but, unfortunately, the relation between them has been most neurotic. It has been like a marriage where the mates, though aware of needing each other, do not really understand each other and, therefore, cannot co-operate. Disappointed, they go their separate ways though, for public consumption, they continue to profess great mutual respect. The offspring of such a badly managed union might be likened to a bastard child: namely, our present-day efforts at integrating psychoanalysis and education. Like its parents, this child is torn apart by unresolved contradictions; it is too sickly to succeed and too schizophrenic to realize what ails it.

None of this would have happened, if Freud's advice had been taken seriously. While he rejected as unfeasible the psychoanalysis of all children, he did feel that educational reform would require bringing psychoanalytic insight to all teachers. By knowing themselves; by having freed themselves of their own anxieties and prejudices; most of all, by having regained their repressed childhood memories and understood what shaped their own infancy and childhood, they could create a needed educational system. Children participating in it would neither be repressively molded nor be handed down old fears and resentments. The reason Freud's advice was not taken is that both psychoanalysts and educators were carried away by the methods of psychoanalytic treatment—directed toward uncovering the unconscious—and neglected the overall, humanist psychoanalytic view of man as he develops from infancy to maturity. Thus they turned to the methods of psychoanalytic therapy of neurotic adults and sought to apply them, more or less intact, to the education of normal children, though such methods are contrary to those of education. Overimpressed by psychoanalysis as a method, they ignored its goal which Freud himself posed clearly: "where id was there shall ego be."

By applying the model of psychoanalytic uncovering and freeing of the unconscious—which is good for therapy but not for education—they achieved an unhappy result. That is, the influence of psychoanalysis on education is an attitude that seems to run something like this: "Since freeing the unconscious does not seem to help in cultivating the ego, let's promote the id"—though this was never openly stated, nor clearly recognized. It is an attitude that reveals itself most typically by calling creative what is basically an expression of the id, such as the scribbling of the small child. One fools oneself and the child into believing that something which has meaning as id expression is therefore ego and superego correct—that is, contains a meaningful message to others—though it's not. Now, there is nothing wrong with the child's being able to mess and smear with paint. It is very good for him to enjoy such freedom. Only we stunt his growth if we view the activity as creative, instead of recognizing it as a satisfying experience. Even when his later scribbling or drawing has become self-expressive, it is still solipsistic. Only through a slow process of education or self-education, through observing and appreciating the efforts of others, through self-criticism and the application of appropriate standards, is mere self-expression transformed into personally meaningful and socially valuable artistic accomplishment.

This process parallels what students of language have described as the progress from a mere signal to a readily understood sign into meaningful communication. A signal expresses some global feeling, nothing more. It becomes intellectually useful—a subject for thought and some minimal interaction—when various signals become differentiated; when signs referring to discretely designated objects appear. Out of such commonly understood signs comes the development of communication which is the expression of complex ideas that are meaningful to others. Through meaningful communication with the environment, through messages sent and received in acts of mutual response, a human ego slowly develops.

This model of a slowly developing ego is very different from any that reactionary educators today seem to favor, be it that of conditioned responses reinforced by punishment, or the notion that the best education is one that ignores both ego and id and puts the child under the total domination of a rigid superego. The latter efforts are reflected in the philosophy of a Dr. Rafferty. That people such as he have any following may, perhaps, be understood in part as a reaction to the hedonism that has both attracted and disappointed so many Californians who felt that their state could automatically ensure the good life. Nothing automatically assures ego growth, neither reward nor punishment. It occurs only through having the right experiences at the right time, in the right sequence and in the right amount. The nonsense of such educational obscurantists does not really concern us. Only our own does. And what I call our own nonsense is the belief, for example, that either education or psychoanalysis can proceed without taking due account of the individual's social origin and the implications for his state of ego development.

I feel free to call this nonsense because Bernfeld, writing the very first psychoanalytic treatise on education in 1925,[5] realized long ago how different are the methods of education and psychoanalysis. The task of education is to induce the child to accept and perpetuate the very best in existing society. Psychoanalysis, as therapy, is a process in which the individual fights free of much that society has imposed on him. In short, education tries to perpetuate the existing order of the outer world; psychoanalysis to revolutionize the existing organization of the inner world. Hence their methods are opposite though their goals may be similar; namely, to enable men to create and live in a truly humane society. How understandable then that an education that tries to apply the principles of psychoanalytic treatment, rather than reach for its goals, must fail. That is why some of the best educators who become interested in psychoanalysis stop teaching and become psychoanalysts. This was certainly true for the very first psychoanalytic educators, such as Bernfeld, Aichhorn and Anna Freud. To practise analysis and education just does not seem compatible.

Interestingly enough, the same seems to be the fate of recent educational reformers. To cite only one example, there is Kohl[7] who, as soon as he succeeded with some inspired teaching of his 36 Negro children, gave up classroom teaching. I believe it was not because the existing educational system makes good teaching impossible, but because he failed to understand the real problem. He succeeded in interesting his pupils in some learning, but the issue was not to get them to learn what he could make interesting to them. The issue was to use education as a means of reorganizing their personalities so that learning would become a way of life for them. This he did not achieve. In fact, neither he nor the rest of us have solved the problem of how education can serve to reorganize the child's inner world. This education cannot do unless it applies the full psychoanalytic model of man, and not just id or super-ego psychology.

Freud seemed to believe, and so do I, that this can happen only if the teacher first reorganizes his own inner world and rids himself, among other things, of his own archaic anxieties. Most of all he needs a true understanding of the human personality, both intellectual and emotional, and of how and why personality is formed. Only then can he educate the student with due respect for both his inner world and the demands of society. Only in this way can the cultural heritage be transmitted so that it becomes a well integrated part of the personalities of the next generation and not a crippling process that fails to educate because it is an external imposition of society.

How then, does the inner world of many teachers impede the learning process in children today? To begin with, let me stress that all efforts to educate have a great deal to do with superego demands. Sublimation does not take place because of the ego alone, as we seem to want to believe. Witness the fact that our underprivileged children, who know full well that it would be ego-correct to learn well in school since they would like better jobs, cannot do so. The reason is that, in the arduous tasks of learning, their ego is not supported by the libidinal energy that powers only the id or superego. Or to put it more succinctly: all education is based on the reality principle. Therefore, while those who live by the pleasure principle can use an educational experience made enjoyable to them, they remain essentially uneducable and un-educated, though they may acquire bits of knowledge and skills. This is so because the experience of pleasure, even around intellectual matters, does not change the pleasure principle into the reality principle.

While Bernfeld's was the first psychoanalytic treatise on education, Aichhorn was the first who tried to apply psychoanalysis as a means of education. He wished to educate children who had never internalized the demands inherent in education, or had come to regard them as alien.[1] His first task, therefore, was to make available to them those inner mechanisms which alone power the educational process. The wayward youth he worked with were neither like our underprivileged youngsters nor our delinquents of today. But they resembled such youth today in being lost to education because they, too, did not function by the reality principle. Some were impulse-ridden, others extremely negativistic. All were disillusioned about themselves, about society and, hence, also about education. Unlike most of our underprivileged today, most of them were very much part of the middle class in orientation. Aichhorn discovered that before any of them could profit from the treatment methods of psychoanalysis they would first have to be changed into neurotics; that is, develop an overstrong superego. Only then were they treatable and, by the same token, amenable to education. They had first to be helped in establishing an overstrong superego with in-hibitions, anxieties and guilt before psychoanalysis as a means could be helpful for them. And this finding of Aichhorn is even more pertinent today.

Of course there are quite a few neurotic children in our classrooms —particularly those of our good middle-class schools, including our private schools—who profit nicely from psychoanalytically oriented procedures. On that basis we can conclude that the same method also works for our delinquent and underprivileged youth. But Aichhorn knew better nearly half a century ago.

His classic *Wayward Youth* was written before psychoanalytic ego psychology became central in psychoanalytic thought. That is why he felt it was necessary to make delinquents neurotic before they could profit from psychoanalytic therapy. While this may still be true for therapy, I doubt it is required for education which does not presuppose that a neurosis exists.

What education does require is a full understanding of the student: how he functions in terms of his personality development; the nature of his superego or surrogate; his view of himself and the ways of mastery he has acquired; what his aspirations are. Thus, if we wish to educate him, as opposed to trying to pound information which is of little use into him, we must know where he comes from, who he is and where he wishes to go.

How absolutely necessary it is that the teacher have this knowledge about his pupils remains unrecognized for historical reasons. In the past, practically all of the school population and even today, a sizeable part shares with the teacher both psychological origins and goals. And when this is so, all goes smoothly. But where differences exist, what the differences mean for education, and how they account for its failures, are not only unrecognized but make learning impossible. Moreover, until recognized they cannot be made the basis of educational planning and procedures.

These oversights are what bedevil so many of our attempts to educate the underprivileged. We resort to half measures because we do not rec-ognize the Janus-like character of education: it must reach the child not only where he is, but as the person he is, in order to guide him to where he is not. Modern education seems to recognize only the second of these goals. At least it seems reluctant really to meet the first re-quirement. But without the first—as Dewey knew, and Pestalozzi before him—the second will never be achieved.

Our textbook writers, for example, have finally recognized that stories about nice, white, blond, blue-eyed middle-class children are good material for teaching reading to nice, white, blond, blue-eyed middle-class children. That does not make them good readers for underprivileged Negro children. But the much vaunted new readers for Negro children still veer away from large parts of Negro realities both in illustration and text. No kinky hair there, no Negroid facial features. Their pictures show nice Negro children enjoying the corner drugstore, not trying to pilfer from it. They do not show or tell about living in overcrowded homes, about not knowing who one's father is, or of being subject to gang rule.

But even if teachers like Kohl,[7] or Ashton-Warner[3] whom I shall shortly quote, begin where the child is socially, racially, emotionally, it is still not enough, though very much a step in the right direction. It is not enough because their Janus faces look only at where the child is or was. Even if they look also at where he should go, they do not concern themselves with the vehicles that can take him there.

Let's look at how Ashton-Warner taught her Maori children who are probably even more outsiders of their New Zealand society than are our underprivileged Negro children. In her novel *Spinster*,[2] her heroine is a teacher who realized that these children wrote exciting stories of their own, only the titles of their stories were less apt to be "Fun with Dick and Jane" than "I'm Scared." So when one of them was encouraged to write her very own story she wrote: "I ran away from my mother, and I hid away from my mother. I hid in the shed and I went home and got a hiding." A six-year-old wrote: "Mummie said to Daddy give me that money else I will give you a hiding. Daddy swear to Mummie. Daddy gave the money to Mummie. We had a party. My father drank all the beer by hisself. He was drunk."

A comparison of these stories, and their matter-of-fact acquaintance with deep emotions about real life as it proceeds in their homes, with those told in the primers of our own up-to-date efforts suggests why Ashton-Warner's Maori children learned well with her. They did so because she taught them where they were. She recognized that an appeal to the emotions can succeed where an appeal to the intellect fails. In this sense she applied, whether she knew it or not, the psychoanalytic recognition of the importance of the emotions in all human efforts to achieve.

And so did Kohl, and many others like him. Only in the long run it worked as poorly for the Maori children as for the culturally deprived children in New York. They enjoyed learning what they enjoyed, and when they no longer enjoyed it, they stopped learning. What these inspired teachers overlooked—and inspired teachers they were—is that nowhere will the vast majority of teachers be inspired and inspiring;

that an educational system resting only on what the inspiring teacher can do must end in failure. And if they think, as Kohl seems to, that by changing the system they will be able to supply all our slum schools with inspired teachers, then they believe in the millenium instead of planning for reality. It is thinking of teachers as being near perfect human beings and, in essence, not so different from the thinking of the recent past when teachers were expected not to drink, smoke or, if a woman, have sex. Yesterday's educational system which asked such perfection of its teachers wanted no real live human beings for its classrooms, but angels from heaven. These requirements for perfection have changed radically, and the ideal teacher must no longer be the puritanic virtues incarnate. But we are equally self-defeating since we also expect him to incarnate a set of virtues, ones only found in the rarest of teachers, and even they seem unable to sustain such qualities for more than a handful of years. To base educational planning on perfect teachers and teaching is to cheat the overwhelming majority of all children who in reality will be taught by average teachers.

What is also overlooked is that much of learning is not just a pleasurable experience but hard work. And there is no easy transition from pleasure to hard work. If one has learned to enjoy both, then one can combine them. If not, one can do only the first and not also the second. Or to put it psychoanalytically: we do not reach ego achievements on the basis of id motivation alone. Id motivation gains us only what in some fashion pertains to the id. The voice of reason is very soft. It is easily drowned out by the voice of our emotions. If our teaching is based on pleasing the emotions alone, their noisy clamor will drown out the quiet voice of reason any day of the week.

How then do we learn? We learn best when the ego is functioning well, that is, when it is able to serve id, superego and the demands of reality all at once. Whenever it does not, there is conflict. And such conflict, where not resolved, as in sublimation, etc., detracts from the ability to learn or makes it completely impossible.

So while we can learn, on the basis of our emotions, what for one reason or another we want to learn, that's all we can learn. Such learning can and does take place on the basis of the pleasure principle. That is why educators who reach their students this way, as Kohl did, are amazed at how fast and how much their children learn. They also quit in disappointment when everything breaks down, which is what happens as soon as learning can no longer proceed on the basis of the pleasure principle only.

All other learning, which means most of formal education, can occur only when we have learned to function on the basis of the reality principle. Because learning that gives no immediate pleasure or satisfaction requires that we function on the basis of this principle: that is, we can accept present and even some future displeasure in the hope of gaining greater satisfaction at a much later time. With modern education, this later time becomes very late, perhaps some fifteen years later. Indeed, the more the reality principle is taxed, the more likely it is to give way. When this happens, the pleasure principle again becomes dominant unless the superego is very powerful, which it no longer is for most of our children. That is why the longer the period of schooling, the greater the rate of the dropouts. This applies to our nice middle-class children, even to college students, who will then be more likely to seek the easy way out that drugs seem to offer.

Here, let's not forget that not so long ago, fifteen years was half the span of a man's life. To be able to postpone reaping the harvest for such a span of time needs very powerful domination over the pleasure principle by the sense of reality. The longer the span of time spent on education, the more dominant the reality principle must be for any learning to take place. This, in terms of educational practice, is what is meant when teachers speak of the need for discipline, attention and concentration.

Fortunately for education as it now exists, most middle-class children still enter school with the reality principle dominant, with the ability to postpone pleasure for a long period well established. Because of this we can still believe that our system works, and that all children are fed into it to their profit. But it still works for proportionately fewer and fewer and, constantly, still fewer. This is partly so because the time spent on education has increased. But, more important, this is so because we no longer live with scarcity but in theoretical affluence. An economy of scarcity, at least in modern Western society, makes the reality principle seem the only way of assuring survival. But the image of the affluent society does away with a good deal of such an outlook.

When one's entire life was swept up with the idea of working now for rewards in the hereafter, as it was at least through colonial days, postponement of pleasure was in the very nature of things. But even then, such unchallenged ascendance of the reality principle had to be supported by the immense pleasure people expected to gain. Only the hope of paradise made it possible for such prolonged waiting for satisfaction; as only the fear of damnation could account for such a powerful superego.

Most of us no longer put store in such beliefs and no longer can or want to base education on superego anxiety. We know how crippling a price of inhibition and rigidity it exacts. What do we do, then, for those children whose school behavior shows they have not given up the pleasure for the reality principle? We either start them even sooner on a learning track they have no use for, and which, hence, is quickly ignored. Or else, we try to teach them as much as possible on the basis of the pleasure principle or on what little of the reality principle they have made their own. Only neither learning goes very far, though some achievements may look startling at a given moment.

Obviously a valid application of psychoanalysis to education would require us to assess the degree to which a child coming to the school has made the reality principle his own. And if he has not done so enough, then all educational efforts must be geared towards helping him to accept it as more valid than immediate pleasure.

This can be done, though it is difficult. And, the older the child, the more difficult it becomes. But I should at least mention that any ability to delay satisfaction of present desires must build on repeated experience that because of the delay, the satisfaction will be even better in the future. The injunction not to grab and eat a cooky right now will be effective only if the child gets a great deal of praise and affection for postponing. And that will help only if his hunger has always been satiated most effectively and pleasantly in the past and will be again in the very near future. No praise will work while the hunger remains, no demand will be effective without the conviction that postponement will most likely net him gains of satiation and praise, while grabbing now will bring satiation only. On the other hand, no postponement will be possible if the child's experience is "what I don't get now I'll never get."

That is why it is so often observed that the underprivileged child can learn only if the teacher's attention is focused on him all the time so he gets the reward of praise the moment he achieves. Too much of his life consists of the experience that if he doesn't grab it now—be it praise, attention or other rewards—he won't ever get it. This is another reason why an education that takes so many years to achieve results (jobs, money) fails to reach children who have no reason to believe that future rewards can result from energy spent now.

For example, in my efforts to teach teachers this seemingly simple principle I have nearly always been up against their puritanic ethic according to which waste is sinful and will be punished by scarcity in the future. This adherence to an over-rigid reality principle has served them well, has permitted them to go through college and become teachers. What they have long ago forgotten though, is how early their adherence to the pleasure principle proved ineffective, compared to the gains they achieved by modifying it in accordance with the reality principle.

But the children they now teach have experienced all their lives that "if I don't grab it now, there will never be another chance." So when the teacher distributes paper and pencils to them, they grab and, in the teacher's view, are wasteful. What the teacher does not realize is that these children, by "wasting" supplies and always asking for more, are trying to find out if supplies are sufficient, if they will be able to get more later even if they don't grab it now. Not to speak of how exciting it is for them to have all their fill, even if only of clean paper or pencils. Because it is only on the basis of such pleasurable satiety that we can afford to postpone. Thus while the "wasteful" children want to learn if there is any validity to the reality principle, the teacher prevents their learning it because he wants them to be living by it already. Most of the experiments children engage in to find out if the reality principle is truly preferable are more complex, but they are all essentially of this nature.

Once the teacher begins to consider the pressure these children are under, and what can be done about that, instead of worrying about the pressure he feels under, he will find his own ways to relieve the children's pressures on him and everyone will be better off. To understand that and act on it requires no unusually inspired teachers, but only ordinary ones who have been helped to understand what is best for everyone in the classroom. And this we can do, when we are no longer neurotically bound to our old prejudices about what is the teacher's role and what is the child's. We can do this when we start to consider instead what human beings are like and why they act the way they do; when we start to realize that the satiation of many needs must precede any learning of how to live by the demands of reality, theirs and our own. By the time we reach that goal of education, these two realities are no longer so different.

BIBLIOGRAPHY

1. Aichhorn, August. *Wayward Youth*. Leipsig: International Psychoanalytic Publisher, 1925.
2. Ashton-Warner, Sylvia. *Spinster: A Novel*. London: Secker and Warburg, 1958; p. 11.
3. ————. *Teacher*. New York: Simon and Schuster, 1963.
4. Bernfeld, Siegfried. *Psychology of the Infant*. Vienna: Springer, 1925.
5. ————. *Sisyphus*. Leipsig: International Psychoanalytic Publisher, 1925.
6. Freud, Anna. *Psychoanalysis for Teachers and Parents*. Stuttgart: Hippocrates Press, 1930.
7. Kohl, Herbert R. *36 Children*. New York: New American Library, 1968.

CHAPTER 24

How Can the Educational Process Become a Behavioral Science?

LAWRENCE S. KUBIE

IS IT REALISTIC OR EVEN DESIRABLE to attempt to turn education into a behavioral science? This question itself is based on several dubious assumptions, as, for instance, that only an "exact" science is Science. Yet "exact" is at best an inexact and relative concept; and Science remains scientific even when it accepts wide variations in the precision of its search for evidence. For it is the search for approximate evidence as a method for approximating closer to reality, never anticipating or insisting upon absolutes, which characterizes sciences.[15] Nothing excludes education from searching in this scientific spirit.

Another assumption which underlies this question is that any attempt to turn education into a behavioral science will destroy its humane quality. Yet psychiatry, medicine, the law and social work have had to learn how to become scientific without becoming dehumanized: i.e., how to preserve the precarious but essential balance between objectivity and empathy. This elusive goal can never be achieved perfectly; the battle for it must be waged continually by every medical scientist and every new generation of physicians. There is no reason to believe that scientists in education could not achieve the same essential fusion of empathy and objectivity as medical scientists.

The only substantial doubt about the possibility that education can become one of the behavioral sciences centers around the elusive nature of the basic data. This will be considered fully below.

The effort of education to become scientific will be complicated by the fact that the relationship between pupil and teacher, like that between patient and doctor, begins before they meet. These relationships are colored and shaped by residues from earlier ties between the child and his first authority figures: residues which are transplanted unwittingly into the patient-doctor or pupil-teacher relationship.

In education, as in psychotherapy, this transplantation of affects occurs on conscious, preconscious and unconscious levels. It has always played a major role in determining both the successes and failures of the educational process. Yet educators have never even acknowledged its existence, much less attempted to influence it.

The patient-doctor and the pupil-teacher bonds have many qualities in common, yet are not identical. Among the relevant differences is the fact that a patient is driven to seek help by pain or discomfort or disability, or a vivid fear of future disability. The pupil, on the other hand, is not driven to seek education by immediate discomfort. Moreover, the penalties which he will pay for remaining uneducated seem remote and uncertain, if he thinks of them at all. This is another challenge to research-minded educators: finding new ways of educating and stimulating the young to anticipate needs which will exist in the future.

In approaching these problems, the history of the evolution of medicine offers education many parallels which could guide its future development. Education should adapt to its special conditions some of the instruments of growth by means of which medicine evolved into a biological science out of its tradition-bound and half-mythological past. By doing so, education will be able to go more swiftly through a parallel evolution to become a behavioral science. The transformation of medicine into a biological science took centuries. If education today will apply to its unsolved problems the tools of modern behavior observation and research (including especially psychopathology), it can achieve in decades what medicine took centuries to accomplish. The recent technical developments which make this possible will be discussed below.

Such a development must start with the development and use of new methods for the perception of precise, reportable and reproducible observations. Our unaided perceptual processes are fallible. Therefore the scientist's slogan is Abraham Kaplan's adaptation of Nietzsche's dictum that science "comes of age only as it abandons the doctrine of immaculate perception."[1] In fact, progress cannot start until the scientist finds out how to locate and correct the errors in his own perceiving, recording and reproducing of primary data.[5,6]

It is precisely in these three basic ingredients of science that the breakthrough has come. New techniques are increasing the precision of basic perceptions and the accuracy of recording and reproducing them. Measuring and counting are also becoming possible; but it is not desirable to introduce these into a new scientific field before the first steps have become part of that science's accepted daily practice. Premature counts and measurements of dissimilar imprecise and heterogenous data which are then treated as though they were homogenous and precise, can only lead to fallacious conclusions. Therefore the counting and measuring of inaccurate recordings of imprecise observations are misleading. Now that greater precision in the gathering, recording and reproducing of primary data has become possible for the behavioral sciences, basic progress in education is only waiting for educators to master the new techniques.

One further general observation should be made about how education can become a science. The question was asked and answered by the great French physiologist, Claude Bernard, in the 19th century. He pointed out that the scientist, the philosopher, the theologian and the mystic are alike in having to work on the basis of their hunches, feelings, biases, prejudices and guesses. He added that what sets the scientist apart from the others, however, is that he looks upon his "hunches" as starting points for investigations, not as the end point of an inquiry. This is the spirit in which the educator of the future must approach his task.

In all psychologies the data to be observed and studied are evanescent moments of behavior, here briefly then gone. Since each moment of life leaves traces of change, these moments can never be recaptured precisely as they had been. In the past our efforts to study these transient moments depended upon our inaccurate reports of inaccurate recollections of inaccurate perceptions of something in which the observer's perception and recall were always vulnerable to distortions by the quality and degree of his emotional involvement.[7,9] Consequently the primary data of all behavioral research consisted of fallible reports of fallible recollections of fallible perceptions. This is a shaky foundation on which to build any science; and under these circumstances it is astonishing that the psychologies of the past (including psychoanalysis) were able to make any progress at all.

Today we have one-way screening windows, tape recorders, moving pictures in black-and-white or color with or without sound, TV cameras with acetate tape and monitoring screens. These can store and reproduce any moment of behavior for immediate study or for repeated later study. They can reproduce the interactions between two people or among several, and the sequences of events in these interactions. Statistically adequate, representative or random samplings of these reproductions of human behavior can now be restudied many times, both alone and with others, so that the errors introduced by the transient mood or lasting bias of any one observer can be balanced and corrected by the moods and biases of others. Furthermore, the subject himself can now add to these data his own recorded introspections and free associations, and also his own subsequent reflections on all of this. Added depth has been provided recently by the use of concurrent video-taped recordings of subject's free-associations, as he views his own image and hears his own words, all of which provides much subtle, additional data.[6]

These gadgets make possible a new precision in the study of ourselves, which in turn prepares the way for a new era in the study of the normal psychology, psychopathology and psychoanalysis of others. The same equipment can serve the same purposes for education. Educators must master the necessary techniques and apply them to the study first of themselves, and then of interactions among pupils and teachers, between teacher and teacher, and between pupil and pupil in the educational situation. None of this is easy, but all of it is possible.[4,14,16] Such studies will bring profound changes to many of the preconceptions which all educators bring to their tasks.

Perhaps the unique thing about science is the way in which it uses a day-by-day study of its own errors as its major technique for moving ahead. An experiment that gives negative results (i.e., that proves that a theory is wrong) is not as gratifying to the investigator as the experiment that proves that a theory is right. Science makes its major advances over the rough cobblestones of thousands of experiments with "negative results," thereby eliminating false clues by proving a theory wrong and preparing the way for the experiment which establishes the accuracy and adequacy of some other theory. This is the positive value of the study of error. It is a dismaying fact that the humanities, religion and education have paid so little attention to this.[15] Only the two disciplines in which death is the price of error—to wit, medicine and military science —have deliberately based their progress on studying their own mistakes openly in the presence of colleagues and students. Education must follow this example.

Among the various techniques for the study of the errors of human living, psychoanalytic psychiatry plays a special role; since psychoanalytic psychiatry is the study of man's failure in living and of his failures to learn from his errors and their repetition.[6,22,25] (The many controversies about psychoanalysis as a therapeutic technique have no relevance to this fact.[20]) Educators should long since have realized that repetition does not lead automatically to the elimination of error, that practice makes imperfect far more often than it makes perfect, that the repetition of error in large full classrooms is no help, that drill and grill are not the ultimate tools of learning. One cannot study errors in the abstract. This can be done only by the microscopic dissection of successful acts and of the individuals who carry them through and then by comparing these data with comparable studies of acts and individuals that fail. Progress in education requires patient studies of concrete examples of the processes and conditions of succeeding and of failing, based on undistorted recordings of both. Psychoanalysis and education must converge in the study of these problems.

In the past the psychiatrist shared responsibility for the dichotomy between psychiatry and education: because he lived in the special world of the psychiatric hospital, apart from the rest of the world, including the educator. To a remarkable degree the psychiatrist of today has emerged from this ivory tower. It is the officialdom of education who now maintain an aloofness from science in general, and especially and lamentably from the behavioral sciences and psychiatry. This aloofness is limiting the educator's personal growth as an individual as well as the maturation of his whole field. If the educator is to enter the stream of science, he will have to accept the challenge of the behavioral sciences, especially psychoanalytic psychiatry.

It has often been said that psychotherapy and education are related, and that falling ill is a mislearning and getting well a corrective learning. These oversimplifications are partial truths. They can be useful, nonetheless, if they remind us that advances in our understanding of health require parallel advances in our understanding of illness. This is the role of "pathology" in medical progress, which provides education with another illuminating analogy.

In education both the "practitioner" (i.e., the teacher) and the investigator will have to become familiar with the clinical manifestations of the neurotic process from infancy to maturity, including especially its subtle, subclinical manifestations, and their impact on the learning process. We cannot hope to improve the educational process until we develop clinically sophisticated "'pathologists" of the learning process. This is why the psychiatrist must come to understand education, and why the educator must come to understand psychopathology. If solutions are to be found to the basic unsolved problems of education, the future will have to see close integration of these two disciplines,[2,8,10,13] And the educator of the future will have to study carefully the process by which the psychiatrist struggles towards maturity both as a person and in his technical field. If he feels offended by this challenge from an outsider, I hope that he will study my parallel challenges to my own colleagues.

As long as the study of medical "pathology" was only a postmortem search for traces of past disease in dead organs and tissues, the practicing physician, the physiologist and the pathologist had relatively little to do with one another. As it became clear that this separation hampered the progress of all three, they became so closely integrated that today courses in normal and pathological physiology are almost indistinguishable. Each has learned from the other; learning about health from the study of illness, and about illness from the study of health. This brought changes not only in the personal relationships between the practitioner of medicine and the student of pathology, but also in the organization within medical schools and teaching hospitals.

If education hopes to launch a forward movement like that which the systematic investigation of failures[15] launched in medicine, similar changes will have to come in the relationship between the teacher (i.e., the "practitioner" of education) and the scientific investigator of the educational process and of its pathological distortions. In time this will also alter the formal structure of schools. In medicine this step gave birth to a new subdiscipline called "pathology." Education will also have to conceive and produce its parallel subdiscipline of educational pathology. Experienced teachers will withdraw from teaching (i.e., the "practice" of education) to become pathologists of education. They will need special postgraduate training in the techniques by which educational failures can be investigated systematically. Such training will, at first, have to be given in centralized institutes for educational research. This will gradually spread and become interwoven into the structure of all schools, much as departments of pathology have become familiar in all medical schools and teaching hospitals.

Such a development is not always happily welcomed. In medicine it was once regarded with critical apprehension. We must anticipate comparable reactions in education. Yet the educator, like the practitioner, will continue to be the dominant figure, just as the department of medicine remains dominant in medical education. This is because the practice of medicine challenges all the contributing sciences with the ultimate tests of their ability to use their knowledge of human biology accurately and effectively. These tests consist of the ability (a) to identify early subtle deviations from normal development, and also the subsequent distortions of further development which result from these earlier deviations; (b) to identify the conditions which are necessary for the initial appearance of these deviations and also for their continuation; (c) to predict the courses of these processes of illness, and to anticipate changes in them; (d) to alter their courses; (e) ultimately, to prevent the initial deviations. Thus, the clinical discipline of medicine with its emphasis on the identification of the processes of illness, therapy and ultimate prevention constitutes crucial tests of our knowledge of human biology. This is why in every medical school the clinical departments constitute the points of convergence and ultimate tests of the preclinical sciences.[17,24]

In the field of psychological medicine, the behavioral sciences must accept the same searching challenges: the identification of processes of psychological illness, their prevention and their cure. Together these are the ultimate test of our knowledge of human psychology. Consequently, a department of clinical psychiatry is to a school of psychological medicine what a department of medicine is to a medical school.[17]

The organization of education as a scientific discipline will have to proceed along comparable lines as it pursues closely analogous goals: (a) The educator must find out not only how we acquire new information, but also how, when, why and under what circumstances we fail to do this. (b) He must discover how and under what circumstances we are able to use bits of new information freely and creatively. (c) He must find out how and why even successful students lose their native ability to use new data freely and creatively during the course of the educational process itself.[12,21,26] (d) The educational scientist must discover under what circumstances it becomes imprisoned between conscious and unconscious restrictions and distortions.[16,26] (e) He must learn how and why there is some loss of freedom in the mere act of translating preconscious processes into conscious symbols.

In short, the investigator of educational pathology will have to study the influences which masked, universal and highly variable neurotic processes exercise both on learning itself and also on the creative capacity to make fresh combinations of new data.[9] Precisely because masked neurotic processes are universal, and also because they begin to invade human life in early years, they distort from the very start the spontaneous learning process. Consequently, the psychiatrist and the educator will have to join in the study of the influence of the early manifestations of the neurotic process on the vicissitudes of the educational process from infancy on. Once launched on this joint study, they will soon come up against the fact that traditional educational procedures tend to strengthen and intensify these neurotic obstacles.[9]

Here we find another significant analogy to the evolution of the primitive art of medicine into a biological science. People were trying to heal themselves and one another long before they were making systematic attempts to investigate how effective or ineffective their healing efforts were. Efforts to heal long antedated the effort to do research. Consequently, medicine made no significant progress for centuries. Early medical theories were products primarily of the temperamental and philosophical vagaries of their authors, who either submitted blindly to precedent and tradition or else, equally blindly, rebelled against them. Occasionally it would happen that some primitive theory turned out to have been correct; as long as medicine made no systematic study of its methods and their successes or failures, however, this was only an accident.

Let me repeat that it has been true of medicine, as it has been true of all sciences, that progress has come primarily through the study of errors. Medical advance began when doctors turned to the autopsy table to face their failures openly in the presence not only of their colleagues but also of their own students.[18,22,25] Challenged by these failures they developed more precise methods by which to study them, and then to rectify and avoid them. Before this, physicians had been medical theorists and practitioners but not medical scientists.

This slow climb to the extraordinary achievements of modern medicine required humility and honesty. Unhappily, nothing comparable is occurring in education. Education has not developed a similar tradition of daily self-evaluation in the clinic of the school. It has not developed a specialized subdiscipline of trained self-evaluators (i.e., educational pathologists). Education, therefore, has developed no new methods of self-evaluation, and has had no explosion of new data, new methods, new theories comparable to that which has happened in medicine. Nor will this happen until education parallels these aspects of medical history by developing its own techniques for the unsparing study of its own failures; by training its own specialists in the use of these techniques; by organizing, staffing and financing its own special departments of educational pathology as integral parts of schools from kindergartens to colleges, universities and post-graduate schools. Without these developments, education will remain a profession with many practitioners and many theorists, but no scientists. (This is close to the point of view recently expressed by John Walton.[30])

Some will object that education need not do all of this itself, that it does not need to have its own educational pathologists in its own department of educational pathology. Here again this medical analogy should supply the answer. Consider what would have happened to medical progress if, without studying their failures, doctors and hospitals had simply sent away those patients whom they could not cure[10] as, in fact, did happen in the past. Clearly no one would have learned anything; not the medical administrators, not the clinicians, not the laboratory men, not medicine as a science. Instead, the convenient expedient of expelling their failures would have produced illusions of triumphant mastery; illusions which could then be supported by building statistics out of the skewed samples which remained. If any doctor counts only those with whom some special technique is effective, he can delude himself into believing that he has found a universal method, and that it is the patient's fault if he is unappreciative enough not to get well. Yet this is precisely what education has done in the past.[23]

When a school failed with a child, the child was usually "flunked out," with a strong tendency to blame the child and his home. With rare exceptions this still occurs, from the lowest rung of the educational ladder to the top. Automatically this practice creates in any system of education a trend to illusion-building. As long as schools continue to dismiss their failures without studying them, improvement will continue to be impossible for teachers as individuals, for schools as organized cultural instruments, and for education as a discipline. Furthermore, when a school system goes beyond this and dismisses all who do not make high grades (as in some vaunted British and Continental schools) and then concludes that it has found the way to teach, it will be deluding itself even more completely. In reality all it will have discovered is how to teach a small, weighted and nonrepresentative segment of the total student population, a sample which wittingly or unwittingly had been selected precisely because it could use these special methods efficiently. Under such circumstances educators cannot explore and therefore cannot understand why any method may work with one small group and not with others.

The conclusion would seem to be inescapable. If education is ever to become one of the behavioral sciences, educators must stop dismissing their failures without studying them. In order to study their own failures, school systems must have their own departments of educational pathology.

Persistent skeptics, of whom there are many, will nonetheless persist in asking why education must do all of this itself. Why must it do its own research, develop its own methods, train its own scientific investigators, staff and finance its own departments of educational pathology? To this a relatively recent period of medical history suggests the answer. There was a time when departments of medicine consisted only of practitioners. Then so-called "clinical pathologists" and "clinical physiologists" and expert laboratory technicians were added. Their limited role was to make special chemical and cellular studies of blood, other tissues and body products.

Most practitioners continued to view with skeptical scorn these laboratory helpmates and their practical applications of basic science. Consequently, for a long time all basic research was carried on separately in the "preclinical" departments of physiology, biochemistry, pathology, bacteriology, immunology, etc. This cleavage between the preclinical and clinical disciplines fostered attitudes of mutually hostile criticism. The clinicians remained naive about preclinical science and failed to use its methods wisely; and the preclinical investigators were naive about clinical problems and failed to inform and guide their studies of health by investigating those experiments of nature which we call disease. They were too naive about disease to derive their problems from the clinic.

In the course of time, however, all of this changed. Internists, young and old, turned to the preclinical sciences; and the scientists of the preclinical departments sought more clinical training and experience.

Each began to incorporate the experimental data and the techniques of the other. Today we find clinicians in all preclinical departments, while in departments of medicine we now find physiologists (sometimes called clinical physiologists), geneticists, biochemists, physical chemists, physicists, mathematicians, statisticians, electronic experts, electron microscopists, microbiologists, computer experts, etc.

A parallel development must occur in education. It can never hope to mature as a science as long as it remains the poor relation of other sciences, dependent on crumbs of abstract wisdom from contentious, experimental, clinical and theoretical critics: to wit, the Rickovers, Conants, Bruners, Kubies and other outsiders.

How, then, can experienced teachers be trained as specialists in the pathology of education, if this is to be the first step in the evolution of education into a behavioral science? Their training will certainly require a new curriculum, which will include all theoretical and experimental elements of the behavioral sciences, culminating in clinical psychology and the psychopathology of the neurotic process. It will also include theoretical and technical data from psychiatry, clinical psychology and psychoanalysis. The curriculum will differ from each of these in the "clinical" data used. These will be derived largely from a wide range of classroom and playground experiences, rather than from hospital and clinic. Early in his training, the educational scientist will also need to be exposed in clinical settings to the manifestations of psychopathological processes. Later, however, the classroom will provide him with a type of experience analogous to that which the clinic and the hospital provide for the behavioral scientist in psychopathology.

The development of techniques for the investigation of what goes wrong in education will evolve out of existing techniques of social, clinical and experimental psychology, psychophysiology, psychiatry and psychoanalysis. Therefore the new behavioral scientists in educational pathology will have to master these first. His curriculum will also include those relevant aspects of human biology which require the use of modern techniques of electronic and computer research, research in afferent psychophysiology, in cognitive processing, in automatic and general muscular discharge, and in communication both within the human machine and between such machines. The departments of educational pathology would also have to be equipped to study the influence of economic, racial and national variables. Therefore, among the research pathologists in education there would be subspecialists in cultural anthropology, social psychology and psychiatric social work.

This constitutes a formidable list of disciplines. It would take any man a lifetime to master them all. Fortunately this is not what is needed. Education as a behavioral science must include them all; but each individual educational scientist will carve out of this only that portion to which his interest and his native endowments propel him.

Gradually, as trained specialists acquire maturity through experience,[13,24] as education becomes a mature member of the behavioral sciences, and as departments of educational pathology grow up in our first-rate schools, their tables of organization will come to resemble the tables of departmentalized organization of our hospitals.

I have already indicated that educators must be ready to study not only the variables in the students to be educated and the variables in the methods used, but also the variables which occur in themselves as teachers. Mature scientists in education will not repeat the mistake of a women's college which threw out an able psychiatric advisor because he dared to raise questions about the influence on students of latent psychopathological traits in the faculty. (In that instance, his specific question concerned the subtle influence on young women college students of a faculty composed largely of spinsters.)

By now it will be obvious that I am convinced that training for research in educational processes, and especially in educational pathology, is the most pressing need of education. I believe that training of educational administrators, which Dean Sizer has recently emphasized,[28] should follow much later. Even in medicine, for instance, it has only been since World War II that we have begun to train hospital and medical administrators and to award advanced degrees in this field. This development started after medicine had passed through all of the necessary earlier phases of scientific development, which education has not yet begun even to contemplate. Well-trained administrators are invaluable in the forward progress of any mature science. When they are introduced too early they tend to limit and restrict those initial investigative flounderings which are essential for creative discoveries. Later they can facilitate the applied research which is done by the scientists, and also the systematic testing of the applications of new hypotheses and new methods. In this way, if temperamentally adventurous and if trained to welcome changes (even when changes make their own tasks harder), administrators can help to implement the work of the investigators and to explore and test the practical consequences of their findings. These are valuable contributions. But administrators as such never break new ground. Without investigators to make discoveries, administrators cannot turn education into a behavioral science. Therefore, at this stage in the history of education, to place primary emphasis on the training of administrators would be like training a horse who has no cart to pull.

Finally the study of current failures can be carried on only where they occur; i.e., in the schools themselves. Here we face what is probably the most stubborn of all obstacles to change. Schools are as human as the men and women who staff them. Many a man feels secretly that it would be fine for someone else (indeed, almost anyone else) to be analyzed as long as he himself escapes that ordeal. Similarly, each educational institution feels that it would be an excellent idea for other schools and colleges to study their mistakes of theory, technique or personnel. Headmasters, department heads and university presidents have stated forcefully the importance of such studies; yet each backs away from the suggestion that he should expose his own institution, faculty and students to investigation. This is not said lightly. It is a condensation of fifteen years of frustrating personal experiences at the highest and most sophisticated levels of scientific education.[3,12,21]

Let me be specific about this. In 1953 and 1954, the *American Scientist* published two papers called "Some Unsolved Problems of the Scientific Career."[3] Among other points, these papers (and later ones as well) challenged educators and schools to try to find out what destroys the creative potential in many of their most gifted students, including those who successfully complete their training with high honors. (This continues to occur even later, in highly gifted faculty members.) With generous enthusiasm, several great scientific institutions requested permission to reprint many thousands of copies of the original articles. Furthermore, they responded to its challenge by admitting freely that they destroy many of those they attempt to educate. In conferences and in extensive correspondence, presidents, deans, department heads, research fellows and graduate students agreed that this was a vital challenge and that the problem should be studied. In subsequent years, three leading scientific schools went so far as repeatedly to invite psychiatrists and psychologists to make a preliminary survey of the local scene and to submit detailed plans for such investigations. Yet nothing has happened. The necessary studies have not been made anywhere. In part, at least, this seems to be because each school wants the studies to be done, but each one wants the studies to be done on some other school, not itself.

It is not hard to understand why this is so. All such investigations must begin by studying not only methods, but people: the young people who are trying to learn and the older people who are trying to teach and those who are doing research, as well as the interactions among them. It is only after a meticulous study of many individuals that comparisons of methods can be fruitful. Yet just here is the primary obstacle. People shy away both from self-examination and from exposing themselves to others. Schools do this, too. Yet it is not equally clear why an easy way around this obstacle continues to be rejected.

On several occasions, privately at meetings with educators and in writing, it has been suggested that the privacy and anonymity of each school and of each individual could be protected if a group of interested schools would unite to organize, staff and finance a special inter-school agency. Its sole function would be to carry on just such investigations as these, but with the explicit provision that when reporting its findings this inter-school agency would never identify any school because identifying a school would lead to the pinpointing of individuals. A further stipulation requires that the inter-school agency must never report to anyone or to any school administration, whether publicly or privately, its findings on any individual in any way that would make his identification possible. Thus all information about any individual, school or organization would remain "privileged."

Such a protection of individual privacy would be more than a humane duty. It would also be essential for the strategy of effective research. Unless each school and each individual felt absolute confidence that this right to privacy would be respected and his identity guarded absolutely, much vital information which the investigators sought would be withheld. Therefore from kindergarten to the highest post-graduate echelons, the study of the pathology of the educational process cannot succeed unless this principle is obeyed strictly with respect to all students and all staff. Though strict observance of this rule will make such studies difficult, cumbersome and costly, it will permit the pooling of data from many unnamed schools and unidentified individuals. It would thus be possible, therefore, to gather useful data, and from these to formulate useful hypotheses to test. Only if studies are carried out by an inter-school agency operating under these restrictions will educators gradually be able to discover how and why their best efforts are hampered and distorted so often and so unexpectedly.

In exploring these problems one other difficult issue must be faced. It is traditional to assume that education and psychotherapy should and can be kept separate from each other. Yet we cannot pretend that the student, whether child or man, can master new data in the absence of inner peace, or that he can use new data accurately, freely and creatively without psychological health. Nor can we assume that a man's intellect can mature if the personality as a whole lags behind, or that a man can become wise by acquiring facts apart from the far subtler process of emotional maturation.[2,13] As a total experience consequently, education from its inception must assist each student in the struggle towards that maturity which means progressive freedom from the tyranny of the buried residues of childhood. This will require the use of procedures which are derived from psychotherapy but which are not identical with it. Used for preventive purposes, they become part of the mores, procedures, organization and staffing of education as a scientific discipline. Yet this challenge runs counter to the prejudices of most educators, partly because it lies outside of their experience and competence, partly because its consequences add to the complexities of their life and job. Nevertheless, educational administrators will have to learn to understand and ultimately to implement this. The old reluctance to accept the unity of psychotherapy and education will have to be replaced by an open-minded, joint exploration of how to integrate them.* Our endowed preparatory schools could well start to move in these directions now.

Finally, I remain convinced that such developments as these will require the backing of a National Institute for Basic Research on the Educational Process, paralleling the National Health Institutes and especially the National Institute of Mental Health.[19] Whether this would be a separate institute, a subdivision of the NIMH, the Children's Bureau or the National Institute of Child Health and Human Development is a practical matter to be considered on purely tactical and strategic grounds. Because our knowledge and our techniques in these areas are still elementary, such an institute should be a place where men could carry on their investigations without having to offer any immediate services to anybody. That is, they should not have to teach anyone but themselves and their staffs. Their experimental school should be used for the testing of theories and methods, much as the Rockefeller Hospital of the Rockefeller Institute for Medical Research was used to test theories of disease and of therapeutic procedures.

Again paralleling the early history of the Rockefeller Institute and Hospital, such a National Institute would exert an influence throughout the world not primarily or solely by making startling discoveries, but by setting higher standards of sophistication and maturity for all investigators into human education. It would exercise a further influence by sending some of its trained investigators to other educational laboratories in other educational centers. Because the educational field lacks sophisticated clinical investigators of the pathology of education, as well as laboratories, techniques and functioning departments of educational pathology, such specialists would at first have to be trained in the National Institute. These specialists would then be placed in scattered areas to carry out their investigations in schools which serve student populations from different cultural, racial and national heritages,

---

* Elsewhere I have emphasized the point that when the lessons learned from psychotherapy are used for preventive purposes, schools do not become therapeutic institutions. The prevention of fission is not identical with fusion after fission has taken place.[9,10,14,16]

different local traditions and different economic and climatological challenges.

This would be another way in which our schools would come to resemble our best teaching hospitals in that teaching, research and the constant study of error are carried on alongside of intensive and expert patient care. No one need fear that this would make guinea pigs of our school children. Here again the experience of medicine is illuminating. Almost everyone knows that patients receive the most skillful care in hospitals which have programs of training and of research. When patients themselves discover that they are part of a research program they are pleased and proud and reassured. They do not feel that they are being used as guinea pigs. This fantasy is entertained chiefly by those who have never had any contact with such hospitals, nor any knowledge of what an active training and research program can do for the spirit of treatment or of education in any hospital or school.

In brief, this is a blueprint for the future development of behavioral scientists in education, for the development of education itself into a behavioral science, and for the development of schools into self-critical educational laboratories. All of this must be sparked, led and supported by the National Institute for Basic Research into the Educational Process.[19]

BIBLIOGRAPHY

1. Kaplan, Abraham. "The Philosophical Point of View." *Psychiatric Research Reports* #6, American Psychiatric Association, October 1956, 199. "Application of Basic Scientific Techniques to Psychiatric Research." *Western Regional Research Conference*, U.C.L.A. School of Medicine, Los Angeles, California, January 26-27, 1956, 211.

2. Kubie, L. S. "The Problem of Maturity in Psychiatric Research." *Journal of Medical Education*, 1953, 10:11.

3. ————. "Some Unsolved Problems of the Scientific Career." *American Scientist*, 1953, 4:596; and 1954, 1:104.

4. ————. "The Forgotten Man of Education." *Harvard Alumni Bulletin*, 1954, 8:349.

5. ————. "An Institute for Basic Research in Psychiatry." *Bulletin of the Menninger Clinic*, 1956, 6:281.

6. ————. "The Use of Psychoanalysis as a Research Tool." *Psychiatric Research Reports* #6, American Psychiatric Association, October 1956, 112.

7. ————. "Research into the Process of Supervision in Psychoanalysis." *Psychoanalytic Quarterly*, 1958, 2:226.

8. ————. "The Neurotic Process as the Focus of Physiological and Psychoanalytic Research." *Journal of Mental Science*, 1958, 435:518.

9. ————. *Neurotic Distortion of the Creative Process: Porter Lectures, Series 22.* Lawrence, Kansas: University of Kansas Press, 1958. (V. especially chapter 3.)

10. ———. "Is Preventive Psychiatry Possible?" *Daedalus*, 1959, 4:646.
11. ———. "The Relation of the Conditioned Reflex to Preconscious Functions." *Transactions of the 84th Annual Meeting of the American Neurological Association*, June 15-17, 1959, 187.
12. ———. "The Fostering of Creative Scientific Productivity." *Daedalus*, 1962, 2:294.
13. ———. "Editorial: The Maturation of Psychiatrists or The Time That Changes Take." *Journal of Nervous and Mental Disease*, 1962, 4:286.
14. ———. "The Unsolved Problem in Education." *Maryland Conference on Elementary Education*, Baltimore, April 11, 1962, 36.
15. ———. "Medicine as a Spiritual Challenge." *Journal of Religion and Health*, 1963, 1:39.
16. ———. "Research in Protecting Preconscious Functions in Education." Papers and reports from the Association for Supervision and Curriculum Development, Seventh Curriculum Research Institute, Washington, D.C., December 2, 1961. *Transactions of the Association* in April 1964, p. 28.
17. ———. "A School of Psychological Medicine within the Framework of a Medical School and University." *Journal of Medical Education*, 1964, 5:476.
18. ———. "Traditionalism in Psychiatry." *Journal of Nervous and Mental Disease*, 1964, 6:511.
19. ———. "The Need for a National Institute for Basic Research on the Educational Process." Hickory Hill Seminar, Washington, D.C., October 21, 1963 (unpublished).
20. ———. "The Scientific Problems of Psychoanalysis." In *Scientific Psychology*, Benjamin B. Wolman and E. Nagel, editors. New York: Basic Books, Inc. 1965, p. 316.
21. ———. "Unsolved Problems of Scientific Education." *Daedalus*, 1965, 3:564.
22. ———. "The Cultural Significance of Psychiatry: the Potential Contribution of Psychiatry to the Struggles of the Human Spirit." 1965. Distributed by Publication Office, Friends Hospital, Philadelphia, May, 1965.
23. ———. "The Ontogeny of the Drop-out Problem." In *The College Drop-out and the Utilization of Talent*, L. A. Perin, L. E. Reik and W. Dalrymple, editors. Princeton: Princeton University Press, 1966, p. 23.
24. ———. "Reflections on Training." *Psychoanalytic Forum*, 1966, 1:95.
25. ———. "A Look into the Future of Psychiatry." *Mental Hygiene*, 1966, 4:611.
26. ———. "The Utilization of Preconscious Functions in Education." In *Behavioral Science Frontiers in Education*, Eli M. Bower and William G. Hollister, editors. New York: John Wiley & Sons, Chapter 4, in press.
27. Paredes, A. L., and Floyd S. Cornelison, personal communication.
28. Sizer, Theodore R. "The University: Key to Reform of the Schools." *The Johns Hopkins Magazine*, 1965, 2:4.
29. Tausig, Theodore, and Sandra Schaefer, personal communication.
30. Walton, John, "Why Universities Are Failing the Schools." *The Johns Hopkins Magazine*, 1965, 2:23.

CHAPTER 25

Psychoanalysis and Public Education

LILI E. PELLER

WE HEAR FREQUENTLY about the educational crisis of today. The situation in many schools is tense, indeed, and, in some, even desperate. But many teachers and administrators feel that any help or inquiry offered by an outsider—like a psychoanalyst—may perhaps be helpful in the long run, but for the present it only increases tension.

Psychoanalysis as an approach, a method for understanding human behavior in all its manifestations (normal and pathological), has so far seen its main task as helping children to adjust to school and helping teachers to understand children who have special needs. These are tremendously important, yet psychoanalysis can fulfill a broader task; it can help define the function of the school, specifically as applied to the role of learning in the development of child and adolescent.

A look at the history of education reveals it has fostered both great changes and great conservatism. One special difficulty today is the survival of outmoded practices despite lip service to "new" slogans. Compare today's incessant talk about "motivating the child to learn" with how little is actually being done about it.

When living conditions as well as psychological insights are fairly stable, then we may confine ourselves to thinking of minor improvements. When societal changes are as radical as present ones, however, my opinion is that a thorough-going analysis is the primary need. But this is not a unanimous opinion, as Conant, e.g., demonstrates:

When someone writes or says that what we need today in the United States is to decide first what we mean by "education," a sense of distasteful weariness overtakes me. I feel as though I were starting to see a badly scratched film of a poor movie for the second or third time. In such a mood, I am ready to define education as what goes on in schools and colleges. I am more inclined to examine the present and past practices of teachers than attempt to deduce pedagogical precepts from a set of premises.[1]

261

Though I disagree completely with Conant, his sarcastic statement can be helpful as a warning. "Eternal vigilance" is needed in many areas, including the use of technical or idealistic terms as a means of avoiding the necessity of solving real problems. I do not agree with him that any discussion of principles must be sterile.

Schools are set up to teach content (information, and its organization; skills; development of specific abilities and talents); they also invariably convey and implant attitudes. The latter function is at least of equal importance with the former.

Formal education, as we know it today, had its start after the industrial revolution. The principal tasks were to teach the skills of literacy to all young children—not because the children needed these skills, but because experience had shown that the skills needed in adult life were more easily taught to children than to adults. Justifiably, it was taken for granted that children were unwilling to take in what the school offered, and would, therefore, have to be forced to go to school and to learn. It was expected that the great majority of pupils would leave school after a few years. This was the situation in Western society, roughly up to 1900.

And these were the attitudes such a school implanted: the ability to work with regularity, punctuality, reliability in details; deferring to rules; keeping order. These attitudes must rank high in an industrial society and the schools were effective in conveying them to the young. In past centuries in the Western world and in the underdeveloped countries* today, the school is asked to promote attitudes ("virtues") which the society needs more and more, but to which the everyday conditions of life are rarely conducive.

At the turn of the century, school psychology appeared and articulated the principles on which the schools had traditionally operated:

1. The child's intellectual development is normally independent of his emotional development. School starts at an age when a child can function as an independent unit for several hours a day. The school takes him over for these hours and looks after his intellectual development. His emotional needs and development are left to the home, the family.

2. Rewards and punishments that have proven effective in motivating children are used. If subtle rewards and punishments do not work, then a fuller dose will.

3. Children don't like to work or to learn. The school must, there-

---

* In backward countries the lack of these virtues is keenly felt by those who seek to assist their industrialization. Ironically, their absence is often connected by these same people with hereditary factors.

fore, "make" the child learn, and frequently check whether the portion of learning planned by experts has been taken in.

4. Making the child do things he dislikes—sitting still and keeping his hands in a certain position, being quiet when he wants to talk, even standing in line and just waiting—all these were truly and honestly believed educationally beneficial to the development of character.

5. It had been "established" by experiments with rats and squirrels that human reactions were determined by habit. There were "laws of learning," including the "law of frequency" which held that the more often an act (behavior) had been performed, and the more often a specific response had been elicited, the greater was the probability that it had become a part of the child's expectable behavior.

6. The other great power shaping the child was imitation. The child learned by imitating what he saw and heard, and he was most likely to imitate what he had observed most often.

The organization of learning was based on these views which supported the main reason for sending children to school: attitudes as well as skills needed in adulthood are best acquired in childhood.

Then came John Dewey's work. Childhood was seen by him not only as a preparatory phase, as a kind of dressing-room where human beings entered in an unkempt condition and which they left groomed and trimmed and thus properly equipped for later life. Childhood as a specific period of human life, with specific needs and values, had been discovered.

In addition to being able to take in attitude and skills, children have potential abilities and talents which can be evoked and nourished in the "early formative" years but are much harder to elicit later. In other words, in childhood it is easier both to put things in and to awaken abilities and bring them out than it is to do later. With progressive education it became the school's task to promote the spontaneity, the freshness of youth—a very new function indeed!

Today it is easy to smile at the romantic exaggeration of progressive education, but the fact is that it changed not only the schools but the teachers of the young. Elementary-school and nursery-school teachers generally began their careers with very different ideas from those with which they started their preparation for teaching. They changed in both what they wanted to accomplish and how to organize their classrooms.

To the functions of instilling into the child what he will need in later years and of protecting and nourishing what he brings with him, we today must add a third function. Most children, especially in the urban society of our times, need supervision and something to keep them busy outside their homes for long hours and long years. That this third point is sheer expediency may make some consider it wrong to ascribe to it the same dignity as that of the other two, but not recognizing this necessary "custodial" function interferes with the other things schools are supposed to do.

While educators and psychologists may differ about the most efficient way of learning, I see much agreement on the issue that the school's primary function is to teach. But there is no intrinsic value in longer hours spent in school. Indeed, the prospect of shorter hours is conducive to both better learning and better teaching. For the custodial function, other facilities are needed, clubs, youth centers, where youngsters are supervised and find worthwhile things to do.

Right now I see our teachers in public schools spending their time and effort on things which are not at all in the line of efficient teaching. I visit schools for various age groups fairly often and am often moved by the resourcefulness and dedication of individual teachers. But their number is in inverse proportion to the school's size. Now we also have a great variety of effective methods and ingenious teaching aids. The Armed Forces during the war years often accomplished teaching tasks in a fraction of the time deemed necessary before. But in our school system, neither outstanding teachers nor their methods come to our attention often enough because teachers are expected both to teach and to keep under control as many children for as long a time as they possibly can.

Too often today teachers as well as students "serve time." In the elementary grades, for example, teachers often use the first half-hour of the day—a time of great anticipation on the part of the child—to do their administrative work while supervising their class. The children do "busy work," things they could do at home or any time; those who are finished are expected to sit still or to read. In the average junior-high-school class, one must note how much time and effort the teacher is able to give to teaching those who want to learn as compared with the time that goes to subduing those who must sit in class and do not want to learn. A high-school diploma may mean that a student has learned certain things but it may merely testify to the fact that he sat still and kept out of trouble for thus and so many hours and years. In college some students may prefer to study certain subjects on their own and to report for a test; they are forced to attend classes and to sign their name to prove that they were bodily present for so many hours.

I do not dispute that at present children and adolescents (and society) are better off if they spend a number of hours in a place where they find something worthwhile to do than if they are always left unsupervised. But it is inefficient, inexpedient and undignified to confuse the function of promoting the best work, in any field of thought, skill or art, with the function of supervision, of custodial care.

Let me now briefly state the principles of psychoanalysis as they relate to development in the schoolchild and the adolescent (Although psychoanalysis has charted the very young child's development in far greater detail than it has that of the schoolchild or adolescent, our knowledge of older children is by no means scanty.):

1. The child's intellectual and emotional development are closely interdependent. Attempts to foster the one without caring for the other are self-defeating. The young child's need for a fairly stable tie to a mothering person has been greatly stressed in recent years, but the corresponding need of the school-age child for a stable tie to a super-ego figure has not found as much attention as it deserves. The school-child lives in a far broader social world than the preschooler and his needs, therefore, are not nearly so absolute. Yet a stable tie to some-body who knows what he does and how he fares, and whom he likes and/or respects, is vital to his social development. This need, to a certain extent, can be met in the family. Beyond that it must be met through membership in an informal or semi-formal, stable, small group. Does the responsibility for providing a friendly guidance person belong to the school? Is the school as we know it today equipped to fulfill this function?

2. Fairly stable ties to contemporaries are probably of equal importance. In our physically mobile society, the necessary ties to play-mates are often broken to children's detriment.

3. Seeing himself as a person who is worthwhile, competent, "good" —a positive self-image—is as indispensable to the child and adolescent as it is to any of us. Erikson has excellently stated the adolescent's need for ego identity with which even the young child observes himself, observes the reactions of others to him, the likeness and the difference between himself and others. He compares himself and his looks and behavior and possessions with others. This early self-image—in part realistic, in part grossly incorrect—develops in the adolescent into the sense of identity based largely on belonging to a group that enjoys acceptance and status. I think of ego identity as a bond to an ego ideal that either supports or interferes with whatever the child undertakes. The willingness of a six-year-old to listen to his teacher, to trust the child who sits next to him, to do his homework—all these and a thousand other daily requests are shaped by the image the child has of himself. On these three vital emotional bonds—to a superego figure, to contemporaries, and to the self-image—intellectual development, the unfolding of talents, the acceptance of values are all predicted.

4. During all development, activity replaces passivity of various kinds. The young child learns to manage his body, he learns to do things for himself, his understanding and his foresight grow. In the schoolchild these trends continue. It follows that the areas where the child makes choices should always be widening. Sound education must encourage physical and mental self-activity. Some schools do, but the trend in public schools is toward administrative units of such size that conformity to strict rules must take precedence over anything else.

Consider the network of petty rules imposed upon high-school students regarding attendance, use of library, trivialities like permission to go to the bathroom or locker. The suppressed but boiling rage is expressed in attacks upon teachers and in destructive acts upon school property. These outrages would not happen if there were not a general deep resentment among the majority of students and teachers who are cooped up in schools totally inadequate for their physical needs, let alone the intellectual and emotional needs of growing children.

5. Most educators seem convinced that children do not like schoolwork. It is interesting that diametrically opposed conclusions have been drawn from this conviction. The traditional school believes in the necessity of a complex system of forcing children to attend school, of assigning what has to be learned on a time basis and of checking regularly to see whether this has been done. Progressive educators, on the other hand, believe that learning should be postponed and the child's burden of academic work lightened. They also believe that children will gladly learn something if its usefulness for the child can be demonstrated (e.g., being able to write or read a note, to count pennies and nickels for a purchase). Above all they believe in the great value of those children's interests that are spontaneous phenomena of natural growth, uncontaminated by social factors or pressures of any sort. While these notions are partly correct, they are far too narrow.

It has been my experience that our clearcut differentiation between "play" and "work" is not valid in the child's world, unless one takes these to mean "what I want to do" and "what you want me to do." The crux of the matter is that educators corrode and destroy the child's desire to learn and to work by the forest of their regulations ("Do this now—in this way—in this place—in this sequence") and by their basic fear that children will not learn what they must unless continually supervised, prodded and pressured.

My experience with children, in groups and individually, with teachers and student teachers, has been that most children can really like or "go for" most of the things that we adults want them to learn, provided the framework is right and the teacher interested in his teaching.

The child's desire to approach and to enter the adult's world is tremendous. It often hitches on silly things, but it is so powerful that it can be redirected and continue to be a strong incentive. The child wants to be able to do what an older or admired companion does, or what a respected counsellor or teacher seems to value highly. In short, social pressures and influences fashion the interests of children as well as of adults.

There are the "component drives" which seek gratifications, e.g., curiosity, the desire to explore, the wish to acquire and to have as much as or more than one's neighbor, the drive to achieve mastery. Children start elementary school around the age of six, i.e., at the beginning of latency. This is the age when they have a grasp of reality and when compulsive traits come to the fore: the child likes to accumulate things, to measure what he has, to compare today's hoard with yesterday's, etc. He likes to repeat things, to embellish and polish a performance. Indeed, if the choice is up to him he often likes the very smoothness of rote learning.

Tests have an important function: students want to know where they stand. But again, tests can serve as a measure against children or as a tool which works with them. If tests are given at predetermined, regular intervals they will often not show the expected regular increase in knowledge and skill. Learning occurs in spurts, not in regular steps.

Under simple (above all, primitive rural) conditions it was the task of the school to stimulate, to bring the child into touch with the tools of information, of learning. In a world where information (newspapers, journals, books, TV, radio, records) is over-abundant, the school's task shifts to giving assistance in ordering the data which the learner has. Today's children are not only the workers and breadwinners of tomorrow, they are also the future participants of fast increasing hours of leisure. For a constructive use of leisure a variety of talents, interests, and versatile skills need to be nourished in childhood and adolescence.

As I have said, school may be called upon to foster attitudes that society needs, but that conditions in everyday life do not favor. In the early industrial era, the ability of growing segments of the population to produce a specific output over prolonged periods was needed. The school promoted this ability, this attitude toward work while contemporary conditions did not. Today regularity, order, cleanliness, conformity to rules may need reinforcement, but they are not the school's main task. A very different attitude is now needed. Many people are uninterested in their work. The social conditions favor this attitude of uninvolvement, which is conducive neither to good work nor to mental health. School could counteract this aloofness, but not by rigid timetables or external controls, which work against the investment of real interest. A school that leaves choices of many kinds to the student makes learning more efficient. I plead for such a school not only for its efficiency but because the experience of commitment to serious work is more significant than any learning content.

BIBLIOGRAPHY

1. Conant, James B. *The Child, the Parent, the State.* Cambridge: Harvard University Press, 1959.

CHAPTER 26

Who Owns the School in Our Changing Society?

ALBERT J. SOLNIT

IN RAISING THE QUESTION, "Who owns the school?" I want to consider four problems. In doing so I am using "ownership" in the sense of who decides how to use the school and what its influence is now and in the future. The school is a "corporation" which has many stockholders at different levels as well as several levels of management and executive leadership. "Ownership" can be defined in terms of: possession, occupancy, usefulness, and that with which you live and work. It involves the buildings, the brick and mortar and soil; the people who live and work in the buildings; the activities in which they participate—what they do together, the results from what they do together, and the pressures under which they live together in the school community. The four problems are:

1. How does the student use his ownership of his school and how can his ownership be clarified and strengthened?

2. How can the parents of students exercise their options and sponsor their school in a manner that enriches the school community? This ownership allows the parents to pay back to the school the debts they incurred as a result of their own education. This, of course, also permits the school to ask how it can compensate the parents for the poor or unsatisfactory educational experience they had in their own school.

3. How do the teachers and their administrative colleagues exert their ownership of the school community? Is their investment one that enables them to grow professionally and to fulfill themselves in one of the great callings that human civilization has created? What interferes with the faculty's fierce and prideful ownership of their school?

4. How does the community express its sponsorship and its pride and fears about the schools it owns?

The pressures brought to bear upon the individual student, his responses to them and the desirable and undesirable influences resulting from them should be considered in terms of the aims of formal education. It is assumed here that the major aim of education is to prepare each student to be able to live his own life in a constructive and socially productive manner, and to be able to minimize the tendencies to become a victim of his environment and its pressures. In short, our educational activities should be designed to help the student live his life rather than be lived by it. This aim can be achieved through three sources of pressure, which are, simultaneously, sources of power. These enormous sources of stimulation represent energies to explore and understand the environment; to clarify and resolve conflict, to permit the individual to adapt to his environment while reshaping it. At the same time, these resources represent the pressures to conform, to limit and to regulate the expression or discharge of the vital energies necessary for growing, developing and expressing one's self.

These pressures and powers are: First, the child himself and his ambitions to grow up with a good self-opinion as warranted by his achievements and sense of direction. Second, the parents and their expectations that their children will realize their own potential, fulfill the parents' hopes and gain the community's approval. And finally, the teachers and their ambitions to help the children succeed as adults by acquiring the tools that can provide access to knowledge, understanding and the judgment necessary for constructive social planning. The educator aims to facilitate this climb to adulthood along lines that encourage self-expression and courageous social adaptation. Moreover, he has the ambition to fulfill himself as that professional representative of society who shapes the child's education into an essential lifeline along which desirable cultural traditions and tools can be transmitted. The teacher's function—his power and the pressure he brings to bear—stems from our society's charge that the educator promote each child's active learning appropriate to that child's development capacities and his social and cultural background through exploiting the available resources in the school and its community.

In the case of the first source of pressure and power, the student, one is dealing with pressures to produce or conform, and with the power to express, seek, probe and master. In addition, each individual student offers various combinations of these influences in different proportions, with different shades of emphasis and with ever-changing relationships between these forces. Among the child's most dynamic sources of power are his impulses, his drives and his unfolding capacity to become a unique person who has borrowed from many models and yet retains his own individuality, whether dramatic, ordinary or uncommon,

Sylvia Ashton-Warner in the introduction to her remarkable book, Teacher,[1] said:

What a dangerous activity reading is, teaching is, all this plastering on of foreign stuff. Why plaster on at all when there is so much inside already. So much locked in, if only I could get it out and use it as working material and not dried out either. If I had a light enough touch it would just come out under its own volcanic power. And psychic power, I read in bed this morning, is greater than any other power in the world. What an exciting and frightening business it would be, even that which squeezes through now is amazing enough. In the safety of the world behind my eyes where the inspector's shade cannot see, I picture the infant room as one widening crater loud with the sound of emptying creativity. Every subject somehow in a creative vent. What lovely behavior of silk sacked clouds. . . . An organic design, a growing living changing design, the normal and healthful design. Unsentimental and merciless and shockingly beautiful.

Of course the younger child is more eruptible and more direct in showing his colorful, pathetic and humorous side. He also caves in more suddenly when caught between the pressure of his own drives and intense feelings and the demand that he become a member of a civilized group of peers and take up the tools of communication, symbolic expression and mental reflection. In the midst of this crucial transformation of volcanic energies, the young student also experiences romantic love and fearful hatred for his teachers and others who constitute his new community. Most of us remember the passionate day dreams of those early days of kindergarten and the first and second grades. "If only she will wait until I grow up, we could get married," said one little boy about his teacher. Of such romantic love, displaced from the home, is the stuff that passionate education is made.

However, though the love is unique, the learning performance may be average. This may be when the expectation of the parents and the dedication of the teacher add up to "this child is underachieving." But who is underachieving? The child? The parents? The teacher? The child's society? His community? His culture? There are no ready answers, only those that are worked out in a manner that reflects the uniqueness of each child working together with his teacher and his parents.

I am reminded of a "Peanuts"[2] cartoon strip in which Lucy says to Charlie Brown, "You got a C in History, that's only average." Charlie Brown retorts, "So what, I'm an average student in an average school in an average community." And then he adds, "What's wrong with being average?" Lucy, hoping to have the last word replies, "Because you're capable of doing much better." For a change, Charlie gets the last word: "That's the average answer."

The older child, with increasingly independent ways of acquiring the basic skills and knowledge and the growing importance of his peer group, is not nearly so vulnerable to his own impulsive reactions and energies. Though he may yield to and depend upon the pressures of his peer group, his own conscience is relatively well developed if unstable and often too strict. His basic skills of reading, writing and reciting are by now well established. In junior-high school he begins to hear about the work market or college, about the fearful consequences of not being in the right group, or of being caught in a track from which he can't escape.

Meanwhile, the world about him exhorts him to follow the laudable aims of "Peace on Earth, Goodwill to Man," while this same world demonstrates a glaring discrepancy between what it professes and what it permits or encourages. The pressure is on. The widening functions of school include special clubs, civic or community projects, and the acquisition of musical, artistic and many technical skills. There are many other opportunities to practice becoming a part of a group of peers that increasingly guides itself in the busy school week and week end.

Adults are concerned that if they don't demand or coax, students will not participate in these less formal aspects of the school program, let alone initiate or organize such activities. It's like the familiar story of the child who didn't talk until he was five or six years of age. He seemed bright enough, was developing well and understood everything, but he never would say a word. One day at breakfast he suddenly said to his mother, "For heaven's sake, why is the cereal so cold?" She was ecstatic. He spoke well; he pronounced his words clearly, the grammar was correct; and he even sounded like other members of the family. Instead of answering his question she said, "But why, why didn't you ever speak until now?" And he thought a moment and said, "Well, up until now everything was perfect." The child responds to the felt need of his reality. But these conditions must be met. Otherwise, the child reacts as in the story about the boy who tried to face the social reality, and when it wasn't tolerable, substituted another reality.

This story concerns a little boy who was scolded by his older sister for taking thirteen candies. He said, "I did not take thirteen candies. I can count, too, you know." His sister said, "Come now, you did take those candies and you weren't supposed to." He said, "I took only three candies." His sister, older, unremitting in her aims at discipline through scolding, and counting on her brother's dawning capacity for guilt, said,

"I know how many you took. I counted them and it was thirteen." His tolerance of self-disapproval having been exceeded, he said, "If it was thirteen, I didn't take any at all!" Sometimes we adults don't leave room for the child to turn around before he goes forward.

The reality we are examining today is that which is found at just the right distance between too much pressure and too little pressure, between an easy conformity and a needlessly slavish non-conformity. It must be found between the large number of viable alternatives that enable the child to be his own person and yet to retain the richness and pride of his own cultural heritage. The adolescent has a particular need to be active in helping us—or showing us the way to a brave new world. And yet the adolescent's approach has to represent his way of gaining some distance from his parents and other adults without closing off his own pathways to the return road to a new relationship with his parents —a form of comradeship in which mutual respect is an essential feature. The adolescent's line of development enables him to explore, experiment, rebel and march forward in order to have time to seek and find himself and his world anew. It is true that a local election today would not permit our junior- or senior-high school students to vote, but they should "own" part of their school and their community. They should find opportunities to form a collaborative alliance with their instructors as well as their peers, if they are to help us find the right distance between the choices mentioned above.

Educators—the school—can help students exploit or resolve many of these inevitable pressures in the service of mastery, sound learning and balanced personality development. As we formulate the principles that will summarize our understanding of this process, we should keep in mind several assumptions:

1. That the inner or development pressures and drives of the student and the pressures and power that stem from the environment are dynamic, multi-influenced, unfolding and changing, at times predictably;

2. That the family is also a changing, developing social unit, the bedrock of our culture;

3. That the world is changing so rapidly—our communities reflect the impact of the realities of nuclear energy, space explorations, rapid transportation and communication—that the need to find the constructive or safe distance between self-expression and self-control is critical;

4. That a school without conflict is neither possible nor desirable, since the student is able to achieve understanding and mastery by facing and working through conflict (If there's no heat, there'll be no light!);

5. That as the family and faculty have their limitations, so has the

student; an essential function of education is to help the student define and cope with both his limitations and his assets;

6. That there is an inevitable discrepancy between what the child achieves and what he, his family, his instructors, and his peers expect of him. What is crucial are not these discrepancies but rather their degree and characteristics, and the resources that the student develops in coming to grips with them;

7. And, finally, that children learn from each other as well as from the teacher, which in part is implied in the aphorism, "When there's too much teaching being done, there may not be enough learning."

In assisting the child's coping with the many pressures which impinge upon him, educators must constantly and critically examine the priorities of the curriculum and the other demands that the school supports or sponsors. Purposeful revision should be a continuous ongoing process.

In terms of the pressures experienced by the educators, it is essential to keep in mind the special risk all teachers face. They are exposed to the temptations involved in communicating with the student at his level, at the same time that they represent the guiding adult model. That is, in developing empathy for the child and in providing a part model for him, the teacher may regress to childishness. This is a necessary risk associated with effective communication with the child since the teacher, a unique authority and guiding adult, identifies with the student in order to influence him educationally. Such a partial identification with the student enables the teacher to exert an organizing and regulating influence on the student and his behavior in the school. This, in turn, reflects the student's partial identification with the teacher.

There is a very knotty problem in this. If the teacher does not understand the child, cannot empathize with him, and cannot put himself or herself into the student's shoes, then the alliance of student and teacher necessary to promote teaching and learning will not evolve. On the other hand, the risk is that the teacher will regress to the level of the child. This requirement and risk are one feature of the educator's work that makes each day so exhausting and so challenging. The teacher has to allow himself to regress a little in order to understand what the student is trying to indicate as a preferred way of learning. Of course, the age of the child, as well as his characteristic ways of learning, determine the degree and kind of pressure and stimulation that this demand creates for each teacher.

Although the teacher has 25 or 30 children in his classroom, he gradually makes a silent but unique arrangement with each child. As the school year progresses, these unique arrangements allow him to establish the teacher-student alliances that enable children to learn individually and as members of a class group. This alliance is a cumulative one which crystallizes into the awareness by the student that he feels a sense of ownership, pride and responsibility for his teacher and his class. Thus, the teacher is increasingly aware, again in a cumulative way, of the uniqueness of each child in the classroom and of the class as a group. The teacher, at some point, feels the crystallization of a sense of ownership, pride and responsibility for each of the students in the class and for the class as a group. The parents, through their active interest and participation in the lives of their children and school, also achieve involvement and ownership.

Therefore, one of the most important clarifying questions to raise is, who owns the school? The students must own part of it. Otherwise they are not going to be able to use pressures within themselves, and those stemming from their family and their school experiences, to enable them to learn, to cope, to become more independent and to find the right balance between conformity and non-conformity.

How do the students own the school? The answer comes from considering the child's developmental characteristics and tasks. Obviously the kindergarten-age child is going to own the school somewhat differently from the high-school student. The younger child is going to be much more tentative. He will indicate that he would prefer to own his home rather than the school. Perhaps his primary task is to achieve the separation and the beginning investment in school, which will yield long-term dividends in an ownership of "stock" in his school.

As the student grows older, he gradually realizes that in order to continue to own part of the school and to own ever-increasing amounts of it, he has to acquire the tools that the school provides so that he can also be increasingly free to express himself and exert his influence. Therefore, as the student moves into the first and second grade, his ability to learn and to use the symbolic expressions inherent in reading, writing, recitation and in the use of mathematical language and concepts, will become the means through which ownership is expressed.

Then the student and students will begin to form into a group, and into different groups. Groups begin to form in nursery school and take increasingly clear shape in each succeeding grade. The power of the group reaches a new height at the beginning of junior-high school when the student-groups often tell the teacher what they want and what they think they should have. Although they are not quite old enough to have that authority, they may have developed a variety of ways of attempting to assert their aims and wishes.

Assuming that the learning of formal material is proceeding at an expected pace, the functioning and experience of the peer group now begins to be a primary interest, psychologically and socially. Evidence of the teenager's interest in ownership of the school becomes manifest through many of the peer group activities both within the school curriculum and in extra-curricular settings. This is seen in pride in class performance, self-government, athletics and cultural or special skill clubs. What had started out as a huge effort to achieve separation from the home also aims toward retaining ownership in the family at home, at the same time as learning and development have proceeded in a relatively balanced manner with the resultant acquisition of ownership of the school.

The degree to which our students express pride in their school and the degree to which they feel they can fruitfully influence their school is a reflection of how well the social, educational and biological pressures in a school community are being exploited constructively.

As this intellectual, social and emotional investing has taken place, the students will pay greater attention to the rules of this complex school community life with its increasing degree of specialization. They seem to ask: How can one get along? From whom can one expect what? And what can one share with his peers which can no longer be shared with adults?

And then the adolescent makes his contribution. How do the faculty's attitudes and practices help him? How is he enabled to use his own biological and psychological pressures, and the pressures created by the demands and opportunities of the school, to further his learning and his search for the adult he will become? This question can be fruitfully paraphrased as: How does the school enable the teenager to acquire an active and appropriate amount and kind of ownership of his school community and experiences? In high school the student begins to think of achievement in the context of a permanent pattern for himself. He becomes aware of the expectation from himself and others that the capacities to form human relationships and to work may forecast his own future patterns of work and human relationships. As the expectation of industriousness and of long-term personal relationships with peers of the same sex and opposite sex develops, there also emerges the expectation of dependability. One can gradually know what each person or group represents and others can know what one stands for along certain lines. This is a prolonged dynamic process often changing in a spectacular and dramatic fashion as the adolescent explores, experiments and tries new ways to get along. This is accompanied by the eventual expectation that there will emerge an adult whose work and personal relations can be considered characteristic for that person.

Meanwhile, what is going on at home? What are the needs of the parents, the family? They have to cope with their own aspirations for their children as well as with their perception of how their offspring is impressing the community, including the school. Parents also have to cope with the fact that they are losing their little child and gaining an individual who is unique but who, at the same time, reminds them of themselves, sometimes reproachfully.

The concept of self-esteem is one particular inventory item that is shared by the parents, the student and by the school faculty. What is the nature of the student's development and school achievement that alters and influences the family self-esteem as a group within their own community? How is this reflected in the relationship between the parents and the faculty and between the parents and their own children? This question should be examined in detail.

And finally, what about the school faculty and administration; how do they own the school? Sometimes educators think they own too much of it and wish someone would help them shoulder the weight of it. They have needs, also, and do not feel they have proper ownership in the school if they feel overworked and underpaid. If their social status is one which they feel is an inaccurate reflection of the self-esteem they should have, their pride in ownership will be jeopardized. If they think of their own needs in terms of what is practical, of an accurate assessment of their worth, and in terms of the support of their community, they can estimate the difficulties in serving as a model for their students. How can the students reach a level of accurate, therefore healthy, self-esteem, if the teacher's self-esteem is distorted? Distortions of self-esteem in the teacher or in the student create unhealthy and destructive pressures in the school community. This brings up certain basic considerations. The ratio of teachers to students, salaries and future opportunities for advancement are among the most important factors that can promote or sap the educator's self-esteem.

In regard to the school faculty, how do they work together with children in tailoring curriculum so conformity and non-conformity are well balanced? The most crucial area in which beliefs about conformity and non-conformity are dramatized and demonstrated is the degree to which the teacher can tailor the curriculum and the individual learning experiences of each child in the classroom who needs such modifications. Obviously, such tailoring is limited and is brought to bear where the child indicates he is overwhelmed by those pressures that other children use to advance learning and mastery. Most learning in which such pressure is being used as a source of power rather than as an obstruction is accomplished silently, without tailoring, with the student as a member of a group; as a member of a group that learns and communicates together, and that uses the teacher as an instrument for their learning.

Does the atmosphere of human relations created by the students and teachers enable the students to become involved in social action, whether it be entertainment, recreation or the practice of political responsibility? Certainly those conditions which promote understanding and tolerance for the explorations and experimentations of adolescents are the same conditions that promote a pride in the alliance that the teacher is able to form with his teenagers.

To know who owns the school and what makes it go, one should ask: What is the fun of it; what is the work of it; the ownership of it; the memories of it; the love of it;; and the resentment and rebelling against it that improve it? "It" refers to learning and the school with plenty of go, and yet with plenty of time for dreaming about what comes next.

BIBLIOGRAPHY

1. Ashton-Warner, Sylvia. Teacher, New York: Simon & Schuster, 1963.
2. Schulz, Charles. Peanuts. United Features Syndicate, 1965.

Index

DATE DUE

APR 12 73			
SEP 2 7 1980			
FE 22 88			
AG 08 '90			
MR 11 '91			
AG 30 '03			
JA 5 '05			
GAYLORD			PRINTED IN U.S.A.